Setting up and Managing a Legal Practice

Fourth edition

Other titles available from Law Society Publishing:

Client Service for Law Firms
Heather Stewart

Conveyancing Quality Scheme Toolkit (2nd edn)
The Law Society

Managing People in a Legal Business
General Editor: Jill Andrew

Marketing Legal Services (2nd edn)
David Monk and Alastair Moyes

Practice Management Handbook (2nd edn)
Edited by Peter Scott

Precedent Library for the General Practitioner (2nd edn)
Martin Smith

Titles from Law Society Publishing can be ordered from all good bookshops or direct (telephone 0870 850 1422, email **lawsociety@prolog.uk.com** or visit our online shop at **www.lawsociety.org.uk/bookshop**).

Setting Up and Managing a Legal Practice

Fourth edition

Martin Smith

The Law Society

© Martin Smith 2012

ISBN-13: 978-1-907698-37-8

First edition published in 1995
Second edition published in 2002
Third edition published in 2008
This fourth edition published in 2012 by the Law Society
113 Chancery Lane, London WC2A 1PL

Typeset by IDSUK (DataConnection) Ltd
Printed by Hobbs the Printers Ltd, Totton, Hants

The paper used for the text pages of this book is FSC certified. FSC (the Forest Stewardship Council) is an international network to promote responsible management of the world's forests.

Contents

Appendices

Preface to the first edition

As a 16-year-old Classics student at King Edward VI Grammar School, Stourbridge, in the West Midlands, I began to wonder what I might do with three 'A' Levels in Latin, Greek and Ancient History. Apart from possibly being an archaeologist grubbing around ancient relics in Greece or Rome, or being a Classics teacher, nothing immediately sprang to mind. My Classics master came up with various suggestions, one of which was law.

'Classics', he said, 'produces a logical mind which is ideally suited to law.'

I decided to bounce the idea off a Scout leader whom I knew and whose opinions I respected.

'What do you think of the idea of me becoming a solicitor?' I asked.

'Now there's a job', he said. 'Money for old rope! They get paid a fortune, they don't start work most days until 10 am and their secretaries do most of the work. You see them in the mornings in the magistrates' court. They haven't got a clue what the case is about and their secretaries sit next to them passing them all the right documents and telling them what to say next. If only I had my time over again, it would certainly be something I'd like to get in on.'

This, I thought, is the job for me. If ever I meet up with the latter individual I will strangle him!

Some years later, when I was aged 22, I went for my formal interview in front of the Law Society. The general view in the queue of young hopefuls was that the interview was a pure formality and no one had heard of anyone who had 'failed' the interview and had been refused admission as a solicitor as a result. When it was my turn to go in, I went in front of three dark-suited, austere individuals who asked me a series of questions including why I wanted to be a solicitor. Ever one to tell the truth and shame the devil, I recounted the advice of the Scout leader. It may perhaps have come as a refreshing breath of stark truthfulness in what had probably been an afternoon of platitudes and well-rehearsed statements of entering an honourable profession and helping to underpin the fundamental principles of justice, law and order in a civilised society, but if it did, the three austere gentlemen betrayed no sign of it. Rather a look of horror and disbelief crept over their faces and one gentleman looked over his bifocals and said, 'I think that far from finding it is money for old rope you will feel you have earned every penny that you make.'

The moral of this story is threefold.

Firstly, even a crusty old Classics master has words of wisdom to pass on.

Secondly, never trust anyone's advice at face value, no matter how apparently learned, or wise, not even your old Scout leader.

And, thirdly, not everything uttered by the Law Society and its officers is complete rubbish.

This book is dedicated to these people, but first and foremost it is dedicated to my dear wife, Rachel, without whose unstinting hard work, help and encouragement when it was needed most, the practice of Martin Smith & Co. would have died shortly after birth.

Martin Smith
November 1995

Preface to the second edition

The legal landscape has changed greatly since the publication of the first edition. Legal aid is now the province of the few and looks set to disappear totally before too much longer. The pressures on practices and on lawyers are as great or greater than they have ever been. In times of trouble people seek the safety of numbers which in turn means that fewer solicitors are likely to want to start a practice of their own.

Nevertheless, the reasons for setting up a new practice remain much the same. It may be as a result of redundancy, political infighting within an existing practice or a divergence of philosophy, resulting in one or more players deciding they could make a better living doing things their way instead.

Given the difficulties which those brave souls setting up a new practice face, the need for guidance through the morass of obstacles has never been greater and it is perhaps surprising that this book remains the only work which deals with the entire range of problems confronting a new-born practice.

I have been much heartened by those who have contacted me in the six years since the first edition came out to say that they found the book a huge help. One common theme was that it was like having a friend along the way to whom they could turn for help. They would look in the book and there were the words of advice and encouragement for which they were seeking.

Much has happened in those six years. My practice has flourished and the 13-year-old son who drew the cartoons is now in his final year at Cambridge. Life hasn't always been easy though; I and my family suffered a terrible tragedy. My son Stephen fell out of his bedroom window in an awful accident at home and was killed. There is no crueller burden which fate can lay upon the shoulders of any human being than the death of a child upon a parent. It is something from which there is no recovery, just adjustment to a new and painful state of affairs.

If at any time of your practising life you feel you cannot go on, when you lose a large client or are under investigation by the VAT people, just take a small crumb of comfort to keep you going. Think of how much worse it could be and that if that Martin Smith and his family can keep coming in to the office day after day and produce the goods for the clients then what's a little VAT investigation between friends?

This second edition is dedicated to Stephen, whose life brought us so much happiness and laughter and whose death brought us so much pain and so many tears. But he wasn't a quitter. He kept going at everything he did. So have we, and so must you.

Martin Smith
November 2001

Preface to third edition

In 1995 when the first edition was published I dare not hope that some 13 years later not only would the book still be in print but also the demand for it would continue to be such that I would be requested to write a third edition of it. This is all the more surprising when I recall that the Law Society had strong reservations about publishing it in the first place when the advice from outside reviewers of the project was that trying to produce a single book covering the myriad tasks that needed to be completed in order to set up a new practice was well nigh impossible. It was felt that there was just too much ground to cover satisfactorily and any book that attempted to do so would result in inadequate guidance being given. The ongoing demand and the requirement for a third edition provides the evidence necessary to refute this suggestion.

That in itself is very gratifying. What is even more gratifying is when I hear directly from those people who have parted with their hard earned cash and who take the trouble to track me down and to thank me personally for producing a book which gave them so much help at such a worrying and uncertain time.

I hope the third edition in its expanded form continues to provide the same level of help and support to new readers. The book now comes with a CD-ROM containing useful precedents for customisation by the user. Gone are the amusing cartoons that appeared in the earlier editions. Perhaps it is a reflection of the more serious environment in which new practices are set up and struggle to cope but I hope the book will prove as useful as ever to those bold enough to start a new practice.

I dedicate the third edition firstly to my wife Rachel who has in one capacity or another given over 20 years' service to Martin Smith & Co and its clients and taken a full part in generating the experience which is now disseminated to others the profession through the third edition. Secondly, I dedicate it to my three children James, Stephen and Emily, all of whom have worked within the practice at some time or another although as described in the preface to the second edition regrettably Stephen is no longer with us. Thirdly, I dedicate it to my latest grandchild Charlie Smith who at five months old still hasn't made up his mind what he wants to do for a living. At least if he has he hasn't told me. Whether he or brother Jack will take up the family tradition in the law and – who knows – start their own practice – remains to be seen.

Martin Smith
September 2008

Preface to fourth edition

It is heart-warming to think that the book is still held in sufficient regard that a fourth edition is considered worthwhile. Even more heart-warming is when I am contacted by those of you at the coal face to say how the book has been of help to them. Practice has always been tough, and every year new challenges arise and with them the anxieties of whether those challenges can be met and the problems overcome. I hope that the fourth edition of this book continues to help practitioners make the right choices for them and to ensure that our profession provides the public with a first class service and a reasonable living for its members and their families.

I dedicate the fourth edition to my two latest grandchildren, Adrian and Cake Tin – the names have been changed to protect the innocent and to provide amusement.

Martin Smith
April 2012

Acknowledgements

It is often said that there are always plenty of candidates willing to take the credit when things go right, but very few volunteers to accept blame when things go wrong.

This book is unique for two things. Firstly, there is no other book on the market at the time of writing that assists solicitors with the formidable task of setting up a new practice.

Secondly, it is unique in that it disproves the earlier theory. The blame for any of the book's shortcomings belongs entirely to me. The persons listed below have given their time and skills freely and unselfishly, and as a result have turned the book into a much better work than would otherwise have been the case. In no particular order, they are:

Nick Hughesman of Lyall Youngman, Chartered Accountants, who prepared the business plan and assisted with accounts matters.

Vic Lyall formerly of Lyall Youngman, now retired, without whose assistance there may not have been a solicitors' practice on which to base my experiences.

Angela Deacon, Jennifer Israel, and the sundry *sole practitioners* and outside consultants who made time in their busy lives at the Law Society's request to read early drafts and contribute their comments.

Andrew Park who helped with the chapter on computers and computer systems.

Pat Skipwith, surveyor, who helped with matters relating to planning.

Carl Upsall of the Law Society whose good humour, tact and diplomacy was of vital importance when stamina and energy levels in the production of the book were running low.

No.1 son James Smith, who at the tender age of 13/14 managed to turn my raw material into polished cartoons and still found time to do his homework.

My wife, Rachel, who despite her myriad other tasks both at home and in the practice devoted endless hours to typing and amending the text.

My very grateful thanks go out to each of the above.

To Victor Lyall

A first class accountant called Vic
Met a lawyer both stylish and slick
Who said, 'I need a place'
Vic said, 'I've got some space
You'd better move in a bit quick.'
Some seven years later up there
Although at first sight it's unfair
The world had moved on
And Victor had gone
But the sly stylish lawyer's still there.

Second edition

My grateful thanks are due to the following for their help in compiling the Second Edition:

George Rendall of QuarryHouse Systems for his help with the section on computers.

Mario Koureas and Keith Ballard of Hetherington & Co for their assistance in revising the business plan and the VAT and tax sections.

Jane Withey of the Law Society for maintaining morale when energy levels became low.

Their input has made for a better work than would otherwise have been the case.

Third edition

Thanks go once again to:

George Rendall of Quarry House Systems for his very considerable help with the chapter on computers, IT and the like.

Simon Blackett and Marie Gill of the Law Society for their help and encouragement throughout.

Fourth edition

Thanks go once again to:

George Rendall of QuarryHouse Systems for the generous amount of time given to ensure the accuracy and relevance of the chapter on computers and IT systems.

Simon Blackett and Sarah Foulkes of the Law Society for their help with and encouragement in development and production.

My wife Rachel Smith for her help with the accountancy and book-keeping sections.

1

Setting up your practice

Setting up – the first steps

People start new practices for all sorts of reasons. They may have been made redundant from industry or from private practice, they may have been victims of partnership splits or they may simply have decided that they like the idea of their name in lights and running their own show. Very often the reasons for starting a new practice in the first place will govern whether the practice will be that of a sole practitioner or whether it will be a partnership.

Sole practice or small partnership?

The majority of people will probably try, at least in the first instance, to set up in practice with someone else. Unless the proposed partner or partners are themselves already working together and are splitting off from an existing partnership or are close friends, the parties, in the main, rapidly reach the conclusion that the risk of things not working out is too great. The old legal adage that partnership is like marriage is only too true in this situation. Before you go into partnership you need to know your proposed partner extremely well. There must be a high degree of trust, mutual respect and confidence, and these qualities must be present in such quantities that they will enable the parties to stay together during the very difficult and worrying early periods, as well as sustaining them later when – it is to be hoped – their hard work will result in success. These times can be just as dangerous as the early periods, since one party may credit themselves with being the architect of the success and may wish to enjoy rather more of the spoils than the others.

No one can help with these decisions any more than a marriage guidance counsellor can when you are thinking of getting engaged. The only advice that I can give is to make sure that you know your future partners as well as it is possible to know them. There may be several of you intending to start a new firm. If there are any parties who are well known to one partner but not to you, ensure that you meet them and their spouses, and see them in a domestic setting as well as in a working environment on as many occasions as you can manage. Do not just rely on your partner's judgement. You should all meet as often as you can, since people react differently when in the company of others than in a one-to-one situation. You must talk about all aspects of setting up a partnership together so that any possible differences of opinion will come out at this stage, rather than 12 months down the line. This process has seen off many a proposed partnership before it has started, which is probably no bad thing since they may have been doomed from the outset.

If there is no one in whom you have sufficient confidence to go into partnership with, you have four choices: stay where you are if that is possible and make the best of it; join another firm as an employee if you get the chance; leave the profession altogether; or set up as a sole practitioner. It is probably true to say that the majority of sole practices result from the first two options not being viable and the third being an even more daunting prospect than the fourth.

Sole practice – advantages

The single most overriding benefit of being a sole practitioner is the freedom you have from day one to run your practice exactly how you please. You have no partners to worry about, you do not have to think about the possibility of people plotting your downfall or arranging your sudden departure while you are away on holiday, no one chases you for your time sheets or billing figures, and there are no 'office politics'. When I was a partner in a City firm, I remember attending a partners' meeting at which we spent two hours debating whether the firm should use window envelopes or plain envelopes. The manoeuvres which took place before changing one's car would have impressed a cabinet minister angling for an increase in his spending budget. Plot and counterplot would be hatched, with alliances being made so that one partner supported another partner's similar application three months further down the line and all being timed to coincide with the firm's greatest month of positive cash flow, and preferably the senior partner's absence on holiday. As a sole practitioner, such decisions, whether trivial or momentous, can be taken in seconds and implemented within hours. Even with a partnership of two, the constraints are immediately in place, with your partner's feelings to consider. As a sole practitioner you have a completely free hand.

Sole practice – disadvantages

The downside of being a sole practitioner is the feeling of isolation, the fact that you have no one – at least in the early years – with whom you can discuss either business or legal problems. You have a strong sense of vulnerability since there is no one to look after the practice if you are ill. The feeling of being overstretched is even more apparent as a sole practitioner than as a partner. You may have to be in six places at the same time.

A surprise in store is that some lenders in conveyancing transactions will discriminate against you as a sole practitioner, despite the fact that your insurance arrangements may be the same as everyone else's. There is not much that you can do about this, other than take on a partner. Almost without exception you will be good enough to act for the household name lending institutions, but a tiny building society will refuse to let you process a mortgage on their behalf and you will lose the business to a competitor. All you can do is try to persuade the client to get their mortgage through a different lender, one that will let them use the solicitor of their choice. Some professional indemnity insurers also discriminate against sole practices and often will not quote terms at all or quote at such ridiculously high levels that you could not possibly accept them.

Nevertheless, when the rewards come you will have the satisfaction of knowing that the credit belongs solely to you. Of course, your staff will have helped and no doubt there will be clients who have put their trust in you and there will be others who will have assisted, providing the breaks when you needed them, but the applause is all yours! Your clients have come to you with their business because of their respect for your ability, skill, integrity and reputation and that, more than anything else, is immensely gratifying.

Limited liability partnership

A further option open to solicitors since 6 April 2001 is the limited liability partnership (LLP). The Limited Liability Partnerships Act 2000 created a new form of legal entity that exists as a separate legal person distinct from its members, liable only to the extent of the amount of the capital contributed to the LLP. If the LLP becomes insolvent, a court can call back funds withdrawn within two years of the commencement of the winding up to prevent partners from removing funds, but otherwise the usual unlimited liability consequences of a practice going bankrupt would be mitigated. However, solicitors must comply with the Solicitors Regulation Authority (SRA) Handbook (**www.sra.org.uk**) – see in particular Chapter 1, outcome 1.8 – and strict rules are imposed on solicitors limiting their liability to clients. To some extent, the advantage of an ordinary partnership keeping its finances secret from the public are lost as LLPs will have to make an annual return and have their accounts audited in the same way as companies. The statutory accounts and other information in the annual return will have to be filed in Companies House and will therefore be open to public inspection.

Solicitors in small partnerships will have the benefit of being exempt from the formal audit, in the same way that a small company does at present. A small partnership for these purposes is one where the turnover is about £1 million or less. Such entities will be able to file modified accounts giving only a brief summary of their accounting position. My view is that, unless you are likely to be turning over say, £500,000 per annum in your first year, the suspicion with which you may be regarded by prospective clients if you are an LLP may outweigh the advantages. There are, of course, solicitors' practices which become insolvent, but provided you keep a close eye on the figures for your practice, take corrective action as you go along and do not overstretch yourself, there is no need to think you are likely to become insolvent. Live within your means, do not take too many risks and get your practice established first. You can think about changing to an LLP if things take off and you start to see a substantial turnover of business. It is also worth sitting down with your accountant and discussing the idea, to get another view.

The advantages of limited liability for smaller practices may be more illusory than real. Landlords and banks may refuse to deal with LLPs without having personal guarantees from the partners. Until there is a history and track record, so that the benefits and pitfalls become apparent, an LLP should not be something undertaken without very careful thought and a lot of advice.

Once the practice is thriving, turnover starts to increase and the potential liabilities rise with the increase in the size of the practice, an LLP is something on which to take some heavyweight advice. I would suggest this is unlikely to be within the first two years.

Solicitor Sole Practitioners Group

All sole practitioners who are members of the Law Society are eligible to be members of the Solicitor Sole Practitioners Group. The group exists to represent the interests of sole practitioners in the Law Society and to provide support, both locally and nationally. Further information can be obtained from **www.spg.uk.com** (see Useful contacts).

You may also find the Solicitors' Assistance Scheme (see **www.thesas.org.uk**) useful. Under the scheme, experienced practitioners will offer help and advice to colleagues when they encounter professional difficulties.

Alternative business structures

Since October 2011 it has been possible to start a new firm as an alternative business structure (ABS) or convert an existing firm to an ABS by introducing non-solicitors into the ownership side of the firm.

What is an ABS?

An ABS is a firm where a non-lawyer or a separate entity such as a company is a manager of the firm or owns part of it. It can also be managed or part owned by an entity such as a company where the entity is controlled by 10 per cent or more of non-lawyers. A non-lawyer is defined as someone who is not authorised under the Legal Services Act 2007 to carry out reserved legal activities.

Advantages of an ABS

You can effectively go into partnership with someone from outside the profession and they will have the status and rewards of a partner. This might be an unqualified spouse who works in the firm, a valued unqualified employee or someone from an entirely different walk of life – an accountant, estate agent or surveyor, for example, opening up the prospect of an entirely different sort of practice that offers a one-stop service to its clients. A wealthy financial backer may invest capital into the firm in return for a say in its management. These are new and exciting challenges and opportunities for the profession. It remains to be seen how enthusiastically solicitors and other lawyers embrace them, or whether they prefer to stick with what they know.

Disadvantages

The one-stop-shop type of service is a new concept. How will the public respond? Will insurers and mortgage lenders take to them or view them with suspicion? For the first time, non-lawyers will have a degree of control over a legal practice. Will your competitors use this to their advantage? You can perhaps hear them now: 'Can Bloggs and Co give you truly independent advice when they know that if they upset their financial backers their funding might be withdrawn?'

Setting up as or converting to an ABS is a major step and needs a good deal of thought before proceeding. There are detailed regulatory requirements which must be complied with and which should be researched as part of the decision-making process. See the Law Society's practice note of 4 May 2011 on alternative business structures.

Franchising

Another new concept for lawyers' practices to consider is franchising. Franchising gives the franchisee the power of the franchisor's brand and access to benefits such as bulk buying, bulk negotiating power with insurers and lenders, and so on, in return for a price, usually an agreed percentage of the firm's turnover. Franchising has changed the face of many types of businesses, for example, opticians and chemists. Will it do the same for the legal profession? We shall see in due course. Certainly, some franchisors are putting huge resources into their attempts to bring branding into the legal services market and are threatening to wipe non-franchised firms off the map. They may make a fortune and change the legal landscape for ever or they may fall flat on their faces and lose huge amounts of money. Time will tell. Meanwhile, I suggest that if you are just starting up you are better off leaving any thoughts of a franchise until later as you will have enough to think about in the early stages. You can take a look at it 12 months down the line when both your firm and the legal world have settled down a little and things are a bit clearer.

Setting up – Solicitors Regulation Authority requirements

In order to set up a new practice, whether as a sole practitioner or a partnership, a solicitor is required to wait until he or she has been admitted for three years or, more accurately, has been entitled to practise for a total of 36 months within the last 10 years. There must be at least one person who is 'qualified to supervise'. This is defined at rule 12 of the SRA Practice Framework Rules 2011 and in most new practices it will be either the sole principal or one of the partners. In each case the person qualified to supervise must have completed the training specified from time to time by the SRA. The SRA has the power to grant waivers in respect of the training requirements in suitable cases. (Note that after 31 March 2012 the obligations in the SRA Authorisation Rules for having a compliance officer for legal practice (COLP) and a compliance officer for finance and administration (COFA) will apply to sole practitioners: see **Chapter 7**.)

Whether setting up early on in your career is a good idea is a matter of opinion. Solicitors who have only been in general practice for, say, two years with law as their first career, are likely to be aged between 26 and 30. Even if they have the management experience to run a practice and to be able to arrange the finance, their experience is likely to be fairly narrow. When any one of the various crises that can arise in a small practice does so, and there is no one else to turn to for help and advice, panic may set in. Having said that, the younger you are, the more energy and drive you tend to have, with fewer family responsibilities, and so you may find more time than others to devote to making a go of it.

Training requirements

You must also qualify for the title of 'qualified to supervise' for the purposes of the SRA Practice Framework Rules 2011, even if you have no one to supervise at present. The training presently specified is attendance at, or participation in, any course(s) or programme of learning on management skills for a minimum of 12 hours. Solicitors who have attended Management Course Stage 1 (the seven-hour course compulsory for those in their first three years following admission) and Management Course Stage 2 (the five-hour optional course) satisfy the requirement. The nature of the training is deliberately flexible. It does not have to be Law Society accredited and will count to continuing professional development (CPD) requirements in the same way as other accredited or non-accredited courses (as the case may be) do.

Where to locate

Where you decide to make your 'home' is an interesting aspect of setting up. The importance of getting it right varies from nil to absolutely crucial. It you have a large client following, your clients will probably want you to be fairly close to them. If you have a commercial following, in practice you will probably have to locate in central London, or, if you are setting up in the provinces, in the nearest large commercial centre. Many clients still have a certain snobbish attitude towards their solicitor's location. If the image you wish to project is that of a highly organised, switched-on commercial firm, you may have difficulty in obtaining instructions from commercial clients if you are located in an unfashionable and run-down suburb or a country lane. Clients will expect you to be in the thick of it, commercially speaking. It follows that certain key decisions must be taken at this stage. What type of practice are you going to market yourself as? What type of market are you going to aim at?

Locating according to your market

In my own case, I decided to offer a general high street practice, while at the same time marketing the practice towards commercial clients both within the area and outside it. This offered clients the skills acquired through 12 years' practice in the City and the same kind of service they were used to from a City firm, but at substantially less than City rates. Many provincial firms have followed this approach with considerable success. Commercial clients take a fresh look at the fees they are charged and the service they receive in times of recession, and may conclude in many instances they can make substantial savings while experiencing little or no drop in the quality of service, advice and work provided in return.

The danger of this strategy is that of falling between two stools: being unable to compete with City service because of size and resources, while out-pricing oneself from local markets because of the additional resources which need to be available to provide the City-type service.

Again, these decisions must be made by the individual, and it is difficult to advise on what type of market to go for. It will depend on exactly what your own experience is, the type of clients you feel able to attract, whether you have an existing client following and so on.

Locating close to home

If you are setting up in partnership, you may wish to have premises that are more or less equal in travelling time for each of you. However, if you are going it alone, the choice is yours. The availability of suitable premises may make the decision for you – if the only premises you can afford and which are available are 50 miles away, you may have no choice. If you can locate close to home you will have the immense satisfaction of hearing news of tube strikes and travel disruption due to severe weather knowing that you can walk to work when others are not so lucky.

Practising from home

Advantages

A further option is to set up in practice from home. At first sight this has enormous advantages – no travelling, and you will not have to worry about the burden of a lease. The initial capital requirement will be less, and you will avoid a protracted, time-consuming search for suitable premises. In addition, the disadvantage of never being able to get away from work is probably less than one might think. Important clients may ask for your home telephone number anyway and may be offended if you are not prepared to disclose it. In the early days you will probably find yourself leaning strongly in the other direction and volunteering your home telephone number to all and sundry, inviting them to call you at any time, day or night. Once things have taken off, you may not be quite so forthcoming! In the early days you will probably find yourself working in the office or at home, until 8 or 9 pm, and again, it does not really matter whether the phone is ringing at home or in the office. If you are working from home, the two become the same thing.

If you decide to work from home it is advisable to have a voice mail facility and an ex-directory telephone number for your family and friends, so that you are not on call all the time. The majority of clients to whom you will be giving your home telephone number will be business clients, and by and large they respect the fact that you are entitled to time with your family in the evenings and at weekends and will only call you if it is something they are particularly worried about or an emergency.

Disadvantages

A much more important factor will probably be your own attitude to work. Many people find it difficult to work from home at the best of times, particularly with children running about and the television blaring. If the home is a place where you normally relax but sometimes work, and the office is a place where you normally work and sometimes relax, the whole thing tends to work much better. You will be better able to switch off when you get home and feel much more in the mood for getting on with things while you are in the office. To be successful in running your practice from home, you have to be very self-disciplined and have fairly spacious accommodation.

In my view, business clients tend to feel more comfortable coming to see you in an office than they do seeing you in your home, where many feel they are intruding. It also presents a much more business-like image if you are working from office surroundings rather than in a room tucked away somewhere in the house. Make no mistake about it: our business is as much about image as anybody else's. You can still have a professional image, even though you practise from home, but you may need to work harder at it. The Bohemian carpet slippers and Val Doonican sweater look is all very well, but it may not be what a commercial client is looking for.

If you run your office from home, unless you live in the high street, you will not be readily accessible to passing trade, banks, building societies, etc. Some building societies are not prepared to instruct you if you practise from home. You do, of course, enjoy the benefits of not having to pay rent and you may not pay full business rates. Even though this is not an insignificant area of expenditure, it is not one of the most substantial. In our case, for example, accommodation charges, including items such as repairs, heat and light, account for only 10 per cent of total outgoings. Staff costs, by contrast, account for more than 46 per cent. Clearly, these figures will vary depending on how much you pay for your premises, staff and other outgoings. The decision must be between cutting yourself off from the high street or other commercial centre, loss of image, etc., for a saving of probably no more than about 8 per cent (once you have taken into account the additional heating and lighting costs involved in working from home). You may also find that you are required to pay business rates on your home, which would reduce the saving still further.

There is also the danger that when you move house HM Revenue and Customs (HMRC) will claim that you are not entitled to the full principal private residence relief for capital gains tax (CGT) purposes. If, for example, your house has six rooms and you use one as an office, one-sixth of the gain made when you sell your home may be liable to CGT if that one room has been used wholly for business purposes.

The answer is to ensure that no single room is dedicated exclusively to the business. If you claim the running costs of one room as a business expense in your accounts, HMRC may take this as evidence of a room dedicated to business use. It is better to claim a proportion of the costs of heat and light, etc., for part of two rooms rather than the whole of the cost of one.

HMRC might point also to the use of a fax machine to support the contention that the room is for business purposes rather than domestic, but if you can ensure that the room has a dual purpose, both business and domestic, say by putting a cooker or a library of non-legal book in the room, you are likely to be able to resist an attempt by HMRC to deny full relief.

You may be able to claim part of your council tax against the profits of the business. As long as you can demonstrate that the amount claimed is reasonable, there is no reason why such a claim should not be allowed. The best approach may be to put forward a global figure for 'use of home as office', with a suitable breakdown available if required.

There is also no reason why a proportion of the VAT on fuel for heat and light, etc., cannot be reclaimed in the same way if you are willing to take the time to work the figures out.

Fully serviced accommodation

One further option, which is not often considered, is the possibility of renting office space from a business and commercial centre. Certain agencies will rent out fully furnished, staffed and equipped offices on a monthly basis. Included in the arrangement is the option to hire additional facilities, such as a boardroom or a conference room with catering services, for a separate hourly rate. The proposal often includes a receptionist, who may direct clients to a waiting area or answer a telephone for you, and the use of other secretarial support staff. This enables you to have a prestigious address, impressive offices and other facilities at a fraction of the true cost, as the cost is split among all the occupiers of the building. Such an arrangement may seem very effective and whether it is for you will come down largely to the arithmetic. You will need to work out what rent you would pay for unserviced accommo-dation and isolate the cost of the services from the total figure. Then make a value judgement as to whether or not all the extra facilities are worth the premium that you are paying. The facilities acquired by this means will often present a very professional appearance and there is no doubt that it is an easy way to answer a lot of questions. Generally speaking, however, this is a short-term solution and you are better off planning for the longer term and choosing somewhere where you can stay for three to five years. Moving offices is very disruptive and time-consuming, as well as not particularly cheap. Nevertheless, serviced accommodation may provide the answer where you have to move in a hurry, you have a client base which needs servicing from day one and, try as you might, you have just not sorted office accommodation out before you have to move from your existing offices. The quick fix of serviced accommodation may thus provide a short-term answer.

The dangers of signing a lease

The serviced accommodation and the office at home options relieve you of the dangers of signing a lease. Before 1 January 1996, if you signed even a short-term lease, you were liable for its duration, which may have been five, eight or 10 years. While you would no doubt have been able to assign the lease if you had negotiated it correctly, there was still the possibility of no one wanting the premises or of a subtenant running up rent arrears and you being liable if you have given covenants or were the first leaseholder.

After 1 January 1996, the Landlord and Tenant (Covenants) Act 1995 altered the position so that the tenant's liability ceased on assignment for leases signed after that date, except where the landlord's consent to assign was required. However, the landlord can require the first tenant to guarantee the assignee's performance of the covenants, so you will still be liable if you act as the guarantor of the assignee's covenants; it is still the case that entering into any lease is a hazardous undertaking and the shorter the lease the better. It is possible to negotiate a break clause so that, after serving the appropriate notice, you can walk away from the remainder of the lease. It is certainly worthwhile doing so, even at the price of having to pay a higher rent. Beware of the landlord who tries to insist on a mutual break clause allowing him to serve notice early and evict you. Whilst the market continues to be in favour of tenants, do all you can to negotiate a tenant's only break clause.

Sharing premises – an ideal compromise?

Some solicitors adopt the idea of a set of chambers along the lines of barristers' chambers. This has the advantages of a good address (often in an area which you would be unable to afford on your own), the support of colleagues whom you can ask for advice and a cross-referral system whereby a client whose problem is outside one solicitor's field of expertise can be referred to another solicitor in the chambers, keeping the work in house. Each solicitor pays a share of the overheads. The usual feeling of isolation experienced by most people setting up on their own is dissipated.

The disadvantages are that friction can be generated by one party always seeming to refer work to others without the favour being returned, no clear lines of responsibility so that people expect others to cope with their practice while they are away through illness, holiday or other commitments, and one party using a disproportionate amount of common resources. In theory the system can work well, but it needs sensible and reasonable individuals who can get along with one another.

Informal arrangements

The solution which we adopted was similar. We discovered, through a client, that other professional people had surplus office accommodation available within their building. They were prepared to allow us to occupy part of the premises on an informal basis and to share with us the costs of partitioning them off. We also negotiated within an accommodation charge the use of their receptionist, waiting area, photocopier and similar facilities. The arrangement worked extremely well. They were paying for all of those under-used facilities in any event and were glad to have part of that burden relieved by us sharing the facilities. We were not, and never have been, asked to sign any formal agreement and the whole thing was done on a handshake. If you have such an informal arrangement, however, you run the risk of your 'landlord' suddenly asking for the space back, which could a problem.

It also meant that, professionally speaking, we had other level-headed business people with whom we could, on occasions, share our problems, and they could do likewise. From their point of view, they had instant access to free initial legal advice and were only too pleased to be able to recommend their own clients to us as a firm that they could observe operating at first hand that was run by someone they felt they could trust.

Of all the various options available, this is the one I would recommend above others. It is cheap, low risk and good in terms of image, and provides the opportunity for a steady flow of clients via your 'landlord' if the arrangement works well on a personal level. I can think of nothing more demoralising than setting up a practice with no clients from one room of a building where you know no one and where the opportunities to get to know your neighbours are infrequent. Your whole working attitude is likely to be affected without the kind of bustling, confident atmosphere that arises where you share space with other businesses. Whether you have a formal sublease or take up occupation on the risky handshake basis is up to you. Who knows, it might eventually lead to an ABS 'marriage' of the two firms.

Getting your premises' image right

It is also important to make sure that the premises are approachable from the point of view of the kind of client you are trying to attract. If the premises have thick, pile carpets, brass handles on the doors and mahogany panels along the staircase, legal aid clients or first-time house buyers may take one look at the premises and go elsewhere, either because they think they are going to feel out of place or because they are afraid that the fees are going to be astronomic. At the other extreme, if the paint is flaking off the walls, the linoleum has holes in it and there is no shade around the light bulb, your commercial clients are not going to come back for a second appointment.

Bear in mind also the Equality Act 2010 and the possible need to modify the premises to comply with the Act's requirements. You must take reasonable steps to provide a reasonable alternative method for making your services available to disabled people, where a physical feature makes it impossible or unreasonably difficult for them to use these services. What you might be required to do would depend on how practicable it is for you to take the necessary steps, the cost of the work and the disruption to your business. Accordingly, if you are a sole practitioner with one member of staff it would probably be unreasonable to expect you to put in a lift if your premises are on the second floor. However, if you are on the ground floor but there is a set of small steps into the premises, it might be reasonable to expect you to replace them with a ramp. These are things to bear in mind when looking at premises and assessing their suitability. If you are using an agent or a surveyor to help find premises you might seek their advice on this aspect regarding any premises you are thinking of taking.

Choosing the location – check the competition

Location will also depend to a large extent on what competition there is in the area. It is not a bad idea to get out a street map, look in the Law Society's *Directory of Solicitors and Barristers* (or on the Internet at **www.solicitors-online.com**), identify the locations of each practice address and mark them with a suitable fluorescent sticky label. At one time I thought of locating my practice in Enfield. It appeared to be a bustling area, only 15 minutes from home, with good public transport arrangements. After 20 minutes with the map and directory, I had discovered about 16 separate practices all located virtually on top of one another. Consequently, I decided not to move to Enfield!

Considerations of this type may not feature largely if you already have a strong client following and have decided that you can manage without passing trade. Depending on the type of practice you intend setting up, you may not want passing trade, but instead rely on providing a good service for your existing client base while seeking to consolidate it with other clients of similar standing. If you have no, or a very uncertain, client base, I suggest that all work is likely to be work that you cannot turn away unless it is totally outside your field of expertise and you feel you would be a danger to the client if you tried to tackle it. You should also bear in mind that many potential clients who contribute to passing trade will be dependent on legal aid. If you do not have a franchise you may spend half your day explaining that you are unable to help them and referring them on to competitors.

Even if work offered does not look particularly profitable, it is still probably worth doing in the early days, unless it is clear that it will be grossly unremunerative. Even poorly paid work in the first few months will bring in some cash and will help to spread the word that your practice has arrived and is open for business. At a later stage, when the practice has got off the ground, you may want to think more carefully about the type of work you accept.

What to call your practice

The way in which you style your firm is to some extent decided for you by the professional rules. Rule 7 of the Solicitors' Code of Conduct 2007 provided that your publicity, and this included the practice name, must not be misleading or inaccurate. You could not therefore call yourself a partnership or Bloggs and Associates if you were a sole practitioner, unless the practice formerly had more than one principal. You could not call yourself solicitors if none of the principals or directors (or members in the case of an LLP) was a solicitor. Apart from that, you could call your practice pretty much what you liked. The 2007 Code has been replaced by the SRA Code of Conduct 2011 and the relevant part of the Code for these purposes is Chapter 8 and indicative behaviour 8.10, which is very similar to the 2007 Code. So long as you follow the Chapter 8 outcomes you can call your practice by whatever name you wish so long as it does not mislead the public, but see **Chapter 12** as to the marketing and image implications involved in the decision.

You must also use the words 'Authorised and regulated by the Solicitors Regulation Authority' on your notepaper and fax header sheets. See outcome 8.5 of the SRA Code of Conduct 2011 and Chapter 8 generally about what you can and cannot put on your headed notepaper and other forms of publicity such as websites.

The dilemma of taking on new fields of work

Unless you come from a very general practice, or are setting up with others so that the firm is able to handle a range of legal services, you will be faced with the dilemma of seeing work go elsewhere, possibly to a competitor, or tackling work which you may not have done before. There is a fine line between being timid and overcautious and attempting things for which you have no aptitude or competence. As a litigator of 12 years' experience, with virtually none of it in conveyancing, will-making or probate, I had some hard choices to make when I started. It may be that some of those choices were wrong; taking on work that I should not have or turning away work which, if I had had a little more courage and self-confidence, I could have dealt with quite easily – certainly as well as the person to whom the work went. Everyone has to start somewhere and you should not shy away from work when you are setting up in practice simply because you have not done it before. In this respect, the *Precedent Library for the General Practitioner*, 2nd edn (Law Society, 2009) written by myself will get you off to a flying start with all the everyday precedents you are likely to need in one volume, with the highly specialised, and therefore rarely used, material cut out.

Using available reference material

You can now buy books relatively cheaply on subjects that at one time might have been considered specialist areas (including handbooks published by the Law Society – see p.ii for details of the distributors). With the assistance of such learning aids and a decent precedent book (for which see the *Precedent Library* above) you can quite easily carry out a perfectly competent job for the client. The hardest part is in saying 'Yes, of course', when the client asks 'Could you handle this for me?'. No one, not even experts, has all the facts at their fingertips all of the time. They all go off and look things up. The client is not only paying you for the knowledge of your subject but also for your objectivity, level-headedness and plain common sense – and for your professional training in how to consult specialist texts and other sources. Your general knowledge of the law, your years in business and your experience of life will often tell you when something is wrong and when to call a halt to further work until you have found the answer to whatever is giving you an uneasy feeling.

There are also plenty of other people – accountants, friends who are barristers or solicitors and even other solicitors in the area – you can ring up and ask an opinion when something is troubling you. If they do not know the answer they may be able to point you in the right direction. It will not be long before this becomes second nature and you are drawing up wills, administering estates and conveying away quite happily.

As well as being spoiled for choice as regards textbooks on specialist areas, there is now a multitude of courses offered on all types of subjects, pitched at all levels of experience. If you wish to develop an expertise in an otherwise unknown area, you can supplement your reading with a short course at a training centre. As well as helping to absorb and consolidate the knowledge so far acquired, it will confirm what you have already learned and give you added confidence. It will also raise questions you had not considered, making you less likely to stumble into something unexpected at a later stage.

If you have a friend who is a solicitor or barrister who specialises in a particular field you are interested in entering, why not ask if you can attend a trial or a conference with them to gain additional experience? Provided the agreement of the client and other partners in the firm is obtained, there should be no difficulty. Doctors think nothing of standing over an experienced colleague to learn from their skill and knowledge.

Advocacy for the inexperienced sole practitioner

If you have never done any advocacy before, now is not the time to feel shy! You may feel that that this is something you are simply not cut out to do, but you are now facing the stark reality of having to earn your living very much at the sharp end. Put aside your bashfulness and just get on with it. The courts are full of barristers and solicitors not necessarily any more skilled than you, and all earning a decent living out of advocacy. If I did not feel tongue tied, embarrassed and have my pulse racing when I got up to speak in a magistrates' court, I would feel that there was something seriously wrong. I clearly recall sitting behind one of the most experienced QCs in the land some years ago (who went on to become a senior Old Bailey judge) when he was opening an appeal in the Court of Criminal Appeal. I marvelled at the way the words simply flowed without a trace of nervousness and how he seemed totally at ease. One of the Lords Justices then asked him if he had an additional copy of the document to which he was referring and he turned to me to see if there was a spare one on the file. As he did so, I noticed that his hands were trembling to such an extent that his own copy of the document was making a quiet rattling noise. As I looked up at him, I could see that he was perspiring heavily across his forehead and neck despite the fact that the appeal was heard just before Christmas and the courtroom was chilly. If people of that seniority and experience are entitled to work themselves up into a state when getting up in front of a tribunal, so are you! Do not let confusion about how to claim the right level of fees and not knowing the paperwork involved put you off. Get out there and earn the fee first and sort out getting paid later. Five minutes on the telephone with another solicitor or a costs draughtsman will show you how to make your first costs claim. The rest are all the same.

If you are going to court for the first time or after a long absence, try to go beforehand, sit at the back and get acquainted with the court. Always give yourself plenty of time to get to the hearing and never arrive late. As well as creating the wrong impression with the client, your own anxiety level will be much increased.

Higher rights of audience

If you think advocacy is for you why not consider getting qualified to appear in the higher courts? You could do all the training and obtain the qualification before you set up. For most people this is likely to be a time-consuming and costly distraction, but for those who are being made redundant and have been given an extended notice period, it could provide a useful opportunity to add another string to your bow.

3

Finance

One of the key early decisions you will have to make is how you are going to finance the practice, whether as a sole trader or as a partnership. The views of people in business, including professional advisers, can vary immensely as to whether you should try to borrow all the money you will need, as little as possible or none at all, or whether the firm's capital should be roughly half borrowed and half proprietor's funds. Once again, necessity may provide the answer – if no one will lend you the money, you will have to put up your own. On the other hand, if you have no money to put in, you can only begin by borrowing. The merits of these debates will be examined later, but if you intend to borrow money, one thing is certain – you will have to put forward a business plan to demonstrate to your proposed lender (who will almost certainly be a bank, or possibly your future partners in a proposed ABS) that you have done your arithmetic and can make the figures add up. Not only that, the lender will look also at the figures themselves to make sure that they do add up and that the business is likely to trade sufficiently profitably to enable you to repay the money. Even if you are supplying the capital entirely yourself, you must prepare a business plan, no matter how rudimentary, so that you can prove to yourself you can make the practice work and be able to measure as you go along how well or otherwise things are going.

Preparing a business plan with professional help

The majority of people setting up a new business will go to an accountant to prepare a business plan. There is no reason at all why solicitors should feel they need to do it any differently. It is the kind of thing that any competent, qualified accountant (as opposed to a bookkeeper-type accountant) can do for you and the cost will not be exorbitant. You must carry out the necessary research into markets, profit levels, setting-up costs, etc. Although accountants will often have helpful ideas and suggestions, they are really there to present in financial terms the business plan that you have put together in such a way that your ideas make financial sense to a bank. They are not there to do all your thinking for you. Keep the accountant's bill – it will form part of your set-up costs which are tax deductible, and so with luck HMRC will be paying a good 20 per cent of it.

Equally, a bank does not need to know down to the last penny what money will be going through the business. It simply needs to have sufficient information to ensure that the project is viable. Some banks will even help you to put the business plan together, but first impressions are just as important in this situation as in any other. The bank may be one with which you have had no previous connection. In due course you may well be looking to the bank as a source of business. If you go in with a half-baked business plan scribbled out on the back of an envelope, the manager is unlikely to be impressed by the way you go about things, and that impression may stick. If you go in with a properly prepared business plan, which has been well thought out, which you fully understand and which you can explain, this will be the perfect opportunity to strike up a good rapport. It may lead to a long-lasting and mutually profitable business arrangement. Bank managers do not now have the same clout at local level that they used to, but you are going to need to use all the connections you can and if a bank manager advises a friend to consult you, it will be a recommendation which will not be lightly disregarded.

If you are not intending to borrow but to put forward the bulk or all of the capital yourself, your preparations need not be so elaborate. You may be able to get away with the back-of-an-envelope approach, providing you are taking a realistic view of the figures and you are reasonably sure that you have not left anything out.

Example of a business plan

Appendix 3 sets out a very rough business plan which you would present to a bank manager when asking for finance for the new venture. **Appendix 4** sets out a costings plan which shows how much money you will need to get started. You will see that the capital requirement is likely to be in the region of £15,000. The costings plan takes no account of the need for working capital, i.e. the fact that you will have to pay out for court fees, Land Registry fees, wages to staff and other overheads while you are waiting for a job to be completed, billed and paid by the client. The business plan at **Appendix 3** allows for a rather more generous injection of funds than the basic £14,424 cost of setting up in the costings plan. However, if you are going to be starting on your own and will not be drawing anything out of the business for a month or two, you will be getting most of the disbursements from the client before paying them out, so you can start with a little less capital than the full amount shown in the business plan. The costings plan is for a very basic sole practitioner's office and involves no staff other than a secretary. If your spouse is able to help you out with secretarial work or bookkeeping, your staffing costs can be kept very low. Whoever does the bookkeeping must know all the accounting rules – this is essential for any practice but perhaps even more important for a sole practitioner as there are fewer people available to sort things out if they get in a mess.

Clearly, the amounts involved are a very rough guide, just to give you an idea of what items you should be thinking about and what they are likely to cost, but you may decide to go for more elaborate premises or to work from home. You may decide to invest in more advanced systems and equipment right from the start and employ back-up staff right away. All these items will cause the business plan to change dramatically and the items in **Appendix 4** should be used more as an *aide-mémoire* than anything else. It does, however, show you how, with only a fairly modest investment by business standards, you can get the show on the road.

Opening bank accounts

You will need to open a bank account even before you have opened an office. Although at this stage you may not have any client funds to put into it, you will still need to talk to the bank manager about opening a client account. Paying-in books and cheque books will need to be printed.

Even if you have not used the bank to obtain the finance, it is a good idea to negotiate an overdraft facility of about £30,000 in case cash flow does not go quite the way you intended it to. The time to arrange the overdraft is at this stage rather than when you are in trouble. Even a fairly friendly bank manager is unlikely to give you a higher overdraft facility than this initially when you have no trading record. Any trading record that you might have had as a partner elsewhere is not terribly relevant.

Choosing a bank

The choice of bank and its location is very important. If you have a good relationship with a bank already and you are going to be setting up not too far away, you may do well to stay with that bank and keep the relationship with someone you know. The power of the local branch manager has diminished considerably over the years but you will still need to create a favourable impression. Banks keep careful records and a note after an interview that Mr and Mrs X appear prudent and sensible and plan carefully for the future may help get the loan you need on another day. It may pay you to retain your connection with that bank even if you are moving away since you can make your day-to-day transactions with a local branch while maintaining the account elsewhere. If you decide to set up with a bank near your office, you have an excellent opportunity to make a good impression. Banks are generally keen to get solicitors onto their books and you should find a very positive response from any bank that you approach.

Bank charges

Most banks will offer you a year's free banking, which is extremely good news when you are just setting up. Nevertheless, you must enquire what the charges are likely to be once that year has run out, and build the cost into your business plan. Banks are generally now familiar with the practice of some small traders moving their bank account once a year to obtain perpetual free banking. In good times the rate of interest that banks are willing to pay on client account balances can vary quite significantly, although at the time of writing it is almost nothing. Some banks will charge a fee for transfers from client account into office account while others do not. Charges for individual items, such as telegraphic transfers, can also vary appreciably. Some banks have several tariffs, some with a monthly service charge and lower charges per item. There is, regrettably, no substitute for doing the homework and getting from banks their individual charges, negotiating the best deal you can and then applying a notional number of debits, credits and transfers and telegraphic transfers, a notional average client account credit and, therefore, interest sum, and seeing which bank is charging you the least at the end of the day. It is a tiresome and complex exercise, but a necessary one.

Having done your homework, you are then in a position to sit down with the bank manager and talk to him or her in fairly stark terms. If the bank manager wants your account – and we are talking long term, up to 20 years – then you need a bit of flexibility. Again, this is no time to be shy. Equally, it is not the time to be aggressive. Local managers are now, in general, controlled by regional offices and a lot of their discretion has been taken away. There is, therefore, no point in pushing them too hard, but what flexibility there is you should exploit as best you can. You may do better in talking to the regional business manager, i.e. the person who does have the power to be flexible, rather than the local manager who sounds sympathetic but has to break the news to you that: 'The Business Centre won't allow it.'

Your bank as a source of new business

This is also a good time to talk to the bank about any minor legal work it may have. Banks now have what they euphemistically refer to as realisations departments – or a central debt collecting unit – so that individual managers are not free to select a local solicitor to carry out debt collection work. Nevertheless, there are considerable opportunities for bank managers to point their customers in your direction for such matters as wills or conveyancing, and a good relationship may result in new clients. The bank staff themselves will need legal representation from time to time like everyone else, so why not you?

Deposit account

You will probably not at this stage have sufficient time or inclination to start looking at deposit accounts. You are required by the SRA Accounts Rules 2011 to ensure that any money that you are going to be holding for a client for anything more than a few days is properly invested, but it is generally a lot simpler just to ask the bank to place the funds in a deposit account. You are unlikely, in the early few months, to have any substantial sums to hold on behalf of a client, but if you do, the best answer is probably to go into a local building society and undertake the same exercise with the building society as you did with the bank manager. Building societies are also a good source of client referrals and you should not miss the opportunity to make yourself known and to make it clear that you are the introducer of the funds. If at that stage you are not licensed under the Financial Services and Markets Act 2000 to give investment advice, you must be careful not to advise your client to place the funds with a specific building society since you may infringe the Act (see **Chapter 12**). This does not prevent a client from directing you to open the account with a particular building society and you carrying out those instructions. Do not forget that these accounts will have to be reconciled at no more than five-weekly intervals in the same way as the client account with the bank and must have the word 'client' in the title of the account.

Electronic banking and funds transfer have now been with us for some time. If you use this form of banking with your own personal account you may decide to have a facility on your office and client account whereby you can move money electronically from one account to another. If you are fully conversant with these matters, by all means use them if the facility is available as you will save a great deal of time. If you are not, it may be something to put in place later.

Once your practice has built up, especially on the conveyancing side, and you need to send and receive significant amounts of money, you would do well to consider having your own CHAPS terminal. (CHAPS is an electronic bank-to-bank same-day payment made within the UK in either sterling or euros.) All you need is a reasonably new computer and a telephone socket and the bank will supply the rest. It does not need to be a separate computer – the one you use for word processing and accounts will do the job if it has enough memory. The bank will tell you if it has. Of course, banks charge for the system but, assuming you are passing the cost of the bank's CHAPS charges on to the client, a break-even point will arrive at about 10 outgoing payments from the client account each month, depending on how much your bank charges for the use of the system. Thereafter you will actually be making a profit as well as having the convenience of control over what is happening, instead of constantly ringing the bank to find out if it has sent the money yet.

If you continue to make a charge to the client for sending the money, be sure to show the charge as an additional charge made by you rather than as a disbursement. A CHAPS charge made by the bank which you then pass on to the client is a disbursement, but a charge made by you for using your terminal to send the client's money instead of the bank sending it is an extra charge by you, not a disbursement, and must not be shown as a disbursement.

As well as being able to send and receive money electronically without having to wait for the bank to get around to telling you what is going on, you will also be able to move money from client account into office account and vice versa if you have made a mistake.

One shortcoming of the system is that it may not immediately show the arrival of a BACS (bank automated clearing system) payment. This only appears the following day unless the sender has transmitted the funds very early in the morning. More lenders are using this method of payment and the Legal Services Commission also uses it to send the monthly payment. It is to be hoped that banks will adjust their systems to be able to cope with this type of payment in due course.

Borrowing requirement or putting up your own capital

As stated earlier, the choice between borrowing and putting up your own capital may come down to what is available and if you have ready cash from, for example, a redundancy payment or capital repaid from your partnership capital account if you have split from a partnership. It is financially unsound to leave that money in a building society account while you go out and borrow your working capital to set up your firm. The exponents of the contrary view argue that they would never put their own funds at risk. This is a view I have never properly understood, since the bank tends to attack your money and assets if it wants its funds back from a failing business. In my opinion, borrowed money is in much the same category as your own money except that it costs a lot more to get hold of and to hang on to, and people have a nasty habit of asking for it back when you can least afford to repay it! You can always put the funds in someone else's name but, if you became insolvent, the trustee may investigate and drag your nearest and dearest into litigation. Is it really worth it?

It became very fashionable in the 1980s to borrow heavily to finance solicitors' practices since there was a plentiful supply of cheap money and the economy was booming. The idea was that you took the bank's money and made it work to earn greater profits and expand your firm to a degree that would never have been possible without outside finance. In more recent times it has been cheap to borrow money but the banks will not lend. If you are able to borrow at cheap rates do not forget that the rates can go zooming up with very little notice and suddenly the loan will become unaffordable. Do not overextend yourself.

Many firms were caught out quite disastrously in the late 1980s when the recession hit and interest rates went through the roof. Being a cautious individual, I set up my own practice from my own funds. I borrowed nothing from the bank and have avoided using my overdraft facility. The result was an enormous sigh of relief as I watched interest rates climb way beyond any level that people thought they would go.

Many large firms were pulled up very sharply by banks that rather abruptly told them that not only would the overdraft not be permitted to rise any further but it would be called in unless there was an immediate injection of partners' own funds in some very uncomfortable amounts. These are the risks that you run if you use other people's money to finance your practice. A better way would be to adopt a policy of borrowing as little as possible and only for specific areas of expansion or to finance a new car or a computer system. The borrowing should be limited so that you have a definite and workable plan to repay it within, say, a three- to five-year period. In other words, treat it in the same way as buying a washing machine on hire purchase. The monthly outgoings would not be too great, you are not paying substantially more for the washing machine and yet you have the use of it during that time. As practitioners, we are all aware of those households that not only get the washing machine on credit but also the TV, the DVD player, the freezer, the car and the microwave. The income of the household is so strangled that it cannot cope. Any firm in that situation becomes very vulnerable. If the bank decides to pull the rug from under your feet, it can bring the entire practice down.

Putting up your house as collateral

Any bank making a loan for setting up a practice is almost certain to want you to put your house up as collateral and, on the plus side, secured borrowing is always cheaper than unsecured borrowing. Again, if you are using your own money, this is something you need not worry about.

Bear in mind that it may not be just your money you are putting at risk. If you are married, for example, it will be the family's savings. Your partner will need to be consulted on these decisions and indeed give consent, even if he or she is not going to be working in the new firm. It is important that your partner is a willing party to the arrangement and not pressurised into it.

If the house is being put up as security for bank finance, your partner will be required to have separate legal advice on the wisdom of putting the family fortune at risk and will be required to sign documents putting his or her share of the house up as security, especially in the light of the

House of Lords' observations in *Barclays Bank plc* v. *O'Brien* (1993) and *Royal Bank of Scotland* v. *Etridge* (2001). Lenders now will require the other party to be made fully aware of the consequences of using their property as security and the effect of signing the loan agreement. These issues should be tackled at an early stage, not left until the filing cabinets are on order and the estate agents are asking for the first month's rent on the office.

The reality is that the house is at risk anyway, simply by virtue of the fact that you are in business. If the business fails, your creditors will attack your assets and the main one is your house. All you are doing by putting the house up as security is to give the bank a head start on the rest.

4

Professional indemnity cover and insurance

The profession decided to go to the open market in September 2000, and so every solicitor is able to obtain professional indemnity (PI) insurance from any insurance company approved by the Law Society. You are therefore free to shop around for the cheapest quote. The premium will depend on the amount of business you are likely to be doing in the first year and the claims record of you, any partners and possibly fee earners working in the firm. In the case of a new practice, i.e. one with no established client base, the gross fees will be little more than a guess. The cover needed for a new practice depends on the type of practice, what work, if any, the sole practitioner or partners bring into the new practice and the level of fees the client base is likely to generate during the first year. From this, the insurer will be able to assess whether the practice can properly be termed a new practice or a successor practice.

Unless you are quite clearly carving out a section of an existing practice with a readily identifiable fee income, you will probably be classified as a new practice. The insurance market has hardened very considerably over the last few years, and the reality is that many insurers are not really interested in the custom of small practices. Nevertheless, there are still some companies who are and you would be best advised to go to a specialist PI broker that can submit your application to those companies who are likely to be receptive to the idea of having your business. It is also essential to create a good impression with a potential insurer, and a broker can help with advice on the presentation of the application itself to show the market that you are level headed, competent and know what you are about.

After the first year the firm has a track record and the fee income generated in that time is a known quantity.

Although the standard minimum level of cover is £2 million, it is very likely that part of any claim will be borne by you, unless you pay an extra premium to reduce or remove the deductible (i.e. the part you pay) or the number of claims you pay in a year. You should bear in mind how excesses and other terms compare when assessing the merits of one company's terms with another if you do manage to get more than one quote.

You may find that after five or six years of running your own practice you get a rather unpleasant shock. You should bear in mind that for PI claims-loading purposes, you remain liable as a principal even after leaving a firm in which you were a principal. Partners are jointly and severally liable for any acts of negligence committed while they were partners, even if they subsequently left the firm. If, therefore, a claim was paid out in 2011, but the act of negligence to which it relates was committed in 2000 and it has taken 11 years to settle, you are a party to that act of negligence if you were a partner in the firm in 1995. You may have no knowledge that a claim was notified; you may never have dealt with the client concerned and, almost certainly, you were not involved in the settling of the claim, unless your former partners chose to involve you. Nevertheless, the PI contribution payable on your new firm was loaded against you for the following five years and your former partners were entitled to look to you for payment of your part of the deductible. If you are in a position to negotiate when you leave your current firm, it is certainly worth trying to secure an indemnity from contributing to any future insurance excess as part of your leaving package.

Premises and contents

You may think that there is not much to insure and perceive this as an overhead that can be avoided. While this may be true in the first few months, it will be a devastating blow if what little equipment has been purchased is either stolen or destroyed by fire. With the cost of even a basic computer or two, the printer, fax machine, precedent library, desks, chairs and so on, you will be into serious money if you have to furnish an office for a second time. Much will depend on the type of premises you have chosen. If you are practising from home, it is as well to check with your insurers that such usage is covered and you may have to pay a small additional premium. At the very least, the level of cover will need to be increased to take account of the purchase of the additional equipment since otherwise you run the risk of having a claim only partially met on the basis of underinsurance. If you fall to the temptation of not bothering to insure in, say, shared premises, do not give way to the temptation for the second year. The expense is a deduction from profits and, once again, the HMRC is making at least a 20 per cent contribution to the premium.

There is also the question of public liability insurance for your clients and your staff. Premiums for an all-inclusive office policy are very reasonable and you should put a policy in place more or less on day one. This is covered in more detail below.

You may be in possession under a lease which requires you to insure the fabric of the building or provides that the landlord does and recovers the premium from you, but this may not include public liability insurance.

Business interruption

There is no requirement to take out business interruption cover. This is a policy which will provide you with a guaranteed minimum income in the event that you are unable to continue to practise due to, for example, a fire. The ordinary building and contents policy will cover you for the cost of putting the premises back into one piece and replacing the equipment, but if during the time it takes to restore the premises you are unable to trade for a period of, say, six months, you are going to be many thousands of pounds out of pocket. Business interruption insurance will cover this eventuality and may also cover such things as the cost of replacing your files by photocopying other people's documents, the cost of temporary accommodation elsewhere, etc. Whether or not you take out this insurance is up to you. It may be available as an add-on to a policy which is essential and may represent good value for money. The risk to the insurers is comparatively small and therefore the premiums are likely to be relatively user-friendly. The benefit to you if you need to rely on it can be enormous.

You will have to take extra care on the question of disclosure. Insurance companies are very mindful of people operating businesses from home without taking out a business policy. If you have a burglary at home and a fax machine and computer are stolen, insurers may try to argue that they are not covered on a domestic policy. So long as you check the terms of the policy you are buying to ensure the cover is wide enough for your needs and make full disclosure, you should not have problems. When choosing a business policy, pay special attention to the section relating to equipment and whether it covers equipment used at home as part of another office base. Tell insurers that you sometimes work from home and so does your partner; confirm that the equipment there is covered on the office policy and, if necessary, pay an additional premium.

Employers' liability

All employers are required by law to provide cover for any injury to staff at work. The Employers' Liability (Compulsory Insurance) Act 1969 requires employers to arrange £5 million of cover in respect of employees sustaining injury arising out of, or in the course of, their employment. While £5 million of cover sounds a lot, this type of cover is generally available for an unlimited amount as part of an employer's general insurance policy (covering loss and damage to equipment, accidental injury to visitors to the premises and the usual kinds of cover an employer would want or must have by law) for around £500 per annum at the time of writing. You are required by law to display a copy of the employees' insurance certificate in a prominent place within your place of business (although since 1 October 2008 you have been allowed to display your certificate electronically). These provisions do not apply where the only employees in the business are husband or wife, father, mother, son, daughter, brother or sister (unless it is a limited company), but you will still need to have cover for visitors, such as clients.

No matter how safe your office, accidents can happen and you are required by the Health and Safety at Work etc. Act 1974 to report anything more than minor accidents to the Health and Safety Executive, which is likely to be located at the local town hall. The executive will institute an investigation depending on the severity of the incident and any injuries sustained. If it discovers that you have no insurance cover, you are very likely to be prosecuted. This is unlikely to impress other staff or clients. As stated earlier, this cover is comparatively cheap and is available as part of a package deal providing for several different types of cover normally associated with running a business.

Ill health

There are three ghosts which perpetually haunt sole practitioners. The first is the prospect that business will dry up and they will have no clients. The second is that they may die leaving a practice with no one at the helm and their partner and children unprovided for. The third is that they may be struck down with a long-term illness. The first ghost is taken care of in this book. The second can be catered for by life policies, and by making a suitable will (dealt with in **Chapter 15**), and the third can be insured against. Once again, whether you take out such a policy is up to you. The insurance is readily available, but it may be fairly expensive and the majority of policies exclude liability for the first two months or so. If you were suffering from a long-term illness and were unlikely ever to recover sufficiently to be able to make a go of the practice, you should possibly be looking to dispose of it rather than trying to stagger on with some form of long-term insurance. Nevertheless, many practitioners may feel happier with such insurance in place knowing that at least the mortgage and general household expenses will be paid up to a certain level if disaster does strike.

Public liability policy

As well as having cover for accidents happening to your employees you will need to consider your responsibilities to visitors, for example, clients who come to your premises. This cover can be obtained as part of the general office package of insurance at minimal cost and you would be foolish not to have it. If your are operating your business from home, you may find such visitors are not covered under your household public liability section if you have not taken out specific business cover. As described earlier, insurers may refuse to pay out if you have a burglary and it is business equipment that has been stolen, such as fax machines, if you have not told them you are running a business from home.

5

Tools of the trade

Computers

When starting a new business many people, and particularly solicitors, rush out and buy a computer. Those with lots of money rush out and buy several computers. Before you do so, stop and think what you are going to use computers for and who in your new firm will be using them. No practice can survive today without making full use of the power of computers, broadband and email. The digital landscape has now become so complex that few practitioners will have sufficient technical skill and knowledge to be able to set up a new practice without the heavy involvement from the start of an IT expert. Find out from recommendations which firms are good and who will be able to give competent advice on what hardware and software will be required, and satisfy yourself that they can supply and install a working system that will operate properly from day one. Get quotes for the costs, including the installation and testing of the systems, and for the cost of support services for the future. Beware of the broadband trap where your Internet service provider takes two weeks to get the broadband operating and you have no access to email during this time. Have a back-up plan in place so that you still have email and Internet access even if the systems in the office are not working. Most people setting up today have probably grown up with computers, but if you are starting out on your own late in life you must make a real effort to grasp the technology. Do not try to convince yourself that you are past it and too old to learn. Professing a lack of knowledge of computers portrays an extremely negative picture of your business, which could do considerable damage. The old excuse of 'I just about know where the on/off switch is' may be a great one-liner at parties, but it will not pay the bills when you have got work to get out and no one to type it. Your staff will bring all their IT problems to you. You cannot keep calling out the IT people for every minor problem. Quite apart from putting up the costs, you will be without the facilities for several hours whilst the technicians get around to attending to your service call.

If you have a notice period to serve because you are leaving a practice through redundancy, your firm may be willing to send you on a training course as part of the redundancy package. A basic course on the use of Microsoft Word, Excel and Outlook will be of great help. How about a touch-typing course? You will probably collect CPD points as well as learning an essential skill. Once you are set up, things will be hectic and this in-between period is the perfect time to acquire or brush up computer skills. There are various ways to do this: ask your local library or further education college for information on local courses. Training can also be found on the Internet, for example, at **www.freeskills.com**.

If you intend operating from an office but want to have a facility for doing some work from home, take care to ensure that the systems you are operating on your home and office computers are compatible.

There is generally no need to invest in especially powerful computers or bespoke software. Computers today are so powerful and relatively inexpensive that off-the-shelf hardware and software is all you are likely to need. Even so, it will probably pay you to bring in a computer consultant to advise you on what equipment to buy and maybe to set it up for you. Both the software and hardware available today are much easier to set up yourself than they were 10 years ago. If you have the time and aptitude then fine, otherwise pay someone to do it for you.

Your approach will be different if there are two or more partners with an existing client base that you know will move with you, rather than if you go solo with only one or two clients. In the former situation it may be worth taking professional advice from a computer consultant rather than just a sales executive in a computer shop. The advice will not be cheap, but if it looks like you are going to need a full-blown networked system within a matter of days, not weeks, of setting up you will get full use out of the system, bearing in mind that you will probably not be changing it for at least three or four years. A service plan with emergency call-out cover might be a good move too. When you consider how much chargeable time you will lose trying to sort it out yourself it makes economic sense to have a computer engineer readily available to get you back up and running. The cost of the advice and the service cover will need to be built into your set-up costs and business plan.

For those people whose initial venture may be rather more modest, the likely solution will be to invest in something fairly cheap with the intention that it will be obsolete in one to two years. You will certainly need a word-processing facility and something to run your accounts on. You can run both systems on one computer, but there may be an advantage to having the accounts on a separate computer – if someone else is putting the accounts information in they will need their own. If you have secretarial help, your secretary will need his or her own computer.

There is no point in investing in anything more substantial at this stage. You are unlikely to need a case management system at this point unless you have a thriving client base that you are sure will move to your new practice. The Law Society has published several editions of its *Software Solutions Guide*, which includes lists of hardware and software suppliers (the 2009 edition is still available at **www.lawsociety.org.uk/ productsandservices/services/usingtechnology.law**). While these suppliers were not approved as such, you have the reassurance of knowing that they have had to reach certain criteria laid down by the Society before being admitted to the list.

So far as accounting systems go, the advice is very much along the same lines. If you are starting out as a two- or three-partner firm there is going to be a great deal of financial information processed immediately and you will need more sophisticated software. You could have a manual system in operation for the first three to six months and to run the two together, but this is likely to be a duplication of effort if used for anything more than a couple of weeks. Reasonably priced accounting software packages specifically geared for sole and small practices are available. A guide to such accounts packages is contained in the *Software Solutions Guide*. The packages featured range from £1,000 to £9,000, copies of which are reproduced at **Appendix 8**.

The system we have used for 18 years is Peapod Solutions' Strongbox system (see Useful contacts). While it has its shortcomings, it is great value for money and simple to use. The cost will vary on the number of users of the system and whether you have any of the legal forms or case management system add-ons, but you should be able to get a basic accounts system and a day's training for around £2,000. For a small interest charge Peapod will allow you to spread the payments over the first 12 months of trading if you are a new practice.

Whatever the size of your practice it is crucial from day one to have a system for backing up data and a disaster recovery plan (DRP), however simple. The DRP may just centre on backing up data and storing crucial computer disks off site, which for most of us means at home. There will be a great deal to organise in the first few months and if you have a computer malfunction or software fault which loses all your financial information, the resultant chaos may be sufficient to make you want to call it a day.

The importance of getting the accounts system right cannot be emphasised too strongly. It is well worth getting an accountant to oversee the design of your systems and their implementation. Get the accountant to carry out or at least oversee your first month's accounts and the reconciliation of client and office accounts. A mini audit after, say, three months, to pick up any mistakes before they become habit or things get out of hand is also a good idea.

Furniture

As with computers, many people will rush out and buy brand new furniture. They will furnish a waiting room with leather upholstered armchairs and sofas and mahogany desks for partners and try to make their premises look as sumptuous as possible to impress clients. Bearing in mind that many clients are far from impressed by such offices and can actually be put off (see **Chapter 2**), this uses up valuable capital resources which may be put to good use elsewhere or held in reserve for later. If six months or a year into the practice you decide to move, you may find that the furniture will not fit in the new premises, that it is out of place or that you need more of it and your particular type of furniture is no longer made and you have to have other furniture alongside it which looks incongruous.

A much better solution is to buy second-hand. Dealers in second-hand furniture advertise in the Thomson Local Directory and Yellow Pages and are not at all difficult to find. You must take the time to go and look at the furniture before you buy and select the pieces yourself, making sure that any faults are simple to remedy, but it is a small price to pay for the considerable savings you will make at a time when your capital resources are limited and your business is vulnerable. If you decide to buy new, go for the 'budget' range rather than anything too fancy.

Library

While the cost of acquiring individual textbooks is not cripplingly high, comprehensive libraries for solicitors are nevertheless surprisingly expensive. As employees or partners in larger firms, a library is something we take for granted. It will no longer be simply a question of walking into the relevant room and finding textbooks and law reports as far as the eye can see. Having set up your new business there will be, sooner or later, a time when you need to look something up and you will find that your usual textbook is not there anymore. When setting up, a library is a substantial expenditure of capital which cannot really be justified. You must, therefore, be highly selective in what you acquire, and this will depend exclusively on what type of practice you have. If you do no divorce work you do not need a book on divorce law.

The best compromise is to purchase a few new books dealing with those areas of law which you will definitely be practising on a day-to-day basis and to make do with second-hand for everything else. The Law Society's *Gazette* runs regular advertisements for individuals or firms wishing to dispose of major works and also professional booksellers who make their living by acquiring entire libraries from practices that are merging. In this way you can generally acquire the current edition of a major work for roughly half the cost of buying it new.

With these items, you will need to be particularly selective. You could spend over £6,000 or £8,000 on a print work such as *Halsbury's Laws of England* or *Atkins Court Forms* and there may be the odd volume or two missing which will have to be replaced. With a looseleaf (or online subscription – see below), there is also the cost of the updating service, which will be a continual drain on time and money. It can be quite demoralising to find each month a brand new release of the *Encyclopaedia of Forms and Precedents* arriving together with an invoice for several hundred pounds and even more demoralising when you have several such volumes arriving for different major works and it dawns on you that the profit costs produced from the last dozen wills you have prepared have been wiped out. Books must pay for themselves. If you purchase a set of books that sits on shelves and does not help you make money, you have made an unwise investment.

The other extreme is also true. There is no point holding up work for the sake of a book. One case on its own may justify you going out and buying the latest work on that subject.

In the early days you would do well to do without the major works and wait until your practice is such that you can justify in costs terms the substantial capital outlay and the constant drain of the cost of updated volumes.

It was because of these difficult choices that I produced the Law Society's *Precedent Library for the General Practitioner*, which attempts to bring the most useful and commonly used precedents and forms from a wide range of areas of practice into one book and CD at a price within the reach of even the most cash-strapped embryonic practices.

Designing your library

You must also have somewhere to put books. They take up a surprising amount of space and they are somewhat less than impressive if they are just lying in a pile on the floor. They will have to be properly shelved or put in proper bookcases, all of which will add substantially to the cost of providing the library. Before you lay out the money on acquiring 20 or 30 volumes of a work, think first where you are going to put them, and how easy it will be for you and other people, possibly not yet recruited, to have access to them without disturbing other people. Be sure to build the cost of displaying them suitably into your calculations.

Online resources

The works mentioned above are also available as online subscription services, enabling you to search consolidated and prospective legislation, law reports, journals and so on. While they can be just as expensive as the print services, they are more easily searchable, there is no need to collate updates and you can customise your subscription according to your area of practice. At the same time, there is an increasing range of free, up-to-date online material and news available (see under Forms at the end of this chapter). A list of useful links can be found on the Solicitor Sole Practitioners Group website (**www.spg.uk.com/links**).

Staff

Employing your spouse or relatives

As a sole practitioner without a client base you know you can count on, the requirements in terms of staff are going to be very limited. You may be extremely fortunate, as I was, in having the ideal member of staff in the form of your spouse.

Many people have commented that having your spouse working in the business can be a dangerous course of action. While there are clearly dangers of tensions from work being brought home, and family squabbles ventilated in the office, the arrangement of having one's own spouse either as a principal or in some other capacity can generally work well. Your spouse or close relative may also be an ideal bookkeeper. If they are not trained they may be prepared to acquire the necessary skills by going on courses.

First, there is the motivation that the venture must succeed if the family finances are not to end in ruin. Second, people get married because they share common aims and dreams, and in setting up a new practice you are likely to be able to count on each other for 100 per cent support in achieving those dreams. Third, your spouse may be prepared to work above and beyond the call of normal duty. Very few members of staff are prepared to work late in the evening in order to get some essential piece of work out of the way while sharing domestic burdens.

Fourth, your spouse will also have his or her own tax allowance which can be used up against income received by the practice.

The other side of the coin is that if your spouse keeps their own job you avoid putting all your eggs in one basket and are thus assured of at least one income coming in each month. It does also mean that to a large extent you are more exposed. If your spouse becomes ill, or if the relationship breaks down, you will have lost your secretary, bookkeeper and partner in one fell swoop.

Whether you both work in the practice or not, if you have children, school holidays tend to become something of a nightmare. They can be counteracted to a large extent by duplicating the office facilities at home so that work can continue while the children are creating mayhem in the rest of the house. However, it means there is one less person to answer the telephone in the office and do a lot of the running around; there is always something of a sigh of relief once the holidays are over.

Employing the kids

Once the practice is established and your children are in their teens, you can provide them with the perfect holiday job. You can pay them up to their personal tax allowance level so that they have a well-paid job in the holidays and their wages add to your wage bill and reduce your level of taxable profit. The children thus pay for their own clothes, travel and so on and if at university can pay their own accommodation fees. As long as they genuinely work in the business and do a proper working day, not just a couple of hours here and there, this is a perfectly legitimate way to save tax and to give your clients a better service. The children will gain valuable work experience and social skills and will enjoy playing their part in the family business. Their computer skills and natural ability on the telephone may surprise you!

Part-time help

You may find that within about six months of trading there is a sufficient profit pattern emerging for you to recruit a part-time secretary. There are many able people who, for one reason or another, do not wish to take on a full-time responsibility but are quite happy to work four or five mornings a week. It may be a good idea to give preference to those people who live locally. If an emergency crops up and you need them in a hurry, you can always see if they can spare you a few extra hours and they are unaffected by bad weather and train strikes. They are also likely to work for less money than those applicants who spend an appreciable part of their wages on travelling.

Sharing staff

If you have been able to find a corner in someone else's offices under the office space-sharing scheme described in **Chapter 2**, you may have been able to negotiate, as part of the package deal, a sharing arrangement for certain members of staff. In the early days, the value of this facility cannot be overstated. If the staff concerned are co-operative and do not feel that they are being put upon, it means that you have the full-time service of a receptionist and/or telephonist and/or typist with none of the responsibility or full cost. If the arrangement is put to them in the right way, things can work very well. For many people, there is a certain fascination in watching a business grow from absolutely nothing and they take some satisfaction from having given it a gentle shove in the right direction. Believe it or not, there are still many people who will do things without expecting any more reward than your grateful thanks and reasonably frequent expressions of gratitude and perhaps a thoughtful gift at Christmas. Show them that you appreciate what they do and what a help they are and they will do much to assist you.

Expanding

As business increases, the helping hands of such treasures may soon prove insufficient. The time may quickly come when you need to arrange to have your own separate receptionist and telephonist. Do not leave this too late so that a problem arises between your office-sharing 'landlords', their staff and you. If you do, the facility is likely to be withdrawn, and possibly your licence to occupy the premises along with it. If you do not let the problem arise, if business later subsides and you decide to reduce your staffing levels to correspond with the downturn, you will probably find that the same people who helped you before will help you again.

Recruiting – factors to consider

Taking on staff is one of the biggest decisions that you will make. Wages are the single biggest overhead of any solicitor's practice. It is vital that you obtain value for money. You cannot afford to have passengers. It is even more critical in a small business to ensure that you have no more staff than you absolutely need (always allowing a little flexibility to cope with sudden influxes of work and expansion) and to recruit the right people – those who will be a credit to your business and who will work hard. Always obtain references and take them up, but in the final analysis trust your own judgement on whether the individual will fit in. They may not have a particularly good reference from their last employer, but this need not be the critical factor in deciding whether to take them on or not.

Their academic record is likely to be important, but people with straight As and good degrees are not necessarily going to be the best people for your practice. You must imagine that you are a client and they are dealing with you as a fee earner. What sort of impression do they make on you? Would you have confidence in them in dealing with your case? The fact that they can remember huge amounts of information and regurgitate it later is not nearly as impressive as the ability to win a client's trust and confidence, and to reassure the client that they will put everything they can into a case and that they care about the result. Contracts of employment are dealt with in **Chapter 16**, but when you decide to take someone on do not forget to write to them immediately confirming their appointment and when they are to start, enclosing a summary of their job description and conditions of employment. If you fail to do so, the employee may think you have changed your mind and not turn up on the agreed date. Even if they do, you may, by that stage, have forgotten quite what the terms were that you offered them.

Telephone systems

No business today can even begin to trade without having a telephone system in place. You will find it very difficult to operate successfully from home with just one or two lines. It is true that if you have many more you will have lines ringing and no one to answer them, but if you decide to trade from home, to a large extent you are cutting yourself off from expansion. There will be something of a vicious circle. People will become frustrated if the telephone is not answered or if they get the engaged tone. This means fewer clients. If you have fewer clients, you are not expanding and so you confirm yourself in your decision to restrict yourself by operating from home. If you are going to have three or four lines, you will need three or four people to answer the calls. Unless you have an exceptionally large house, you will rapidly need office space.

If you accept the above principles, the telephone system you will require will probably have at least three lines. You may also choose to have an additional private line purely for your own outgoing calls. This applies equally to two- and three-partner firms. If you do have a private line for outgoing calls, remember to ask your service provider to withhold the number so that it is not automatically recognised by the recipient, otherwise the line will be ringing continually when you are trying to have a meeting with a client and you will be unable to filter out calls.

If you go for a main system which can accept at least five incoming lines and possibly as many as 10, you can start, in the case of a sole practitioner, with say three lines on which you can make both incoming and outgoing calls with a skipping system, so that if one of the lines is engaged an incoming call will automatically skip to a line that is free. As the business expands, you can then add additional lines and extensions to the system. Both BT and other major suppliers such as Merlyn or Mercury have excellent systems, so you are now rather spoilt for choice. The simplest approach is to contact their sales representatives for a demonstration of their equipment and you can decide which system is most likely to suit your needs.

Make sure that any agreement you sign does not tie you to the equipment for an inordinate length of time. The shorter the period, the better. It is also probably better in the early days to rent the equipment than to buy it, since you can then take advantage of improved products as well as spread the cost. Most agreements impose no penalty provided you stay with the same company if you are upgrading the equipment. Read the contracts carefully to see what happens if you terminate before the agreement expires or wish to reduce the size of the equipment. Look carefully at the terms of any maintenance contract, which is normally obligatory. Check to see whether you can buy the system outright at some point and what the cost will be. If there is no clause allowing you to do so, try to negotiate such a deal. Keep a close eye on things and after about a year investigate the cost of buying the system outright or of buying a similar system if your existing supplier will not sell it to you. If you have the cash available and are sure the system offered to you is the right one, you could buy a second-hand switchboard at the start, but you should be thinking of retaining it for at least four years for the investment to be worthwhile.

Installing lines

You have rather less choice when it comes to telephone lines and, although BT's monopoly in many areas has ended, there is still very little choice when it comes to the allocation of lines, unless cable companies operate in your area. It is important to ensure that an early approach is made to the area sales department, which will discuss your requirements in detail. You should have a clear idea of how many lines you will need, the number of extensions and the system's eventual capacity in terms of maximum number of extensions before you make contact. Do not forget to allow for expansion, or the separate lines for your private line, fax machine and Internet connection. It is important to ensure that the lines are allocated as far in advance as possible. It is better to have the lines available a month before the business opens than to find that, for whatever reason, you have been let down and you are somehow expected to run a business with no telephones. There are telephone companies who will advise on the type of systems available and will install everything for you, but bear in mind they will have a vested interest in selling you an all-singing, all-dancing system rather than a basic set up which might do perfectly well.

Fax machines

Fax machines were once described by my local district judge as being an instrument of the devil. Faxes are not such a vital tool as they were before email came along and with it the ability to send documents as attachments, but they still have a part to play, especially when the Internet connection goes down. It is not worth buying a cheap or second-hand fax machine. You should either have a dedicated fax line or share it with the broadband connection.

There are many fax machines on the market, offering all kinds of gadgets – they may store messages and only transmit them at off-peak times, remember millions of regularly dialled numbers, store messages even when paper has run out, and so on. Most of these gimmicks are never used in a small practice. Fax machines often come with other facilities so they can double as a copier, a scanner and a printer. It is better to buy a good basic machine that does a good job as a fax even if it does not have the other facilities on it, but the multifunction machines have improved considerably over time. I would start with a multifunction model and expect to replace or supplement it within six months if all goes well and the volume of business demands something with a bit more muscle. Then is the time to look at a higher volume copier with a service plan whilst using the multifunction one for making colour copies when required.

It is not really practical to delay installing a fax since, if you follow my advice and have a dedicated line or one shared with the broadband, you will need to put the fax number on your notepaper. It is best to have all the telephone and fax work carried out at the same time and all the equipment in place before you start trading rather than to try to install the fax after you have been practising for a few months.

Voicemail

You should try to avoid relying on voicemail for the first three months. There is no way around the hard slog of the first year or two and in the first three months, if not a good deal longer, you are going to be working long hours. A combination of your continued presence in the office and a relatively small client base, unless you are setting up with a ready-made one, means you should be able to take most calls yourself. If you have at least one other person who can take messages for you, this should be enough for you to be able to cope with all your calls. If you switch all extra calls over to voicemail people will get the impression you are not available and will go for someone else who is at the end of a telephone more often than you are. Most telephone systems come with a voicemail facility as standard. Once the work has built up you can start to take advantage of it. By then your clients should be confident that they can rely upon you to return calls promptly if they do not reach you at the first attempt.

Email and website

As described earlier, email is essential from day one. Potential clients will look upon a business that is not using email as being something out of the dark ages. Despite the potential for misuse, I would suggest having full email and Internet facilities for everyone from the start. There is a risk of people opening up files with potentially damaging viruses and that your staff look busy when they are actually sending messages to their friends, but it is such a part of everyday commercial life that it has to be a risk worth taking.

Make sure that you have proper security measures in place. The web is seething with phishing emails, where fraudsters send you apparently genuine emails from respectable organisations to try to get you to disclose your personal data to them. This can be passwords, bank details, PINs and so on. Never click on a web link in such circumstances. Go directly to the organisation's website and check there whether your account has been suspended as the email might claim, or go into your local bank branch if the emails says that you need to re-register with them and ask the bank if it really do wants you to do so. Keep passwords secret at all times and change them regularly. Choose passwords containing asterisks or similar or numbers in the middle of words.

Your own website is now an absolute necessity from the first day. Most clients expect you to have a website, as do potential employees. There will be many clients and good quality job applicants who will take a look at the firm on the web before contacting the firm or responding to an advertisement and the website will create the wrong impression if is poorly constructed or not there at all. This is gone into in more detail in **Chapter 6**.

Document exchange

From the outset you should put yourself on the document exchange (DX) system. There are still some solicitors who are not on it and many people setting up feel that it is an expense that they can do without for the first year or so. In my view it is simply not worth trying to make the saving. Most other solicitors are now on it, as are many banks, building societies and so on, and it is extremely reliable.

Notepaper

Your image is important. Two- and three-partner firms may want to have their notepaper designed by graphic designers. As well as layout and design, you may want them to come up with something to make your firm stand out from the rest, such as a logo. The charge involved is not inconsequential. If spread between two or three partners it is bearable, but a sole practitioner is likely to shy away from what is perceived to be an unnecessary set-up cost. That is fine, providing you are going to have a reasonable product. Notepaper is the solicitor's shop window. If the notepaper looks of poor quality and amateurish, it will reflect very badly on the solicitor's practice. I recently saw a newly founded sole practitioner's notepaper which he had designed on his computer and had produced on a laser printer. The quality of the paper itself and the appearance of the notepaper were pretty poor. He offered the opinion that anyone who had a computer with a laser printer and was still paying out money to have letterheads printed 'was a mug'. I made no comment, but I did feel what a pity it was that with only a very small investment he could have substantially improved on the image that his practice projected to his clients and the public at large.

There is no doubt that a good quality product can be produced from laser printers and you may wish to experiment if you have access to one. They are certainly not bad for producing mock-ups and trying out different ideas. However, once you have decided on what the notepaper will look like and you are ready to produce the finished product, it is far better to ask a printer to do it. Ultimately, you may decide that with a few adjustments you can do just as good a job as the printer and, once your stock of professionally printed notepaper has run out, you can always produce your own.

Do shop around and haggle, but make sure you show a specimen of what you have already and ensure that it is clearly recorded in correspondence that any quotation must be for letterheads that are of at least as good quality as the sample provided. Other printers may be able to produce cheaper notepaper, but if the overall appearance is not as good, you want to be in a position to walk away from the order on the grounds that they have not fulfilled their part of the contract.

The set-up costs for professionally printed stationery are quite high initially and the printer will then encourage you to order in large quantities since it brings down the price dramatically. By and large you should resist such offers, particularly if you are a sole practitioner. Larger practices will obviously use more paper, but a sole practitioner may take two years to get through what would be a normal print run for a two- or three-partner firm and in that time you may have moved premises, taken on additional staff and would like to put them on the notepaper, merged or changed telephone numbers, etc. Also, by keeping large stocks of notepaper, you take up valuable storage space and tie up cash. Do not forget to order a few business cards and compliments slips at the same time, but beware of ordering in too large quantities.

Setting up a precedent library

When you left your last place of work and decided to set up on your own, you probably took with you, in so far as you were able, every kind of precedent you could lay your hands on. These might include drafts of pleadings settled by counsel, specimens that appeared in the Law Society's *Gazette*, precedents photocopied from standard but expensive precedent books or a pleading served on you by someone else that you thought looked particularly good. You must always bear in mind the question of copyright. It is not a bad idea to check with counsel that they do not mind you adopting their pleading as a basis for others in the future. With a bit of flattery in the right place as to what an excellent pleading it was, they probably will not mind. Precedents taken out of precedent books that you have not bought yourself may need a little more care. You do not want to start your practice on the wrong end of a copyright action.

Every practice needs to have a precedent library of some sort. This will take two forms: precedents stored on a word processor and precedents contained in textbooks. You may feel that before actually starting work you should rush out and buy masses of material compiled on a disk by other people, so that you can be all set to go on the first day. This is both unnecessary and a waste of time and money. You will probably fill up your entire hard drive with things that you will never use. There is no harm in including a few items, such as a standard precedent for a will, a fairly common form of consent order in a divorce matter and so on, which you are fairly certain you will be using on a regular basis. Other than that it is much better to wait for the occasion when you use a particular Word document, and then you may decide to keep it as a future precedent on your computer. By buying a book containing precedents which cover a specialist area in which you practise, you will obtain the benefit of a ready-made precedent and also help and advice from the author on how and when to use it. Having saved that onto a disk, you will hopefully be paid for that particular job and have the precedent ready and waiting for a similar one in the future. If time goes by and the work is not repeated, you can always delete it. You have still been paid for putting it on there in the first place. By creating a precedent library on your computer's hard drive (or backed up on disk) and then periodically trawling through it to remove those items which you have not actually used again, you will acquire your own database of precedents in an economic and cost-effective way. Other information is much more neatly stored away on a bookshelf and is just as easily accessed as if it were on computer. You may wish to consider indexing your precedents alphabetically. All too quickly you may acquire so many precedents that it takes an age to find the one you want unless you have a paper or an electronic index.

As mentioned earlier, I wrote the Law Society publication *Precedent Library for the General Practitioner* precisely because of the difficulties faced by small practices in the early years when it comes to deciding what books to get when the budget is limited.

Forms

A great many of the forms in everyday use are available free of charge from various websites. The Land Registry (**www.landregistry.gov.uk**) has an extensive collection of forms, and they can be completed on screen and printed off. Likewise, the Courts and Tribunals Service page of the Ministry of Justice website (**www.justice.gov.uk/about/hmcts**) has a substantial catalogue covering several areas of litigation. In addition, Office of Public Guardianship (**www.justice.gov.uk/about/opg**) has all forms necessary for drafting and registering lasting powers of attorney. The Court Service and Justice websites are now interlinked and access to one provides access to both.

Despite this free competition there are still several commercial organisations that will sell you access to their even more comprehensive catalogues either for certain defined areas of work or for wider selections if you want to cover the whole spectrum, but access is not cheap. Similarly, there are several companies that will sell access to sophisticated banks of commercial precedents. As a cheaper alternative you might like to consider my own *Precedent Library*, published by Law Society

Publishing, which provides bespoke precedents as well as links to the publicly available forms on the government websites referred to above and guidance on how to fill in the more involved forms.

Do not be afraid to approach another firm if you need a form in a hurry. If you constantly run out of forms and are always begging them from other people, you may outstay your welcome, but if you enlist other people's help once in a while they will not feel bashful about asking you. Co-operation between fellow professionals is always a good thing and such small beginnings can lead to other things.

6

Advertising

Advertising may be defined as telling people who you are, where you are and what you do. Marketing is persuading them to buy what you are selling once you have told them who you are, where you are and what you sell. You may feel that when you are first setting up there is no point in devising a marketing or advertising strategy, that there is not enough time and that you do not have the financial resources. You are wrong on both counts.

The business of a solicitor is the selling of legal services. To get customers you have to let them know who you are, where you are, what you can do for them and why they should choose you rather than anyone else. If you are able to get the first three across, there is a reasonable chance that they will choose to work with you – at least you are in the running. Even if you are taking with you an existing client base, you will be foolish to rely on that alone because you need a steady stream of clients through the door. Even your established clients will not want to use your services for all their legal requirements. There will be gaps that must be filled.

Where to advertise

Print directories

Where you advertise will depend on who it is you want to reach. For the average, general high street practice, you should consider advertising in the Yellow Pages and Thomson's Local Directory (their online equivalents are at **www.yell.com** and **www.thomsonlocal.com** – see below). The Yellow Pages runs an excellent banner advertising scheme on behalf of the Law Society whereby local solicitors can have their name put in a general advertisement and have a display advertisement for little more than the price of a lineage advertisement. This has been expanded in recent years to offer several different types of banner advertisements, and you may have to choose between a general type of advertisement and a more specialist one (call 0800 371755 for details). Thomson's Local Directories do not run a similar type of advertisement, but since the areas covered by the individual directories are smaller, the same sized advertisement tends to be cheaper.

Local newspapers are another option, but you have to bear in mind that nobody reads last week's news and a local paper will last, at best, for one week. To have any real effect, an advertising campaign in a local paper must be spread over several weeks. You should compare the cost of doing that and the number of people you are likely to reach with what it will cost to advertise in the Yellow Pages or Thomson's – an advertisement that runs for a year. You must also place yourself in the position of someone looking for a solicitor and consider where you are likely to look. In the main, people are likely to look in a dedicated directory rather than a local newspaper; if they see your details in a local newspaper it is likely to be more by accident than the result of a deliberate search for a solicitor there.

Once you have set up and your advertising is having an effect, you are likely to be contacted by all sorts of other businesses suggesting that you place an advertisement with them. Consider each one carefully. My experience is that, in the main, most other forms of advertising do not work. Local authorities will suggest that you have your name in a box on their calendar. Counselling services will sometimes send bereaved relatives brochures and will offer to sell you space in them so that you can assist with the administration of an estate for the people they reach. Again, my experience is that people do not respond to such advertisements.

If your practice is a two- or three-partner firm, your approach may be slightly different. You may have specialist skills within the practice and want to advertise to a particular section of the public, either as well as or instead of a general advertisement. The basic rules are still the same. Who are these people and where are they likely to look if they want to find a solicitor? Will it be a specialist trade publication and if so, which one? How many other people are advertising in that trade publication? How many clients will you need to persuade not only to respond to the advertisement but also to instruct you as their solicitor before the whole thing becomes cost-effective?

Do not leap forth with an entire advertising campaign before putting your toe in the water. Place a few advertisements in a fairly modest way to see what sort of response they bring. If you are deluged with enquiries then you know you have found the right place to advertise, but if there is a deafening silence then it is unlikely that you will substantially improve on the response simply by increasing the size of the advertisement and the frequency with which it appears. On the whole, it is better to be cautious with your advertising rather than flamboyant. This is not to say that you can place a few bits of lineage in a local newspaper and expect the clients to roll in. The size of the advertisement must be sufficient to be eye catching. There is no point in a tiny advertisement tucked away in a directory surrounded by other people's massive advertisements. It would be better not to advertise there at all.

The timing of an advertisement is likely to be crucial. Directories such as the Yellow Pages and Thomson's have fixed copy deadlines and if you miss the deadline for submission of your advertising copy in an annual publication then you may not be able to promote your firm through this medium for another 15 months. You will either have to do without any advertising, find a less favourable publication whose copy date you can make or content yourself with periodic forays into local newspapers. Always remember that advertisements may not work for all sorts of reasons. It may be that you have put the advertisement in the wrong medium, that the advertisement itself is not eye catching, or gives the wrong information or creates the wrong impression, or that the timing of the advertisement is wrong.

Electronic advertising

A web presence is now a necessity. You will need a website as a matter of urgency. Advertisements on sites such as **www.yell.com** generally bring a good response. You can also pay to raise your profile with web search engines such as Google so that if someone searches under 'solicitors in Barchester' your firm will come up as the first entry more often than not. This does not guarantee response, but at least you are then in the mind of your target market. All firms cannot be top of the list all of the time and such enhancing tools are rather expensive, particularly as you pay something every time someone just clicks on your entry. There are specialist agencies that can help you in this area if you wish to pursue it.

Designing your advertisement

Any advertisement must leap off the page (or the computer screen!) to someone who is looking for a solicitor. Put yourself in the shoes of a prospective client. Look at the other advertisements in the particular medium you are considering to see which advertisements you find attractive and ask yourself why. Is it their size, the nature of the services offered, the price or the general impression and friendliness created by the advertisement? What is likely to be attractive to you will probably attract other people. You can go to an advertising agency, but if you are a small practice the fees are likely to be prohibitive. For the time being, you will probably have to be your own advertising executive. Do a mock-up of the advertisement that you propose to put forward and show it to your friends. Ask them what they think of it and what impression is created of your practice by the advertisement. Ask them where they would look if they were trying to find a solicitor cold rather than use a recommended one.

The advertisement itself is crucial. Having made your advertisement sufficiently eye catching that it might encourage prospective clients to take the trouble to look at it, you will have around one or two seconds to sustain that interest before they become bored and start to read someone else's. The message should therefore be interesting, short and to the point.

There is an old saying in advertising that you should never sell the product – you should sell the idea behind the product. If you accept this maxim, you do not simply put in your advertisement, 'We do conveyancing'. The customer does not want to buy a conveyance; what they want is to buy the services of someone who will take the burden and worry of the house-moving process off their shoulders. Accordingly, your advertisement will be more along the lines of, 'We take the pain out of conveyancing'. This is what the customer is looking for. You have hit the right note and they are now prepared to read on. Your references to experience, fast, reliable service and written quotations available the same day will all serve to reassure the customer that you are the firm they are looking for.

If, in your opinion, you feel that the client is not terribly interested in claims to reliability and speed but only in price and will simply go for the lowest quote, you may prefer to centre your entire message on price. In that case, your advertisement is likely to put the price per conveyance (if that is the way you operate your firm) as the most prominent feature. If you opt for this idea, you must be sure that your potential customers are concerned solely with price and not with quality of service – you can be sure that your competitors will be explaining away your very low price on the basis of the low-grade service you will be providing for the low fee charged. Whether the work goes to you or to them is all part of the fun.

Personally, I have never sought to advertise myself as the cheapest firm in town and I would rather be thought of as someone who provides a good standard of work for a sensible fee. In the days of cut-price conveyancing and price wars this may be something of a luxury. If the large retailers decide to enter the fray it is very likely that they will try to take over the market by virtue of price. Most practices will struggle to compete on price and would be best advised to emphasise the quality and reliability of the service they offer compared with the impersonal conveyor belt service of the large retailers for what after all is likely to be a very significant event in their life. Will this approach be enough to see off the big boys? Time alone will tell.

Once the phone has started ringing, with people asking how they enlist your services, there is one crucial question you must ask them: 'How did you get my details?' Introduced at a suitable juncture in the conversation (not too early as it may sound rather unfriendly, and clients want to talk first about their problems before they talk about anything else), it provides key information as to which advertisements are working and which are not.

The answer may be that they have found you in a publication or that they have been recommended by someone else. In the case of a recommendation, it is important to telephone or write to the person making the recommendation and thank them for it. Not only is it good manners but it also makes that person feel that their contribution towards your business is appreciated and not taken for granted, which hopefully will lead to further recommendations. There is no need to send them a gratuity (words of thanks are usually enough) and gratuities can lead to slippery slopes (such as offending against Chapter 9 of the SRA Code of Conduct 2011). However, there may be occasions where people have gone to inordinate lengths to secure the work for you and, in those exceptional circumstances, a modest donation to their drinks collection may not be out of place. Anything more and you may need to examine the Chapter 9 outcomes more carefully.

Where the client has found you as a result of an advertisement, you should make a note of the advertisement. It is also important that your staff make a note of it if they take the call. It is important to know where every single client has come from.

Write down the sources of your business and count them up at the end of the week/month/year. Once you have moved on to, or possibly started with, two or more partners, you undoubtedly will have to write down and collate the information somewhere centrally at the end of the month so that you can get a precise picture of the cost-effectiveness of your advertising. You can start to analyse precisely where your recommendations are coming from, and possibly why, and work out whether further efforts in a particular area will bring yet greater rewards.

Responses

You have placed your advertisement, the prospective client has telephoned you and has started asking questions about the practice, your prices and your experience and may have started telling you some of the problems that they face. So far, so good. You still have not converted the telephone enquiry into a real, live client. All you have is an opportunity to do so and you should not let that slip away. You have paid a lot of money to get this far and that money will be wasted if the client puts down the phone and chooses another firm. Inevitably, you will convert a comparatively small number of your responses, so do not get too despondent if you have a few days or even weeks where none of the people you have spoken to on the telephone actually make an appointment and give you the business. It is, however, an opportunity to review the position generally and to ask yourself if there is something you are doing wrong.

A certain impression will have been created by your advertisement itself. This is something over which you have a good deal of control. As discussed previously, you should consider what sort of image you wish to project for the firm and this image should be contained within your advertisement. What are clients looking for? How can you project this, both in your advertisement and from the moment the telephone rings? Having obtained a certain mental picture of what the firm is going to be like, the client's next contact with the firm is with the person who answers the telephone. You may have a dedicated telephonist chosen for his or her pleasant, friendly and helpful manner, or whom you will have trained to answer the telephone in this manner. If you have a group pickup system so that the telephone can be answered by anyone in the office, it is important to listen to how people are answering the telephone and dealing with clients. There should be a standard response so that the opening words are the same, which is likely to sound more professional than a whole variety of openings. Imagine yourself on the other end of the telephone when you hear a member of staff answering the call and ask yourself how you would react if spoken to in that way.

Telephones must be answered quickly. If a telephone is allowed to ring for any more than three or four rings, it tells the client that the firm is not run particularly efficiently – you have already begun to lose the image battle. Never allow clients, or anyone else for that matter, to be put on hold for more than 15 or 20 seconds. It is far better to explain that the person they wish to talk to is likely to be some time and take their number so that they can be called back. If a caller must be put on hold, they must be reassured that they have not been forgotten and that Mr Bloggs has almost finished and should be off his present call in just a moment. Leaving people on hold also puts you under pressure and clogs up the phone lines.

Winning the client

A caller has now been put through to you. You have about 30 seconds in which the client will decide whether they like you or not, and whether you sound the kind of solicitor with whom they would like to do business. What you say in that time is vital. Again, you must analyse what this particular client is looking for and then match your response to fulfil the need. If the client is looking for a sympathetic ear, no amount of your telling the client how efficient and reliable the firm is will be of the slightest use – they want someone to sit there with their mouth shut so that they can pour their heart out. That is not to say that you must sit there endlessly allowing the client to tell you their entire life story only to find that at the end of a free half hour call the client tells you that you are far too expensive when you get down to the sordid business of hourly rates.

Similarly, the potential client may simply be trying to get free advice, or they may have a serious problem which needs attention. By commenting on specific areas of the problem that they have outlined, you may be able to demonstrate that you have the right legal knowledge and the confidence to deal with their matter without actually getting too involved. The one thing you should be aiming for is to arrange for the client to come into your office at the earliest possible opportunity. It may be prudent to find out at a fairly early stage in the conversation whether the client is likely to be eligible for

Legal Help or will have to pay for the advice. If you have not had to deal with such calls yourself previously and have simply been fed a steady stream of clients, this process may be rather difficult for you, but you will fairly quickly be able to recognise what parts of your conversation put clients off and what elements of it they find attractive. There is no point having a client who is clearly ineligible for legal aid but who feels that your hourly rate is far too high – such clients are likely to be nothing but trouble any-way. Nor is there much point in a long discussion with someone who clearly cannot proceed without legal aid when you do not have a franchise. Nevertheless, there are abrasive ways in which one can put the question of fees (such as, 'Well, I am sorry, but that's my hourly rate. If I don't charge that I go out of business') and more diplomatic ways ('I can appreciate that it may sound a lot, but there is a certain minimum level at which we have to charge in order to make the figures add up. Perhaps we could get together for half an hour and see how far we get with that. Would that help?').

The free interview

You may feel that it would be worthwhile offering clients a free 10–15-minute interview, either as a general policy, possibly advertised, or just in suitable cases where it looks as though the client may not be eligible for legal aid but is unable or unwilling to pay for the advice. If you get the client into the office then in that 10–15-minute period it may become clear that the cost of the legal services may not be quite as prohibitive as first thought or perhaps a conditional fee agreement or insurance might be the answer. At worst, you have lost 10 or 15 minutes of your time, but you have ceased to be a name in an advertisement. The client may have future problems and turn to you for help; by that time funds may be avail-able to pay you privately, or the client might recommend a friend who has lucrative work. Even with clients of modest means there may still be a way forward. You could offer to draft a claim form and get it issued for an agreed fee and the client deals with the rest of the claim themselves as a litigant in person.

Other professionals

Other professionals such as accountants and surveyors are an excellent source of new business. They are people who usually are trusted by their clients and if clients are pointed by a trusted source in your direction they are likely to place their business with you much more readily than some-one shopping around. Before such professionals refer business to you they will need to be convinced that they can do so with confidence. They would hate nothing more than to be the instrument of placing a valuable client in the hands of someone who goes on to make a mess of the client's affairs. 'Fine solicitor that friend of yours turned out to be!' is every professional's nightmare when considering to whom they should refer a valued client. Most professionals will already have their own contacts to whom they refer such work, so you will have to demonstrate that you have something else to offer. Your fees may be more competitive, you may appear to be more switched on and more up to date than the usual lawyer to whom they send such clients or you may simply just be nicer or more approachable.

Where do you start? You may have some work that you can refer yourself. People often want a survey carried out or need an accountant and do not know of one, but the same considerations apply in reverse. If you do not know an accountant already whom you trust yourself, you may need to ask friends and maybe get to meet anyone they recommend. It is generally a mistake to try to formalise an arrangement by just hinting that you are referring someone to them with a view to them returning the favour, but there is no harm in making it apparent that you are eager for new business at an appropriate moment. You might suggest meeting for lunch to discuss ways in which you can help each other.

Your website

We live in the electronic age and every professional firm is expected to have a website. It is your showcase to the world at large and it must give a positive image to anyone who sees it. Your IT adviser can give you details of companies that offer a scheme by which you can design quite a professional looking website by using templates which you then adapt to your own business and write your own copy, all done over the Web, before the site then goes live. Alternatively, you can have a company design it for you, although this will be more expensive

Bear in mind that in the main a website is a glorified advert and the same principles apply as for any other form of advertisement. You would probably be best to employ a specialist company to design it for you. The cost is likely to be £2,000 or £3,000, but to do it yourself is time-consuming and technically difficult. Plan your website carefully, and ensure that the web design company follows your instructions on content. Pretty pictures and the history of the firm are nice, but the primary purpose is to sell the firm and explain what you can do for the customer.

If you decide to produce your website yourself, your IT adviser may be able to help you put together something that looks reasonably professional with the use of various templates. These have a series of pro forma wordings and formats that you can take as your starting point and adapt to your style and your market. The quality of the artwork and design will be far better than anything you could hope to achieve yourself, but it will still be a good deal less expensive than asking a website building company to build you a bespoke site. It will do for a couple of years before you can afford the time and cash to have something grander. When that time arrives do not select a website builder out of Yellow Pages or a similar directory. As with all types of services, get a recommendation from someone or choose a site that impresses you and ask them who designed it.

CHECKLIST

- Work out marketing and advertising plan.
- Set the budget.
- Decide on the type of media to be used.
- Contact media for copy deadlines and prices.
- Design adverts.
- Place in chosen media.
- Check advert has appeared correctly.
- Monitor response.
- Review the chosen media and the content periodically and adjust if necessary.

7

Putting in systems

In this chapter we will look at how to set up the essential systems to help your practice run smoothly: computers, filing, storage, accounts and reporting systems, and back-up and recovery systems.

Computers

The type of practice you were in previously, and what you did in it, will undoubtedly have determined the extent of your knowledge of computers, systems and software. This section is intended for those whose exposure to those areas has been less than they feel is required to supervise the operation of their own office system. If this does not apply to you, please skip ahead to the next section.

As discussed in **Chapter 5**, computers are not the answer to everything: they are a tool of the trade, nothing more. There is still a case for some records to be kept manually. A manual system can be instantly accessible: you simply get the notebook out of your desk and look up the relevant page.

Where computers score over manual systems is in their ability to handle very large amounts of information and to retrieve that information at amazing speed and with incredible accuracy. They are therefore absolutely vital for any practice, however small, and it will be only exceptionally today that anyone will want to start a new legal practice without having a computer system in place from the start. You will find it very difficult to manage to do everything manually unless the practice is going to be very small and likely to remain that way.

The power of computers in respect of both speed and memory has increased dramatically over recent years and shows no sign of abating. The problems of storage and capacity to run complex programs have largely gone as a result. Speed and capacity are now no longer major issues as even modestly priced computers will be able to handle the everyday demands of a medium-sized office.

It will be no use just installing several computers and expecting you and everyone else involved in the practice to work things out as you go along. You will need to analyse exactly what the day-to-day problems are and then apply your mind, or possibly that of a computer consultant, to the question of how a computer may be able to help you. By approaching it this way, you are much more likely to invest in a computer system that will suit your practice rather than ending up with a white elephant. The trick is to have the problems first and then adapt the computer and its software to solve the problems rather than to get the computer and the software and then think what problems you can put it to work to solve. You will also need to think one stage ahead. Look at your business plan and see where you are likely to be in about three years' time and then take a conscious decision that you will either get rid of your computer at that stage and buy a completely different one, or a different system, or buy the kind of computer system now that can be expanded to meet your future needs as and when they arise.

Types of computer system

Computers fall largely into two systems for the purposes of a small practice: stand-alone systems and networked systems.

Stand-alone means precisely that: the computer does not 'talk' to anybody except, hopefully, the person operating it (unless it is connected to the Internet). If you have two or three computers in the office that are stand-alone, they are not linked to each other. Stand-alone systems are, generally speaking, less complicated and more suitable for the sole practitioner. They are simpler to use and cause fewer problems than networked systems, but networked systems can transfer data between computers faster and much more easily.

Networked systems consist of a series of computers and other devices, which are all part of the same system. They can all access the same information from a central point and share central resources such as printers and modems, rather like extensions on a telephone system. Accordingly, if you have several people who will need to use the computer or the same data, either at the same time or at different times, and they each need a computer on their desk, a networked system is the right one for you. Such systems are either a 'peer to peer' system, so that no one computer is superior to the other, or a 'server/client' system, where the server is king and the 'client' computers are controlled by it. About five years ago it was not cost-effective for a small practice to start out with a server system as a server might cost around £3,000 and the added benefits were insufficient to justify the extra cost. Since then they have come down to around £1,000–£1,500, easily within reach of a small firm. The result is that unless it is going to be just you on your own or possibly you and a secretary, you would do well to consider a server/client system, and certainly if there will be four people all using a computer on a daily basis.

Storage and memory

Storage

Information on a computer is stored either on a hard disk or drive, CD-Roms (read only memory), or on a USB flash drive (memory stick).

External hard drives can also be used either to store large files of data instead of cluttering up the internal hard drive or to back up data that is on the internal hard drive. For added security many external hard drives are easily portable so that information backed up on them can be taken home at night and brought back the next day. Memory sticks are means of transferring data; they too are portable and a convenient means of moving about smaller quantities of data or for the close control of particularly important files.

Memory

The memory on computers is measured in megabytes (MB) and gigabytes (GB), one gigabyte being 1,000 megabytes. Memory comes in two sorts, RAM (random access memory) and main memory. RAM is fast but is temporary. All other memory such as the hard drive is permanent and slow. For a small firm of up to three partners using peer to peer systems, you will need a computer with at least an 80–120 GB hard disk. The memory capacity on machines is constantly increasing, with most manufacturers offering computers with hard disk capacity 500 GBs as standard. At the end of this chapter you will find a suggested system for a small practice, with costs, that is likely to meet your needs for a year or two. Computers are changing so rapidly that you should check to see that the suggested system has not become out of date by the time you read this, but it might reassure you to know that we traded quite happily for the first five years on a system which had a tiny fraction of the power of the system in the example. If you do need to increase your memory capacity after you have bought your equipment, an external hard drive is an excellent solution, or you can have an additional internal hard drive fitted if there is the physical space available within the body of your computer.

Operating system

The operating system is the software that tells the hardware what to do. Microsoft Windows is now the most common operating system for computers in the world. Because of its popularity and its user-friendliness, most computers are sold with Windows software already loaded by the manufacturer. The most recent version is Windows 7 and it will be adequate for the business needs of all but the largest of new practices.

PC or Mac?

You may come across computers called Macs. These are almost a different kind of computer and those that have them swear by them. They are particularly embraced by the arts and music worlds. They have a much smaller share of the market than the PC. Most businesses other than those involved in music, art, publishing, films and so on opt for PCs. Unless you are a committed fan of Macs already, I suggest you do the same.

Software

Office suite

You will also need a bundle of interrelated desktop applications referred to as an 'office suite'. Most computers are preloaded with Microsoft Works, which is a very basic office suite. However, the latest version of Microsoft Office Home and Business (e.g. 2010) contains Word (word processing), Excel (spreadsheet), PowerPoint (presentations) and Outlook (emails) at a cost of around £160 inclusive of VAT.

Antivirus

It is vital to have proper antivirus software to protect your data from viruses. Most computers come with a free trial of commercial antivirus software, and you should make sure to purchase the full version before the trial runs out. There is quite a lot of free antivirus software available on the Web that may suit your needs in the early days, after which you should take professional advice on what further protection you should put in place.

Printers

When it comes to the appearance of legal documents or letters, presentation is everything. If you need to send to clients a print-out of a ledger, it is nice to send something that looks professional even if the clients are more concerned with the transactions shown on it. This means you are really going to need a laser printer. You might consider having an inkjet printer as well if you are printing out coloured documents such as lease plans.

Opinions are divided on whether it is better to equip each fee earner and secretary with their own printer. The cheaper option is a higher quality networked printer shared by more than one fee earner. Some say this is more trouble than it is worth unless the people sharing produce very little of their own work directly and so only want to print the occasional document.

Setting up your computer

Having selected your hardware, software and printer, you have them all delivered. Then comes the shock. The courier dumps the whole lot in the middle of your office floor, waves a cheery goodbye and disappears. There is not even a paper instruction manual anymore, as the manual is now loaded onto the computer itself – which is a total waste of time if you cannot get the computer to work!

Sorting out the printer can be the biggest problem. The software on the computer needs to give certain instructions to the printer, so the two need to be able to communicate effectively. Printers are able to operate to different page set-ups (i.e. margins and paper size) and this can lead to initial problems. The printer may need to be told the paper size and repro-duction quality or resolution. Fortunately, many printers today are sold with set-up disks and these considerably simplify the process of getting the printer to work.

By far the best idea is to buy everything from a small specialist com-puter supplier rather than a national discount warehouse type of trader. You can either negotiate a package which includes loading the operating system and software packages onto the machines to leave you with a fully working system or pay them to do it. The typical charge rate for a com-puter engineer is £75 per hour. It should only take 60 to 90 minutes per computer to set up a networked system of two or three machines with a printer or two and an Internet connection. Do not be fooled by the multi-nationals' claims to set up machines and give after-sales service. In my experience they comply eventually with the basic letter of the agreement but support consists of waiting for hours in a telephone queue to be given half a solution to your problem, and meanwhile you are trying to run a business. The extra cost of the retailer setting up the system for you so that it is fully operational and of having someone around who will actually attend your offices to fix anything that goes wrong is invaluable. Like most things, it is best to get a recommendation from someone if you can.

Back-up and recovery

From the very first day you will need to have a system for backing up data so that you will be able to retrieve data quickly in the event of a problem. Data for these purposes will consist of accounts information, client details and the actual work you are doing for clients, such as letters, pleadings and statements. Discuss the accounts side of things with your accountant and then with your computer supplier. There are inexpensive programmes available that can automatically back up your accounts data when you turn off your machine and copy it to a hidden place on your website. Depending on the size of your website and the amount of data you have, it may also be possible to back up and store text as well. Even if it is not, some web hosts will rent additional storage space and will encrypt the information and store it on the server. This system has the added advan-tage of being able to store earlier versions of work as well so you can go back to a document as it was six months ago if you need to. You might also back up your data onto an external hard drive – these come in portable models, which hold up to about 320GB, or desktop models, which can hold even more. The aim should be that if disaster strikes you should be able to be back up and running pretty much at full speed within 24 hours. A disaster recovery plan is now a professional requirement, as well as being sound business practice.

As well as automatic systems for back up and retrieval, you should also ensure that individuals back up their work. Your accounts person should be taking a copy of the accounts data on something like a removable flash drive and taking it home. That way if there is a fire and the information on the computer is lost and, horror of horrors, the back-up to the Web has failed, you still have all the information safe at home. Likewise, remove essential software programs, set-up disks and so forth from the office and take them home.

Most people consider it unwise to email data to your home computer. Emails can go astray and this vital information may come into the wrong hands. Back-up over the Web to the server is more secure because it stays at the server rather than travelling further afield. Back-up onto another hard drive in the office will give you some protection – if the hard drive of one computer fails or the data becomes corrupted it should be safe on the other one. It will not save you if someone breaks in and steals both machines or they are both destroyed by a fire.

Periodically, you should test out the back-up system by denying access to the data by the normal route, forcing staff and yourself to try to retrieve the data by other means. This is the time to discover the data has not been saved because you forgot to pay the subscription to the web host or that the bookkeeper has been ignoring your instructions to create their own back-up because they cannot be bothered. Better to find out now than when you come in one Monday morning to find empty spaces where the computers used to be because there has been a break-in and all your data has gone with them.

Cloud computing

A further option as part of a back-up and recovery system or as a system in itself that you might want to install is cloud computing: but what exactly is it? Some companies install far more computing capacity than they need for their everyday requirements so that they have capacity to expand. Instead of allowing it to sit there idly, some organisations have made their facilities available to other businesses or to the general public. One of the biggest providers to the public is Amazon. Cloud computing enables you to access these facilities in much the same way as you might plug into the electricity grid and pay for what you use. In the case of cloud computing, what you use may be storage capacity or it may be software applications. You have probably already experienced a form of cloud computing in the form of an email account with a web-based email service such as Hotmail, Yahoo!Mail or Gmail. The software and storage is in the 'cloud' and not on your computer. To be clear, cloud computing means huge specialised warehouses with banks of computers linked together and their power and capacity made available to users via the Internet. Ordinarily, your business might purchase half a dozen computers and then have to put the software on them. That software might be Microsoft Office products such as Word or Excel or it might be an accounts package. Each time you take on an additional employee you would have to get another computer and pay for a further software licence for each of the software applications that the employee will use. Every time the software is upgraded you will have to buy new software for each of the employees. As other software programs are written and come on the market you might want to upgrade to different software and again you will have to buy new licences and install each new version on each computer.

As you and your employees use the software you will create files and data. All of this has to be stored somewhere. If you have a central local server it will be stored on that. In some cases it will be stored on the user's individual computer or on an external hard drive. All the information will have to be backed up. It will all have to be protected by means of antivirus software and firewall software or hardware used to thwart people who may try to hack into your systems to access or corrupt your data. Why bother with all of this cost, responsibility, time and effort when all you need to do is to plug yourself into your cloud service provider's facilities to have immediate access to the state of the art software, endless storage capacity and powerful security and data protection tools which a much larger organisation can provide while you would be able to afford to put in place yourself. After all, say the advocates of cloud computing, if you want a pint of milk you do not necessarily go out and buy a cow.

Further, the ability to connect to your provider's cloud is not limited to the office. Any device that can connect to the Internet, be it a smart-phone, a tablet such as an Ipad or a desktop computer at home or in the office, is all you need. For those people who cannot bear to be away from work you could be in your hotel room in Paris or New York with your laptop and call up the document you were working on in your office the previous day and complete the job before going down to dinner in the evening. Just for good measure you might want to check over the files or emails of your employees back in the office to make sure that they have carried out the various jobs that you have assigned to them before you left, before quickly sending them an email pointing out that they have not quite finished them and you want them done before you get back at lunchtime tomorrow. There is no waste because you are charged for whatever you use and how often you use it as if you were on a meter.

So what can go wrong? Well, quite a lot actually. You may have chosen a cloud service provider that is based in a country whose data protection or privacy laws are very different from our own. By checking your employees' emails and the work files that are under their control you may be committing an offence wherever your cloud service provider is based. It is unlikely that an international arrest warrant will be awaiting your return at Heathrow Airport, but most of us would rather stay on the right side of the law, no matter whose law it might be.

What if the system breaks down? What if the data is lost or a hacker gets through and the data is corrupted? By basing all your facilities on your cloud service provider's server you no longer have direct control over it. You cannot send in your IT guy to sort the mess out and you are totally reliant on the cloud service provider's resources. But, say the proponents of the cloud, cloud service providers live or die by their reputation. The cloud service provider that has a major catastrophe and loses its customers' data or suspends all service for a fortnight will be brought down overnight, so that kind of thing will just not be allowed to happen. Oh won't it? History teaches us differently. Remind me again which record company it was who said of an emerging new pop group: 'We don't expect the Beatles to do anything significant in this market.' After all, Northern Rock is never going to collapse and Barings Bank is as safe as houses, isn't it? So, are you better off being a passenger on the unsinkable luxury liner Titanic, leaving all the responsibility and workload to captain John Smith and hoping he manages to steer a clear path around the icebergs, or is it better to be a Sir Francis Chichester, being bounced around on the ocean wave in Gypsy Moth at least having the comfort of knowing that your destiny is to some extent in your own hands and if something goes wrong you can make some kind of attempt to correct the situation? Some people say that migration by all computer users to a cloud system is inevitable, but for the moment my advice is to keep an eye on things and to hold back for present. Let everyone else test out the system, and learn from their mistakes so that by the time you join the cloud the problems will have emerged and solutions found. As always, it is the thrill of making choices such as these that makes being in practice on your own account such fun. Just make sure that you know where the key to the lifejacket cupboard is! And no matter what your decision is, *always back up*!

Accounts packages

There are many accounts packages available that are specifically geared to small practices. They vary in complexity and prices range from about £1,000 up to £9,000. Generally speaking, the more expensive the package, the more it will do for you in terms of management of information and the more matters it can handle. Because of its additional complexity, it will take up more space on the computer. As a small practice I would suggest that those packages at the lower priced end of the scale would be perfectly suitable. These matters and the different accounting packages that are available are covered in more detail in **Chapter 3** and **Appendix 8**.

Our solution to these various difficulties was to have separate computers for the accounts and word processing. This meant that when the point came when we needed the two functions to be dealt with at the same time, the bookkeeper did not have to stop work to allow the typist to produce a word-processed document.

It is, in my opinion, better to start off with a computerised accounts system, but to ask someone experienced with accounting systems to run it for you for the first few months so that any teething problems can be dealt with. Then, if you want a member of staff to run it for you or you hire a less experienced bookkeeper, they will be taking over a system which you know works and have confidence in. It may be feasible to do it yourself at the very beginning, but it will not be long before you will be far too busy to stay on top of it. Better to have someone else to run it from the start.

You can survive without databases, spreadsheets, computerised debt collection systems, conveyancing systems, case management systems, and so on in the early days unless you are starting with an established client base and will have a fairly high volume of work from the beginning. Once you have built up a regular turnover of work then you can decide which additional systems can be applied usefully to particular tasks.

Filing

Another choice for you to make – a manual record-keeping system or a computerised one? We have always managed perfectly well with the manual system described below, but we are probably the exception and if I were setting up now I would investigate a computerised system and either go with that or switch from manual to computerised early on. The later you leave it the greater the amount of data that needs to be transferred from one system to the other unless you phase the old out and the new in, which means that you will have to be able to access the information from both systems for a very long time.

Card system

When I was in partnership, each file had a number; in fact, it had several numbers. As someone who is very bad at remembering numbers, I found this particularly irksome. Each file had a number so that I could find it in my filing cabinet. It had a different number on the accounts system. It had a third number for time-recording purposes. It had add-on numbers to show who supervised it, what type of matter it was and who the fee earner was, and when it was put into store, it had yet another number to enable it to be retrieved from the dead file system.

The reason why files need several different numbers is because each system comes in at a different time. When setting up a new practice, you have a unique opportunity to have one number for a file throughout its entire life since you are starting all your systems in one go. This gives you an amazing advantage over all those people spending collectively millions of hours looking up all the different numbers each time when they want to do something with a file.

To start off, you need a card index box with A–Z dividers and two A5 size books, one of which has A–Z pages on it. You then start numbering your files. If you have taken some files with you from another practice, there is nothing wrong with adopting one of the several numbering sequences and using that as your starting point, providing any new files that are opened are numbered sequentially from the highest number of the existing files. Put all your files in correct numerical sequence in your filing cabinets and then make out an index card for each one. The top line on the left-hand side will be the client's surname followed by any first names and the file number will be in the top right-hand corner. The nature of the matter will then appear underneath. The file is then cross-referenced in the other two books. You will go through your files systematically in this way. If, like me, you took only a few clients with you from your previous practice, this may take a depressingly short amount of time so that when you have indexed all 10 of your files, you can sit down and make a cup of tea!

The index card should then look something like this:

BLOGGS, FREDA (MRS) Re: Road traffic accident	7483

Mrs Bloggs's name is then put under B in the A5 book with 'Re: Road traffic accident' opposite it and at the end of the line the file number 7483. It is a matter for you to decide whether you start your numbering sequence at file no. 1 or file no. 1,000 – in the latter case giving the impression to the rest of the world that you have thousands of files and not just 10! You then turn to the other A5 book and write '7483' on the left-hand side and 'BLOGGS, FREDA (MRS) Re: Road traffic accident'.

Having listed all your files in this way, you can give instructions to your secretary that any new file that is opened must be allotted the next number and when the label is made for the file cover an index card must be created, the two entries made in the two A5 books and the index card put in the appropriate place in the filing card box.

As your practice expands and you have individual fee earners with their own set of files and filing cabinets, it is important to insist that people stick to the system. A great many people try to create their own system, which spells disaster. They will tell you that they find it much easier to put things in their filing cabinet in alphabetical order. Insist they do it your way. The day will come when they are not in the office and you need to find one of their files in a hurry. If the client's name is McDonald, you will not know if it is filed at the beginning of the M section, or in a separate section for Mc or Mac. If the file number is 7483, the only possible place that the file will be is between 7482 and 7484 in the filing cabinet. It may be necessary to check more than one filing cabinet, but the possible places for the file to be become substantially limited.

As a sole practitioner, the buck very much stops with you. If the file cannot be located, it is your fault. If someone else is operating the kind of filing system more appropriate to a Neanderthal, it is your fault. Setting up a new practice, you have the opportunity to lay the foundations of a highly efficient filing system and keep it that way. It is your fault if it goes off the rails because your staff subsequently demolish the system over a period of time.

Having set up the card index system, this number then becomes the number for your accounts system. Occasionally, some computerised systems have to use a certain number of digits, but you can often get round this by putting noughts at the beginning or end of the number. Certainly, with the simpler systems more appropriate to small practices, they have no problem in accommodating four-figure reference numbers.

The same number can be used for a time-recording system and for the dead filing and storage system. We have always had a system whereby a file is moved out of a live filing cabinet into a dead file cabinet. Critics of this may say, with a certain amount of justification, that you are taking up valuable office space and cluttering up the place with a load of dead files. Inevitably, you will find that if you take a file out of a live cabinet when you think it is finished and put it into some kind of long-term storage, within 24 hours someone will write you a letter on it. We keep files in a dead file system where we can have ready access to it for at least a year after we think the matter is ended. It does mean that every now and then you have to go through the cabinets and flush them by taking out files and putting them into dead filing cabinets, but it is an exercise well worth the effort. Then after a further period of inactivity or when your dead file drawers become full, suitable candidates can be removed to longer-term storage and should at that stage be marked with destruction dates. So far as the filing system is concerned, you can maintain the same number right the way through live, dead and storage systems.

Computerised systems

There are several computerised systems on the market and it is certainly worth exploring what is around from the beginning of your practice. A well-known package is ACT! 2008 CRM software. Produced by Sage, the respected accounting software house, it provides a comprehensive record in one place of names, addresses, telephone numbers and the like. It will also enable a record to be kept of all data exchanges with clients and other points of contact so you can keep track of all calls made and received, emails and letters, and other information about your clients in one place. There may be some duplication as lawyers need to keep attendance notes and time records, and other systems may have a facility as well for this data.

Storing

Quite how long you should store files is a matter of opinion. *The Guide to the Professional Conduct of Solicitors 1999* gave certain guidance on the topic (see Annex 12). The position is not specifically covered by the SRA Code of Conduct 2011 but the Chapter 7 outcomes and indicative behaviours require you to have systems in place to comply with data protection legislation. The Data Protection Act 1998 provides that you should not retain data for any longer than is necessary. Most of what is contained in a client's file could be defined as data of one sort or another. The requirements of Chapter 4 to keep the client's affairs confidential also impact on this area. In my opinion, by following the earlier guidance from the Guide you are unlikely to be criticised.

What might be suitable arrangements for one firm in a given set of circumstances may be considered inadequate for a different firm or in slightly different circumstances. Clearly, you will have to have regard for the general law and for negligence claims and the limitation periods affecting them, but it is possible that courts or tribunals will have regard to the guidance previously given in the Guide as a first point of reference.

The safest and, generally speaking, most unattractive option from a practical point of view is to offer the file back to the client. If he or she declines to accept it, there is at least an argument for saying that the client cannot complain if you dispose of it and suddenly it is required. However, it does mean that you have the problem of transporting the file back to the client at some expense, almost certainly to yourself, or asking the client to come and get it.

If you are not going to arrange for the file to go back to the client by some means or another, you will have to store it – but for how long? The real cost of storing documentation is always fairly high, unless you take it home and keep it in the attic, where it is going to be difficult to get at. Clearly, the shorter period of time you store a file, the better for you. However, if you destroy a file too soon, you are taking a chance. It is always difficult to explain to a client why you have shredded the file and the word 'negligent' will constantly be seen to be passing through the client's mind, even if it is not uttered.

Personally, I take the view that comparatively minor criminal matters can be destroyed after as short a time as two or three years (but see Annex

12A of the Guide on the relevance of VAT problems). If the client reoffends, there is every chance you will not be instructed anyway – criminal litigation clients can be notoriously fickle. The chances are that the client will not remember which firm represented him or her and in any event, there will be no need for the file to be retrieved. If there is such a need, key information such as previous convictions will be on record elsewhere. You will presumably have a copy of your bill in the office, which should assist you with the VAT problem referred to above.

Similarly, with conveyancing sale files, the client has disposed of the property and so why is there any need to retain the file for any great length of time? The answer is likely to be the danger of a possible action for misrepresentation against your client by the buyer despite any exclusions you may have put in the contract. If those are going to happen at all, they are probably likely to happen within a period of, say, three years. Clients are unlikely to complain about being misled on what exactly they were buying after that time. The exception to that is defects in title, but in that event clients are probably likely to turn first on their own solicitors and you have the maxim of *caveat emptor* on your side. You may be prepared to take the view that you can dispose of such a file after three years if you are prepared to accept the VAT risk referred to above and six years may be safer. It is a matter for your judgement and a question of how much storage space you have available.

Is it ever safe to dispose of a purchase file? The client may stay in the property for 20 years or more and a defect in the conveyancing work may only come to light when that client comes to sell the property. It may, therefore, only ever be safe to dispose of such a file two or three years after you know for sure that the property has been sold on again, even if that may not be for 20 years. In all other types of cases, you will really have to wait for at least six years. Some people take the view that 16 years is the right period for a purchase file, i.e. the long-stop period of 15 years under the Limitation Act 1980 plus a year for a margin of error. Even this lengthy period has been thrown into doubt by relatively recent cases which suggest that the time limit does not start to run until the discovery of the negligent act, however long ago it occurred, which means an almost indefinite period of risk. Case law such as *Brocklesbury* v. *Armitage & Guest* (2001) and *Cave* v. *Robinson Jarvis & Rolf* (2001) has raised the prospect of there being no safe period for the disposal of old files by holding that those professionals who are unwittingly in breach of duty are in the same position as those persons who deliberately conceal breaches from their clients. Meanwhile, the Court of Appeal has given some comfort in *Ezekiel* v. *Lehrer & Co.* (2000) by holding that the client must be ignorant of the relevant facts. If he or she is aware of them, no subsequent act of the solicitor can conceal them from him or her. The Court of Appeal went on to say that the lower courts should be wary of being too easily persuaded that a claimant has a fresh cause of action just because the solicitor failed to advise the claimant that he (the solicitor) had been negligent.

If you are faced with a client who demands to know why you have destroyed a file at a time that is in their view premature you might want to refer to the Data Protection Act 1998. Part of the Act's requirements is that data should be stored for no longer than is necessary. Data has a very wide definition and is basically information. If it is no longer necessary to keep the information you have a duty under the Act to destroy it. This duty may be in conflict with other duties, but that argument may have to be resolved on another day. Bear in mind that destruction of the file may leave you without any evidence to defend yourself against a claim if one is made. It is a tricky balancing act.

The best time to judge how long to keep a file is when you first put it into long-term storage and the best person to do the judging is the fee earner who worked on the file, unless they are quite junior. At that stage all the relevant factors should still be reasonably fresh in the fee earner's mind. No file should be put into store without a destruction date marked in red on the front. This makes the job of destruction far easier. The selection of files for destruction should only ever be undertaken by a principal, or at least a working party of senior fee earners under the supervision of a principal. If a file has been recalled from storage for any reason, careful consideration should be given to the question of reassessment of the destruction date. It is foolish to leave a destruction date intact if it is clear from further developments on the file that it is not going to the shredder quietly.

Another option today is to scan paper records and store the data electronically. Files need to be prepared so that the paper records to be scanned are sifted and documents which do not need to be kept are discarded. The documents themselves may need preparation to remove staples and paper clips but once this has been done many scanners will automatically process 50 pages at a time. Though initially time-consuming and thus expensive, gone will be the rows of files taking up lots of space either in your own offices or in expensive warehouses.

Accounts

At first sight, setting up your own accounting system seems horrendously complicated, particularly if you have never concerned yourself with the workings of a firm's accounting system before. In fact, it is not at all difficult. Because it seems such a formidable task, it is tempting to go out and buy a computerised system that has everything on it. As discussed earlier, this would be a big mistake. Once again, it would be a case of getting a computer and then trying to see what problems you could load onto it rather than identifying the problems and then finding out how a computer could solve them.

Who should be your bookkeeper?

Unless you are fortunate enough to have a spouse or close relative who enjoys bookkeeping, it is best to employ someone, albeit on a part-time basis. It is normally a bad idea to try to do it yourself. It usually ends in disaster and, in a great many cases, an appearance before the disciplinary tribunal.

If you use a part-time outside bookkeeper, do not just select one from the telephone book. Get a recommendation, preferably from another solicitor with a small practice, or at the very least from an accountant whose judgement you trust. It is an easy matter for someone to get your accounts into a mess and an enormous task getting them straight again. It is no defence to an allegation of breach of the Accounts Rules that it was the bookkeeper's fault.

Another alternative is to use an outside bookkeeping agency. There are a number of companies who will provide a computerised bookkeeping service for you. You send your financial information to them and they do the rest. While at first sight this may seem attractive, it is not particularly cheap and you do not have much control over it. If, for any reason, the bookkeeper needs to have access to the files, the file is likely to be out of the office for three or four days. There is also a tendency to feel that you have covered that particular problem and not to look too closely at what is going on because it is now someone else's problem. If this system is to be used, a close eye should be kept on it, and in the early stage of practice this can be a difficult thing to do. Chapters 4 and 7 of the SRA Code of Conduct 2011 effectively extend the responsibilities for preserving confidentiality to any work outsourced that is critical to the delivery of the legal services. If you outsource your accounts you must make sure that the agency you use has systems in place to safeguard its clients' information and documents. Failure on the agency's part is likely to amount to failure on your part too and will cause you to infringe the SRA Code. The Code also requires you to make documents available to the SRA when requested, so you will need to have contractual terms to cover the position where a client's files are under the control of a third party such as an outside accounting service and the SRA wants to inspect them so that you have the power to require the service to deliver the files up to you at short notice.

Assuming that you are going to do the job in house, you will need to keep the following:

1. A system of slips or vouchers.
2. Ledger cards (one for each client).
3. Bills delivered book.
4. Clients' bank book.
5. Office bank book.
6. Petty cash book.
7. Wages book.

If you are starting with a computerised system, most of these books will be on the system. Even if you have a computerised version of these records it is often useful to have a paper version too. To start with, I would suggest having both and evaluate whether the extra effort of maintaining the paper version alongside its computer equivalent is justified by the amount of use the paper records get and how useful you find them. You will probably only want to maintain the slips, the bills delivered book and the wages book in the longer term.

System of slips or vouchers

You may be familiar with a system of slips. You may have complained bitterly in the past that you cannot get anything out of your cashier's department without filling in a piece of paper first. Now that you are on the receiving end of people asking for things without slips of paper, you will come to realise their value and how they hold the system together. Slips are generally colour coded and you can choose any colour system you like. The four that I have always used are: a pink slip as a cheque request slip (or anything else where money is going out of the firm, such as outgoing telegraphic transfers); a blue slip for any form of money received (including incoming telegraphic transfers); a green slip for transfers, be it between office and client account, one office account to another office account or one client account to another client account; and a white slip for petty cash. All of these should be duplicated by means of carbon paper so that whenever you create an original for the accounts department you can put a copy in the file, even if at this stage of the proceedings the accounts department is you or your spouse sitting in the next room! It is amazing how often the copy comes into its own. By checking the file you can see if you really did send off the application to the Land Registry because there will be a copy of the pink cheque request slip with the Land Registry fees shown on it, etc.

Once the original slip has been actioned, for example, by the drawing of the cheque to which it relates or the conversion of a petty cash slip into money, it should be annotated (e.g. a big tick or crossed through) to show that the necessary action has been taken, so that you do not end up drawing two cheques for the same amount or paying yourself your expenses twice from petty cash. The slip is then placed on a tag and given a number. That number will find its way on to the ledger card in due course.

The following example involving a county court claim illustrates how the system works.

Fill out the pink cheque request slip for the court issue fee (check with the court what the correct fee is first), put the carbon copy on the file and pass the original pink slip to the bookkeeper/cashier (as a sole practitioner this could be you). The cheque is then written out and the slip crossed through and placed on the tag and given the next number, for example, P [pink] 1. As this is a new matter, we will be opening a new client ledger card. This will normally be an electronic entry in your computerised accounts system, but the entries are the same whether it is an electronic ledger card or a paper one. Enter the details on the card, add the date and in the narrative column put 'court fee'. In the debit column of the office account section put the court fee, for example, £100. In an appropriate column on your sheet write 'P1'. This tells you the number of the pink slip used to draw the cheque. In months to come, no doubt during the audit by your accountants, someone will ask you something about the cheque that was drawn. You can then look the matter up on the ledger card, see that the cheque request slip was P1 and dig it out from your bundle. This will give you information such as who requested the cheque to be drawn, the payee and perhaps more information on what the cheque was for than was recorded on the ledger card. The same system applies for each type of slip.

BLOGGS, ALBERT (MR)				FILE NO. 0068	
Re: SHODDY ENGINEERING LIMITED					
Date		Office A/C		Client A/C	
		Dr	Cr	Dr	Cr
1/4/12 Of you on a/c costs	B2				£300.00
4/4/12 Ct fee on summons	P1	£100.00			

The client ledger

You will only need a ledger card system if you are operating a manual accounts system. Most new firms will start with a computerised system and will employ a bookkeeper to set up the initial ledgers and entries. If you do prefer to have a manual system to start with a number of companies have fairly simple ledger cards, for example Oyez or Peapod (see Useful contacts). If you or your accountant can devise your own, you can produce a home-grown version quite cheaply and the remaining accounting books can be constructed from conventional accounting stationery at a much lower cost than purchasing a complete bespoke package. The method is the same whether the entries are on a paper ledger or a computerised one. Use a new ledger for each new client matter, with the name of the client and the details of the matter at the top. Keep the ledgers in numerical order with a new number allocated to each client as the files are opened. There is no need to open a separate ledger for a client until there is a financial transaction in relation to it, the first normally being a payment on account of costs or possibly a court fee or a local authority search fee. As outlined previously, your new system will have the same file number and accounts number.

You will also need a number of nominal ledgers on office account where records are kept of office expenditure, for example, housekeeping, wages, stationery, and so on.

Bills delivered book

Again, the bills delivered book can be a manual or a computerised record, or you can run two together. It is a record of all invoices you raise, showing to whom you have rendered an account, when and for how much. Your computerised system will have a facility for recording much of the data referred to below, but we have always found it useful to keep a manual record as well. You will need an A4 size book with at least seven columns on each sheet, or the computerised equivalent. Head it up across a double page to include the following:

* Year/date.
* Client's name.
* Client's account number.
* Invoice number.
* Fees rendered (gross).
* VAT.
* Net fee (i.e. profit costs).
* Disbursements net of VAT.
* Date paid.
* Method paid (i.e. cheque/cash/transfer, etc.).

As you raise an invoice, fill in the columns with the relevant details, and when the client makes payment, make sure to complete the remaining columns.

Any spare columns can be used for extra information, for example, if the client pays by instalments, payments can be noted down with the relevant blue/green slip numbers recorded. At the end of each month, total the money columns, leave a small gap and follow with the next month's transactions.

We used to use invoice pads which were self-carbonating, using the top copy for the client, one copy for the client's file and the third copy placed in a ring binder marked 'accounts rendered'. The pads were printed with my firm's headed paper details and pre-numbered. We now print off our own but use coloured copy paper for the different uses outlined above and number them sequentially ourselves.

The ring binder with the copy invoices constitutes the bills delivered book for SRA Accounts Rules purposes, but the A4 book will prove exceptionally useful from a management point of view. In addition, you may, as a fee earner and principal, wish to keep a separate list of all bills which go out in your desk drawer. This will not be quite as scientific as the other records, but will give you quite an accurate idea of how well or badly you are doing without having to switch on a computer or interrupt the book-keeper. Also, the fact that the information is immediately to hand will encourage you to use it.

A sample entry would look like this:

Date	Client	A/C no.	Invoice no.	Fees £	VAT £	Net £	Date paid	Fees paid £	Method
1/10/12	Mrs L Jones	6600	2356	120.00	20.00	100.00	10/10/12	120.00	Transfer G23

Clients' bank book

This is a record of all financial transactions regarding clients' money.

Again, you will need a book roughly A4 in size, but wider if possible, with at least seven columns per page. As for the bills delivered book, head it up across a double page as follows. On the left-hand page you will need the following columns:

- Year/date.
- Client's name.
- Client's account number.
- Detail (i.e. how much money received from client).*
- Slip number (i.e. number of blue slip).
- Bank (i.e. amount deposited in client account).*

(* These two figures should be the same!)

The left-hand side of the clients' bank book is, therefore, for lodgements at the bank.

It will be of little surprise, that the right-hand page of the clients' bank book is for payments out of the bank. Head the right-hand page up as follows:

- Year/date.
- Client's name.
- Client's account number.
- Cheque number.
- Slip number (i.e. number of pink or green slip).
- Amount paid out.

The SRA Accounts Rules 2011 require a running total to be shown. At the end of each month, total the money columns and reconcile them with the amount shown on the latest bank statement. The Accounts Rules provide for five-weekly maximum periods in which the figures must be reconciled, but this is really only to allow a little flexibility. It is sensible and generally more convenient to do it monthly.

Office bank book

The office bank book is a record of all financial transactions involving the firm's money as opposed to clients' money. You will need a book of similar size to the clients' bank book but with at least 15 columns, preferably 20, on the right-hand page.

As for the clients' bank book, the left-hand page will be for money received and the right-hand page for payments made. Head the left-hand page up as follows:

- Year/date.
- Details (i.e. who has made payment).
- Client's account number.
- Slip number (i.e. blue slip number).
- Banked gross.
- VAT.
- Net amount.

Head up the rest of the double page (including any of the remainder of the left-hand page still available) as follows:

- Year/date.
- Details (i.e. who cheque made payable to).
- Cheque number.
- Slip number (i.e. pink slip number).
- Gross amount.
- VAT.
- Nominal ledgers.*

(* The remainder of the page should be divided into columns for the following items: stationery, salaries, fax/phone, rent/rates, motoring, books, furniture repairs, insurance, advertising, clients' disbursements, PAYE, VAT payment, practising certificate, PI insurance premium, etc. The amount of space available will determine how many headings you can have.)

At the end of each month, total the financial columns and reconcile the amount with the latest bank statement.

Petty cash book

This is a record of all cash payments made from the firm's petty cash.

You will need a book identical to that used for office bank. Again, the left-hand page is for money received, the right for payments made. Head up the left-hand page as follows:

- Year/date.
- Details (i.e. where money has come from. This will almost always be 'bank' (i.e. cash withdrawn from office account).
- Amount received.

The remainder of the double page can be used for the following headings:

- Year/date.
- Details (i.e. what has been purchased, e.g. milk, stamps, etc.).
- Slip number (e.g. white slip number).
- VAT.
- Nominal ledgers.*

(* As above, the remainder of the double page should be headed up with the various nominal ledgers you feel are appropriate, e.g. refreshments, postage, papers, cleaning, sundries, fares, etc. As before, at the end of each month total the various financial columns and reconcile the total with the amount left in the petty cash box.)

Wages book

This book will be a record of salaries paid to all employees. An A4 size book will suffice, with approximately seven columns per page. One A4 page should be adequate for the necessary information. Head it up as follows:

- Year/date.
- Employee's name/National Insurance (NI) number.
- Gross salary.
- Employer's and employee's NI contribution.
- Income tax.
- Employee's NI contribution.
- Net payment.

At the end of each month, total the columns for employer's and employee's NI contribution and income tax and add the two together; this amount will be the PAYE payable by the 18th day of the following month. You may be able to pay PAYE quarterly rather than monthly, and HMRC's website contains details of how to make payments.

On the subject of wages, you will, of course, have to work out using the various tax tables supplied by HMRC how much tax and NI to deduct from each employee's gross salary. The tables can be downloaded from HMRC's website and are fairly self-explanatory. However, if you are in any doubt, contact your local tax office. It will usually be able to sort out any queries quickly. Do not put off contacting the office – if you are interpreting the procedures incorrectly it is much better to find out as soon as possible.

Reporting systems

Reporting procedures – Community Legal Services Quality Mark and Lexcel

As a sole practitioner starting a sole practice, you may not at this stage be considering the Community Legal Services (CLS) Quality Mark or the Lexcel accreditation scheme (developed from the Law Society's Practice Management Standards). But if you have several staff and the client base to go with them and/or intend to seek a franchise and a Legal Services Commission (LSC) contract, it would be well worth putting in the systems in accordance with Lexcel, both from the point of view of opening the way to a franchise application at a later stage and because they will help the practice to be run efficiently and, hopefully, profitably. The day may not be very far off when, in employment tribunals, Lexcel accreditation is considered evidence of compliance with the SRA Handbook in the context of an unfair dismissal claim and, likewise, before disciplinary hearings. Rather like the Highway Code in the magistrates' court for driving offences, the plea that Lexcel accreditation is voluntary may ring hollow when you are trying to justify something that you have done or failed to do.

From a sole practitioner's point of view, if you have perhaps only one or two members of staff, you may feel that much of the contents of the Lexcel standard is irrelevant. This may be true up to a point, but it should not stop you having some sort of business plan and a marketing strategy. From your employees' perspective, they will feel better for you having a chat with them about their performance over the last year, discussing their strengths and weaknesses and generally making them feel as though what they say and do in the course of their work is noticed and that it matters.

The chances are that if you are starting a brand new practice the last thing on your mind will be a franchise, CLS Quality Mark or Lexcel. However, if the practice is going to start from humble beginnings, you should probably make yourself aware of what those standards are and implement them selectively as time goes on, with those that are most relevant to your particular type of practice taking priority.

Supervision of employees

In a small practice, reporting procedures can be kept fairly informal but should be implemented. It should be you who opens the post, so you should see every letter that comes in, as well as signing, or at the very least, approving every letter that goes out. Bear in mind the provisions of Chapter 7 of the SRA Code of Conduct 2011 which requires you to have a clear and effective governance structure (outcome 7.1) and systems and controls and comply with the principles, rules and outcomes and other requirements of the Handbook where applicable (outcome 7.2) in place to achieve them; failure to exercise proper and effective control over your employees would normally amount to a breach of the Code.

Handing fee earners their post provides an ideal opportunity to go through it and discuss anything that might become a problem. This does not mean that you have to go through every letter in the morning with your staff. Grilling an employee about every piece of post is not only offensive to the intelligence of the employee and will undermine their confidence, it is also an waste of time. If your employee is a trainee solicitor, you will need to have regular meetings in order to comply with the training regulations. Either have a set time each month to talk through any particular problems and ensure that you both feel the level of supervision and degree of responsibility is appropriate, or just address particular issues when suitable opportunities arise – the only danger with the second approach is that time tends to pass faster than both of you expect and there may be a longer than necessary gap between a problem and your discussion.

Encourage an open door policy so that trainees and other staff come to you with their problems rather than you spotting danger signs only to discover that they are the tip of an iceberg, the bottom two-thirds of which should never have arisen and would not have done had you been more approachable. It is very easy as a busy sole practitioner to delegate a matter to a fee earner and then feel that it is their responsibility. It always remains your responsibility and you should know exactly what is happening virtually on a daily basis on any file that you have delegated. Do not be afraid to ask to see the file – files are yours first and foremost. If you ask in the right way and with a high degree of frequency on a variety of files, fee earners will not feel their authority is being undermined. A file examination and discussion will not then be usual and fee earners will welcome the security of knowing that work has been looked at and approved and that they are on the right course. It is also good practice to pass one of your files to an assistant from time to time and ask them to look at it and come back with their views. The interchange of ideas that ensues builds confidence, and a request from you to look at someone's files is then not perceived as an intrusion.

With larger firms, the system becomes much more complicated, as indeed it does once you have three or four fee earners. At that stage it will be necessary to have regular diarised staff meetings, which should be at least monthly if not fortnightly, preferably with each fee earner separately. File lists will need to be maintained and, if not computer generated, to be kept by hand.

At the staff meeting the file list should be reviewed, and after consultation with the relevant member of staff, a view taken as to whether the fee earner is under- or over-employed and work reallocated where necessary. Time records should be carefully scrutinised. Fee earners keen to make a name for themselves may try to persuade you that there is no problem in dealing with the work that you have allocated. The time sheet may show that they are working ridiculously long hours, which is a problem that needs to be addressed every bit as much as the fee earner who appears to be underproductive.

An annual performance appraisal system needs to be implemented. The Law Society's *Lexcel People Management Toolkit* (May 2011) contains an appraisal system that is entirely suitable for the vast majority of practices with only minor modifications. The assessment areas may be amended to suit individual tastes and the attributes sought in a particular employee, but the system adopted has the benefit that it can be applied to different types of staff, so that senior fee earners and secretaries can all be assessed with one type of form with the benefits of both simplicity and fairness. While the system outlined has a number of options, I would suggest that appraisals are carried out on the anniversary of the staff member's entry into the firm and that it should be explained to the member of staff that while the outcome of the appraisal will not be irrelevant for the purposes of pay review, the two are separate issues and the outcome of the appraisal is only one factor in the review of an employee's salary.

Existing franchises and contracts

If you are leaving a firm that has a franchise and a contract and you intend to try to take some of your publicly funded clients with you, you are in for a nasty shock. No matter how long you may have previously held a franchise or a contract, you will not be able to continue to act for those clients until you obtain a franchise and a contract from the LSC for the new firm. The LSC made it clear when introducing franchising that it expected the number of outlets for legal aid to reduce under franchising and so they have; it also made it clear that it was not intending to increase the number of outlets, and it seems likely that for the foreseeable future new franchises and contracts will be rare occurrences. It may be possible to obtain one-off authorisation for the odd certificate, but it is unlikely that you will be able to obtain authorisation for lots of certificates while you are trying to get yourself franchised.

You will have to go through the preliminary audit stage as you did at your old firm, obtain the franchise and then bid for a contract successfully. This procedure is likely to take several months and apart from the odd authorisation for one or two files you will not be allowed to carry out any legal aid work in the meantime. It is likely that in that hiatus the client's enthusiasm for transferring its work to your new firm will have evaporated and the old firm will retain the work. No doubt in the copious amounts of free time that you will have while setting up your new firm you may find time to mount a Human Rights Act 1998 challenge to this arrangement, which is likely to prove a major barrier to anyone with a large legal aid following setting up their own practice, quite apart from the fact that clients, to all intents and purposes, are deprived of their solicitor of choice.

The alternative would be to take your client following to a firm that already has a franchise and a contract and apply for an amendment to the certificate to show the new firm as acting. The other option is to merge your practice with a firm with a franchise and a contract. Depending on the size of the firm that you have left, it is possible that it might have a problem retaining its franchise because it may not be able to meet the supervisor standards if it cannot replace you quickly.

Compliance with the quality assurance standard is a prerequisite in applying for a LSC franchise. As an example, perhaps the first items you will need to attend to will involve writing out a job description for any staff that you take on, together with a contract of employment. A simple way to deal with this and other practice management aspects is to buy a selection of relevant Lexcel toolkits published by the Law Society. These cover client care, risk management, people management, information management, financial management and business planning, and business continuity planning, and each comes with a disk of useful template documents. The toolkits are specifically designed to assist with compliance with Lexcel's practice management standard and the precedents are easily adapted to suit your own firm.

Money laundering

Solicitors, along with banks, building societies and other financial institutions, have been charged with the burden of making life more difficult for criminals by their requirement to comply with a series of Acts and regulations which generally come under the heading of anti-money laundering legislation. Money laundering means the process by which the identity of 'dirty money', that is the proceeds of criminal conduct/crime, and the true ownership of those proceeds, is changed so that the proceeds appear to originate from a legitimate source. Serious consequences flow from failure to comply with the legislation and it can be the case that no guilty intent is required for an offence to be committed. Such lack of intent and a genuine desire to comply with the law will always be relevant to penalty but will not necessarily save you from the consequences of breaking the law.

The Law Society has produced a very helpful practice note on anti-money laundering (AML) to take account of various EC directives and Money Laundering Regulations 2007, SI 2007/2157. Help with interpreting the practice note can be obtained by telephoning the Law Society's Practice Advice Service (0870 606 2522 between 9 am and 5 pm, Monday to Friday).

In addition, a practice note on mortgage fraud covering money laundering issues has also been published by the Law Society. Both practice notes are available on the Law Society's website at **www.lawsociety.org.uk/ productsandservices/practicenotes.page**.

The summary below is intended to give you a start in getting to grips with the legislation and the regulations, but it is not intended to be exhaustive or as a substitute for reading the AML practice note in full and, where appropriate, the legislation itself.

The first step is to appoint a nominated officer. If you are the head of the practice that is likely to be you and I will assume that is the case throughout this section (though see the AML practice note, para.3.3.2). In my opinion, being the nominated officer is a poisoned chalice since everyone else who reports anything suspicious to you will have a defence to any future charge and the burden of responsibility then shifts onto the nominated officer, who will have to decide whether to report any suspicious activity to the Serious Organised Crime Agency (SOCA). Failure to act or act correctly may mean you commit an offence. Your neck is, therefore, firmly on the block.

You are required to have in place internal controls, policies and procedures to deter criminals from choosing your firm for money laundering and to ensure compliance with your obligations under the law. Further details about what systems are required to avoid committing an offence are provided in Chapter 3 of the AML practice note. The nominated officer has responsibility to ensure that identification procedures, record-keeping procedures, risk assessment procedures, internal reporting procedures and training procedures are maintained and everything is properly recorded.

Training

The legislation states that all relevant employees should be made aware of the law and regularly given training on how to recognise and deal with transactions which may be related to money laundering. Section 3.9 of the AML practice note recommends a risk-based approach to who needs what training and when. It is my opinion that in a small practice, the safest way to ensure that you comply with the training requirements is to train everyone, including part-time staff, secretaries, receptionists and accounts staff. Refresher training must also be given periodically and training given to new members of staff on joining. As stated earlier, all training should be recorded. The training should cover at least the following topics:

- What is money laundering?
- What are the warning signs?
- Client due diligence.
- What do you do if you become suspicious?
- What must we all carry out in our day-to-day activities so that they become routine?
- Client confidentiality issues.
- Tipping off offence.
- Making a SOCA disclosure.
- Obtaining consent for proceeding with a transaction or case.

What is money laundering?

Money laundering is not simply the conversion into clean money of the proceeds of a robbery or of drug dealing. It is dealing in any money that is the proceeds of crime. Crime is defined very widely in the legislation so that any money tainted with any form of criminal activity is included. It therefore covers such things as clients who tell you that they do work for cash which they do not declare to HMRC or who tell you about friends or partners who do. Likewise, people who work and yet claim benefits to which they are not entitled come under this heading.

What are the warning signs?

Chapter 11 of the Law Society AML practice note sets out information about warning signs. These include transactions of an unusual nature, transactions with clients you have not heard from before and who you might feel surprised have chosen your firm to act for them, such as where they live a considerable distance away and it might be thought more logical for them to have instructed a local firm. Any transaction involving large amounts of cash should arouse suspicion, as will transactions which are required to be carried through at great speed. Sudden changes in the financing arrangements, the identity of a client or the amounts involved may raise suspicions, or instructions given through an intermediary.

What steps must we all carry out in our day-to-day activities so that compliance becomes routine?

The day-to-day steps will include:

- Checking the identity of clients. See the precedent proof of identity sheet at **Appendix 14**.
- Recording what steps have been taken so that compliance with the regulations can be demonstrated.

- Client care letter. All client care letters should include reference to the need to comply with the money laundering legislation other than where it is clear from the regulations that such identification steps are unnecessary.
- Recording suspicious activity to the Money Laundering Reporting Officer (MLRO) or reasons for not reporting.

Client confidentiality issues

Client confidentiality has proved a very troublesome area recently. Before the advent of money laundering legislation the situation was clear, namely that anything that a client said to their legal adviser was protected by a professional obligation to maintain a client's confidentiality at all times. Exceptions were made where, for example, a client might inform his or her solicitor that he or she was about to go out and commit a murder or other serious crime. It was a judgement call for the lawyer to make on whether the action threatened was sufficiently serious to warrant breach of the confidentiality duty by reporting the matter to the authorities. The Proceeds of Crime Act 2002 (as amended) contains certain provisions for disclosure of information to SOCA. Legal professional privilege still applies to these provisions. For more information see Chapter 6 of the AML practice note. The Law Society has set up an AML directory where solicitors can obtain 30 minutes' free legal advice from other solicitors on money laundering issues. This can be accessed at **www.lawsociety.org.uk/choosingandusing/ findasolicitor/moneylaunderingdirectory.page**. Better to spend £1,000 on legal advice than to pay a substantial fine and/or go to prison for six months.

Tipping off

The money laundering legislation contains an offence of tipping off. Briefly, if you advise someone that you are about to bring the client's or someone else's suspicious activities to the attention of the authorities by making a SOCA disclosure, the offence of tipping off may be committed if it is likely to prejudice the investigation. It follows that if you as the MLRO are making a SOCA disclosure you should be careful about who you inform. Likewise, this should be made clear to relevant members of staff if they report suspicious activity to you. See section 5.8 of the AML practice note for more detail.

Making a SOCA disclosure

Making a SOCA disclosure falls to the MLRO. See Chapter 8 of the AML practice note for detailed guidance. Wherever possible, you should try to submit your report online via SOCA's preferred form. This enables you to submit information securely at any time of day and receive an email confirmation of receipt. If you do not have computer access, reports can also be made by post or fax, but they must still be typed on the preferred form and you will not receive any acknowledgement.

There are rather involved rules as to when and if you can take any further steps in the transaction without having SOCA's permission to do so, and if you find yourself in this position you should check the legislation. In most cases you cannot proceed without permission (see AML practice note, para. 8.3.7).

This summary can only be something with which to get you started. Even the AML practice note produced by the Law Society as an overview of the regulations runs to approximately 100 pages. At least the above summary should ensure that you are thinking in terms of money laundering compliance from day one and know where to look to fill in the gaps in your knowledge.

Appointing a COLP and COLFA

Under outcomes-focused regulation as outlined in the SRA Handbook (**www.sra.org.uk**), all authorised firms will be required to have a compliance officer for legal practice (COLP), who will be responsible for ensuring their firm's compliance with all its regulatory obligations, and a compliance officer for finance and administration (COFA), who will be responsible for ensuring their firm's compliance with the SRA Accounts Rules. The SRA Authorisation Rules for Legal Services Bodies and Licensable Bodies 2011 outline the requirements for these roles. Alternative business structures (ABS) will need to have individuals appointed to these roles when they are licensed by the SRA. The COLP and COFA will be authorised to undertake the role from 31 October 2012 and the SRA will begin the nominations process by 31 July 2012. The requirements of compliance officers are set out in rule 8 of the SRA Authorisation Rules. The Law Society's practice note on compliance officers also sets out the responsibilities of COLPs and COFAs. COLPs and COFAs must record any failures of a practice to comply with authorisation or statutory obligations, and make such records available to the SRA on request.

These matters are dealt with in more detail in **Chapter 12**.

CHECKLISTS

Computers

- Decide how many computers you will need.
- Analyse the tasks you wish the computer to perform.

- Decide how long you need your computer to last, e.g.

    (a) one year, as an experiment and then replace;
    (b) three years, then replace;
    (c) five years, then replace.

    If in doubt, buy something cheap and throw it away after a year.

- Research the market to determine what software is most suitable for your needs, bearing in mind the likely number of clients, employees, accounts, etc. in the period identified above.
- Having selected software, research the market to ascertain which is the most suitable hardware in terms of capacity, reliability, price and back-up services.
- Decide on networked or stand-alone system.
- Obtain references from other firms operating the system and talk to them about suitability, reliability, etc.
- If appropriate, obtain the advice of a computer consultant. If you have the money, get them to install the system and set it up.
- Make your purchase, or lease, depending on overall cost.

Suggested specification for a computer system

An example of a standard entry level computer:

- **Computer:** Acer Aspire X3990 desktop PC.
- **Processor:** Intel Core i3-2120 dual core 3.3GHz, 3MB cache, Intel H61 Express Chipset.
- **Memory:** 4GB DDR3 RAM, DIMM.
- **Hard drive:** 500GB SATA.
- **Operating system:** Windows 7 Home Premium 64.
- **Removable media devices:** DVD writer.
- **Peripherals:** keyboard and mouse (monitor not included).
- **Networking:** integrated network adapter, 10/100 fast Ethernet network card.
- **Interfaces:** 9 x USB 2.0 ports, 1 x HDMI port, 1 x external VGA port.

Cost: **£379.00 including VAT.**

Software

- Microsoft Office Home and Business 2010 – Licence – 1 PC (£160 including VAT).
- 2010 versions of Word, Excel, PowerPoint, OneNote and Outlook.

Printer

- Brother HL-2250DN compact network mono laser printer with auto duplex (£85 including VAT).

Total cost: £464 including VAT.

Acronyms

- DDR3: double data rate 3.
- DIMM: dual inline memory module.
- DVD: digital versatile disk.
- GB: gigabyte.
- HDMI: high-definition multimedia interface.
- MB: megabyte.
- PC: personal computer.
- RAM: random access memory.
- SATA: serial advanced technology attachment.
- USB: universal serial bus.
- VGA: video graphics array.

If you are networking the machines, they will need to be linked together with networking cable which costs approximately 50p per metre plus VAT. A typical charge rate for an engineer to set up the system and test it is £75 per hour and it would take between 60 and 90 minutes per computer. You can link up to 10 computers together in this way in a network but any more than that and you will need a server. This acts as a central repository of information, which is then accessed by each computer, and a central security device controlling access to the resources, as well as to the machines themselves and peripheral devices such as printers.

If you are linking several devices together in a peer to peer system, you will need to use Windows 7 Home or above. The management of the computers becomes more cumbersome in a peer to peer set up. Further, the Windows licence which allows up to 10 devices to be linked does not just refer to computers. You must include any peripherals such as networked scanners and printers in your calculation. The practical limit of the smaller versions of the software is probably three or four linked computers. Alterations to the peer to peer system require each computer to be individually made but with the client/server system you alter the server and the other machines all fall into line.

(All prices as of May 2012.)

Filing system

- Buy card index box and A–Z dividers.
- Buy two A5 books, one with A–Z indexing and one without.

- Go through your current files allocating file reference numbers and entering details on the card index and cross referencing them alphabetically in the A–Z indexed A5 book and numerically in the other A5 book.
- Put files in numerical order in a filing cabinet, highest numbers towards the front.
- Label filing cabinet drawers with the range of numbers contained in each drawer.
- Put up a large notice detailing consequences, preferably fatal, for anyone who transgresses the rules of your filing system!

Storage

At this stage, you should have no files to put into store, unless certain old clients from a previous practice have asked for their papers to be transferred to you even though they are completed matters. If so, label a filing cabinet 'Dead Files' and treat in the same way as a live file, except put the index card into a second card index box marked 'Dead Files' and put the file into the dead file cabinet.

Your card index box will need to be much larger than the one for live matters. As time goes on, more and more files will go from the live system into the dead one. It is usually a bad idea to destroy the index card even if the file itself is destroyed. If someone says you acted for them and wants their file many years later, you may be able to check through the card system and tell them with confidence you never acted for them since there is no card for them and it must be the firm down the road. You cannot truthfully do this if you destroy cards as you go along.

Accounts (assuming you are not going straight for a computerised package)

- Buy:

    (a) pink, blue, green and white transaction slips;
    (b) client bank book;
    (c) office bank book;
    (d) bills delivered book;
    (f) wages book;
    (g) petty cash book.

    You may wish to discuss size of books, number of columns, etc., with your bookkeeper before purchase.

- Make out ledger cards for any existing/transferred files you have, using the file number as the account ledger number.
- Write out headings in your wages book and make entries for each employee (this may not take very long!). There is no need to make out

a section for principals as they are not employees, but you will need to keep a record of what draw you take and when. You will also have to pay a self-employed person's NI stamp (details obtained from your local DSS Office – do not put off contacting it). The wages book may be a convenient place to keep such records.

Reporting systems

If you are starting a sole practice with few or no staff, there will not be much reporting to be done. You might usefully make a diary entry for six or nine months' time to consider what systems you need to implement and plan an action timetable. If you are starting with three or four staff then you will need to:

- Draw up and issue contracts of employment.
- Put in place a staff appraisal system.
- Put in hand a scheme for fortnightly/monthly management meetings.
- Implement a time-costing system.
- Allocate files to fee earners.
- Set date for first partners' meeting, if two or more partners!

Cloud computing pros and cons

For:

- Lower capital expenditure.
- Less or not so powerful hardware is required. You only need a computer advanced enough to run the 'middleware' necessary to connect to the cloud system.
- No individual software licences required.
- Latest software versions always available.
- More sophisticated and more numerous applications than you might be able to afford on your own.
- No need to install or uninstall software.
- Better security because the big boys can spend more on antivirus and anti hacking measures.
- Can be accessed from whatever device you are using and from wherever you are.
- No need to have the same programme installed at home as in the office.
- Forms part of your business continuity and disaster recovery plans since all information can be stored off site.

Against:

- Privacy issues – who is looking at your data? It could be accidentally or deliberately erased or altered.

- Very limited or no access to audit or security logs.
- Loss of control. You are totally reliant on the cloud service provider's resources to deal with maintenance or security issues.
- Tied into a contract. If you are not satisfied with your provider it may be difficult or expensive to move to another provider or out of the cloud entirely.
- Legal issues. Who owns the data – you, the service provider or the owner of the hardware? Can the service provider refuse access to the data if, e.g. you are in dispute over cost or quality of service?

8

VAT and tax considerations

How to register

Registering for VAT purposes is remarkably simple. If you decide to involve an accountant in your initial period of setting up to deal with such things as a business plan to obtain finance from the bank, advising on your bookkeeping system, tax considerations, the ideal year end, the best time to set up and so on, you may also ask them to deal with the registration of the firm with HMRC for VAT purposes. There is, however, no real need to do that, as will be explained.

Do you have to register, and if so, on what basis? If at the end of any month your taxable supplies are or are likely to be above the specified limit for the previous 12 months, you must register. The same applies if you have taken over an existing practice which was required to register before you took it over. The limit at December 2011 is £73,000 (of turnover for the previous 12 months). If you are below that level, you do not have to register, but if you decide you wish to register, HMRC must register you for VAT purposes. You may be wondering, looking at the three files that you have just taken with you from your previous firm, whether you are going to be anywhere near the £73,000 limit. But rest assured you will be. Accordingly, the decision is made for you – you will be registering for VAT purposes.

Cash accounting?

There are several possible bases on which it is possible to register, but only two which are really applicable to law practices: the cash accounting system and the standard scheme. If you are a sole trader or a two-or three-partner firm, your turnover is unlikely to exceed £1.35 million a year. If it is likely to exceed this amount, you cannot join the cash accounting scheme. If you are allowed to, opt for cash accounting. There is only one disadvantage in part payment of VAT (set out below), but it is in other respects preferable.

The principal difference between the two systems is that with the cash accounting scheme you only have to pay HMRC the VAT collected on bills that have been paid. If a client fails to pay your account, you do not pay the VAT element of the account to HMRC until they do, whereas under the ordinary system the VAT must be paid over irrespective of whether your client has paid the bill. Most small practices, therefore, want to take advantage of that benefit and opt for cash accounting. One particular trap is the position where a client pays part only of an account. If that happens, you must apportion the payment between VAT and the rest of the bill. If the bill contains VATable disbursements, it may not be a straight forward task to decide whether to apportion the payment between non-VATable disbursements, VATable ones and profit costs. The regulations require that there be a 'fair and reasonable apportionment'. There is no problem in apportioning if the bill was simply for profit costs and VAT, or indeed if all the disbursements are VATable. The difficulty is remembering to include the VAT element of the part of the bill that has been paid in your VAT return, which, if forgotten results in an underpayment of VAT. Fortunately, some computerised accountancy systems now make the apportionment automatically.

There is no requirement to stay in the scheme for a set period, but you must leave it if your supplies – which in your case are the bills sent out to clients – exceed £1.6 million. You may leave the cash accounting scheme voluntarily at the end of any VAT accounting period if, for example, you do not think you are deriving sufficient benefit from it. You do not need to notify HMRC. You can rejoin at the beginning of any VAT accounting period, provided you meet the criteria at that point in time.

Another advantage of the scheme is that you obtain automatic bad debt relief.

There are complicated rules on when and how HMRC must register a person who applies for registration, but these really need not concern solicitors. The gist of the regulations is that HMRC want to be sure that you really are setting up in business of a kind that is going to involve VAT and not trying to set up a VAT fraud. A simple covering letter to the local VAT office (a phone call to an accountant will tell you which the local one is, or for that matter any local trader will probably do the same) enclosing the application form, imaginatively entitled Form VAT1, is all that is needed. Your letter will no doubt be on headed notepaper of some sort, even if you have not had the final version back from the printers, and will merely say that you are setting up a new solicitors' practice from a particular address, that you intend trading from a particular date and that as you will be making regular supplies of VATable services you wish to be registered for VAT and you have duly completed Form VAT1. Within a couple of weeks you should receive your VAT registration number and you will immediately need to telephone the printer and arrange to add the VAT number to your invoices.

You will need to notify the local VAT office (not the VAT central unit) of any changes in the business. These changes include a change in the name and/or the address of any partner, an alteration in the composition of the partnership or a change in the principal place of business.

All VAT returns must now be filed electronically online. Completing the first few VAT returns will no doubt fill you with dread as you will mostly be relying on information produced for you by other people, but it is you who has to take responsibility for the VAT return. You and you alone bear the responsibility, but unless you are going to repeat completely the work that others have done, which may take several hours, you will have to rely on their accuracy. This is a fairly daunting prospect since the penalties for misdeclaration can be severe, and HMRC is not normally noted for its high degree of tolerance and flexibility. You may, however, draw comfort from three psychological crutches.

First, in a solicitors' practice it is more likely that the error you make will be in favour of the VAT authorities than yourself. The only kind of supply that any solicitor is likely to make is in the provision of professional services to a client. All of those services will be VATable, with the possible exception of carrying out work for foreign clients, and even those services may be VATable. The VAT calculation is comparatively simple and involves adding up the value of supplies made and paid for in that VAT quarter, i.e. totalling up the bills, and extracting the VAT element from those bills and any disbursements that carry VAT. This constitutes the VAT output against which you offset the VAT you have paid out to others, including VAT on counsel's fees. You will need to go through all the monies that you have paid out in the course of your business to see where you have paid VAT and where you can prove you have paid VAT, i.e. you have a VAT invoice/receipt. You then extract the VAT from those invoices/receipts, and that constitutes your VAT input. Subtract the VAT input from the VAT output to arrive at the VAT figure, which will normally be with a sum to pay over to HMRC. In the first quarter you may not send out any bills at all and yet you will have paid out a lot of money in setting up, which includes a VAT element. In those circumstances it is just possible that you will have a credit, but this system of HMRC paying you money instead of the other way round will very rapidly change. If it does not, you are probably best advised to cease trading as you are not doing any business! Bookkeeping can easily be organised to show the VAT position without any special calculation if working on cash accounting, so you can see what your VAT liability is as it mounts up.

Pitfalls

The calculation should be relatively straightforward for a bookkeeper, so that provided you include VAT where only part of the bill is paid and you do not include VAT credits where you should not have had one, you should be alright.

The trap occurs when you forget to include the VAT in your next VAT return when someone pays a bill in stages. The tendency is to include the VAT element in the first payment but not the subsequent payments, or to treat the first payment as a VAT exclusive instead of a VAT inclusive payment. At the time of writing, VAT is currently levied at 20 percent. You should extract VAT from each payment by dividing by six. If, for example, you send a client a bill for £240, i.e. £200 plus £40 VAT, and your client pays you £120 in month one and £120 six months later, you should treat the first payment as one of £100 plus £20 VAT and the second payment the same way. If you credit the whole of the £120 to yourself and do not pay the £20 VAT, you have made an underpayment of £20.

(Although this does not strictly relate to VAT, it may be helpful to mention that if you wish to obtain the net amount from a gross figure, you should multiply the gross figure by five and divide by six. For example, a gross figure of £330 consists of £275 net (330 x 5 = 1650/6 = 275) and VAT of £55 (330/6)).

VAT and vehicles

Another possible pitfall arises where you use a car in the course of the business and claim some or all of the running expenses from the firm. If so, you are probably also setting off the VAT. HMRC will insist that not all of the expense is claimable either for VAT or income tax calculation purposes. It will point to the fact that there will be an element of private use involved and therefore a proportion of the running expenses will not, strictly speaking, be incurred in the running of the business. The procedure in relation to VAT is that you should claim all the VAT on the fuel and running expenses and then surrender the VAT on the private use element according to a scale of charges which varies with the size of the engine of the vehicle. The scale of charges can be obtained from your VAT office.

One option is to pay your own car expenses but charge travel expenses in connection with your business. As you are only charging purely for those costs directly involved in running your business, there will be no private use element to be extracted for VAT and income tax purposes. The problem is that detailed records and receipts will need to be kept to show what the actual expenses are.

However, you may be entitled to claim some of the VAT back on your telephone as it is highly probable you will be making at least some of your business calls from home. Again, speak to the VAT office about what percentage of the VAT it feels would be appropriate for you to reclaim and agree with it what the private usage element will be. By way of example, the VAT office allows me to claim 90 per cent of my home telephone and mobile telephone usage as business use.

The second crutch is that fairly early on in your trading period, i.e. within the first six months, you are very likely to receive a visit from a VAT inspector. Such a visit is not necessarily to be feared. The purpose of the visit is to pick up any errors you have been making before they lead to serious difficulties. If you have been claiming the full cost of the petrol for the mileage covered by your car (as indeed we did) it is far better to find out about it at an early stage where the amount of VAT underpaid is £60 or £70 than to wait until the firm's fleet has risen to several vehicles with the consequential increase of VAT underpaid. Any problems such as this can be ironed out at this stage.

The third weapon in your armoury is that other dreaded annual event – the accounts audit. This is when you pay other professionals a fortune to crawl all over your books and papers to be told just before they present their bill that you have been doing all sorts of things wrong and it is going to cost you the earth to put them right. If this is indeed your perception of the annual audit, try looking at it another way: any lecture that you may receive at the hands of your accountant will be nowhere as severe as the talking to you would get from the Inspector of Taxes or the VAT inspector and if you listen to what you are told, you will avoid those mistakes in the future. The bill from the accountant is likely to be more palatable than the bill you would have got from HMRC had the accountants not taken the time to do the job properly.

Is everything lost and will you be carted off in chains if the accountants discover that you have got your VAT calculations wrong? This depends on the extent of the error. HMRC accepts that people can make mistakes – it is not going to pounce on every underpayment and impose every penalty when you have made a mistake. For that reason, HMRC has a system whereby if you discover an error in your return and if the net amount of your error during that period is no more than the greater of £10,000 or 1 per cent of VAT turnover for the accounting period in which the error was discovered, you simply adjust the VAT and include the correction in your return for that period. You may be charged interest on any errors you disclose in this way. You must also complete Form VAT652 or write a letter of explanation and send it to the VAT Error Correction Team in Liverpool. Provided you follow this procedure, no penalty will be imposed if the error was a simple mistake and the error was not careless or deliberate. Full details can be obtained from HMRC's website (**www.hmrc.gov.uk**). In calculating whether you have gone over the £10,000 limit, you must go back through all previous VAT periods. What matters is whether mistakes discovered in each of those periods that have not yet been remedied when added together total more than £10,000, not whether it is £10,000 in any one period. You can only correct errors that have occurred in accountancy periods that ended within three years by this method.

For these purposes, you can take into account any overpayments, so that if in one period you have under-declared £1,200 and in another period you have over-declared £500, the sum total is a net under-declaration of £700 and you simply add that to your next VAT payment. You must also tell HMRC about it by completing Form VAT652 or by writing a letter of explanation and record the error in your VAT account. You should also write a note about it for your accountants and keep the note with your other accounting records.

If you are over the £10,000 limit or the errors occurred in accountancy periods that ended more than four years ago, you may still make a voluntary disclosure by sending full details of the error in writing to your local VAT office, which will send you a notice of voluntary disclosure confirming the amount of your disclosure and any interest payable. Once you have made a voluntary disclosure of an error, you cannot incur the more serious penalties which are imposed for a 'prompted disclosure'. That is, where HMRC announces that it is going to visit you to inspect your records and at that point you tell them about the mistake because you are worried it will find it. The basic message is, therefore, to tell HMRC if you find you have made a mistake rather than waiting to see whether it finds it first. If you opt for the latter course and you get caught out, it starts to become painful.

Any good bookkeeper or accountant will be fully aware of all of these matters, but as the person responsible for signing the VAT return, the buck stops with you. It is therefore very much in your best interests that you familiarise yourself at the outset with your responsibilities for VAT. Before you turn yourself in to HMRC, clothed suitably in sackcloth and ashes, there is one final thing that you might try to do to get yourself off the hook in the event that your errors exceed the £10,000 limit. Go through all the things that you have paid for, not only in that VAT period but all previous ones, and see whether there is anything on which you have paid VAT that might not have been included in a VAT return. On the occasion when it was pointed out to us that we had breached what was then the £1,000 limit, I went through this exercise and managed to find a seminar that I had attended on which VAT had been charged. The majority of courses of that type do not carry VAT but this particular one did. It was a full-day course and because my bookkeeper had been used to treating these courses as non-VATable, it had not been included in the figures. We were able to write off and get a receipted VAT invoice and the VAT element of the bill was sufficient to bring us back under the £1,000 limit.

HMRC publishes a very useful pamphlet, no. 700/45, 'How to Correct Errors and Make Adjustments or Claims'. It is well worth having a copy in the office, available from your local VAT office or from HMRC's website (**www.hmrc.gov.uk**).

Income tax and the self-assessment system

Each partner of the business must file a tax return for the previous accounting period ending in that tax year. The return will show that partner's share of profits. Partners will therefore have to agree between themselves how the profits will be allocated for tax purposes and how the money will be found to pay the tax due.

For new businesses, the first tax year will be the year in which the business started and its basis period will run from the day on which the business first traded to 5 April of the following year. Thus, in year one, if you start your business on 1 September 2012, your first tax year is 2012/13 and the basis period is 1 September 2012 to 5 April 2013. You will pay tax on the actual profits made in this period.

There is nothing to stop you having a trading year through to the following 31 August 2013, but for tax purposes your first tax year will be seven months long and you will be taxed on seven out of your 12 months in that tax year.

For your second tax year you will be taxed on the profits made over the 12-month period (assuming the accounting date is at least 12 months from the commencement date). In our example, the second trading period would be 1 September 2012 to 31 August 2013. Part of these profits will, of course, have already been assessed in the first tax year and are called overlap profits. This overlap is adjusted either on retirement or where there is a change of accounting period, but the effects are not indexed to take account of inflation. In the early years as profits move from a low base and then rise there may be a tax advantage in adopting an accounting year ending early in the tax year, such as 30 April. However, the system is designed to ensure that nobody avoids tax on any of their business profits indefinitely. If you arrange things so that overlap profits help you when you first start out, the overlap element will catch up with you when you cease to practise or if you change your accounting year.

Individuals should take advice as to the best date for commencement and how long the first accounting period will be, but for the majority, the most favourable date is likely to be an accounting year running from 1 April to 31 March.

The assessment

Tax returns will have to be filed by 31 January following the tax year. The taxpayer must do the calculations and the inspector will then agree or dispute them, but it is up to the taxpayer to get it right initially without the intervention of the inspector. Although in theory the inspector sets the level of tax, the majority of small businesses, including solicitors, submit their accounts and tax returns via accountants, who calculate the amount of tax due. The inspector checks through the figures and if they are not acceptable, discussions take place and an accommodation is reached. The inspector has 11 months after the 31 January filing deadline to raise starting enquiries. Enquiries are bad news and best avoided by getting the return right in the first place by filing full and complete information with the return to supplement the accounts. If an agreement cannot be reached, the inspector raises an assessment and leaves the taxpayer or their accountant to argue against it at a hearing before the tax commissioners. However, in most cases agreement is reached before that stage. You retain the option to have the inspector do the calculations, provided you submit the necessary information sufficiently early.

Time for payment

The relevant tax for the relevant period is in two instalments on 31 January and 31 July each year. A payment on account of the tax due must be paid on 31 January in the year of assessment and a further interim payment will be due the following 31 July (which is in the year following the year of assessment as it is after 5 April). These interim payments will usually be based on the tax payable in the previous year, a bit like an estimated electricity bill or a service charge arrangement on a flat. Then on the following 31 January a further payment will be due. This will be partly a payment on account of the next tax bill and partly a settling up of the actual tax due for the earlier period now that the figures have been agreed, always assuming that the inspector and your accountant have reached the accommodation referred to earlier. Any CGT payable will also be due in the 31 January payment.

Tax planning

If you have been a partner in a large firm, tax planning considerations will be something which will have passed you by. Even in a fairly small partnership, these aspects are usually dealt with by the accountants in conjunction with the senior partner. If you are now a sole practitioner, or perhaps a two-partner firm, you are the senior partner and this is something which you cannot afford to neglect.

You need to establish a tax reserve to avoid getting into difficulties. This should all be part and parcel of your business plan. Keep an eye on what money you are making in a year and only take out by way of drawings at the very most what you would pay yourself if you were an employee. In this way, you leave the tax element still in the business. There is no need to be particularly scientific about this. See how much profit you have made for the month and take out up to 75 per cent of it. If there is no real need to take that much out, leave it in the business. In this way, you will start to build up a credit balance on the office account.

When the balance gets more than your everyday needs, transfer it into a building society account. This will be the office deposit account, but to a large extent it will also be your tax reserve.

In your first year your start-up capital should assume you will not take a draw at all, so in effect you will live off your savings, or borrowed money, until you have a year's trading behind you and can assess what sort of profits you are making. Your budget for the first year will in any event be very haphazard. There will be unexpected expenses, and perhaps even the odd piece of particularly profitable work, each of which will distort your budget. You may, however, feel there are months, especially in the second six months of trading, when you can be adventurous and take a draw.

You will need to be very conservative in your drawings policy for years one and two. Once this somewhat turbulent period is over and patterns are emerging, you can start to exercise a little less caution and still take a draw (although perhaps not a full one) even in a bad month, taking a yearly view of the position rather than focusing on just that one poor month.

If you have a particularly bad month, you will still need to pay your bills. You must bear in mind that you are taking out money which is not really there. Provided you are not drawing out the full level of profit in the better months, things will even themselves out.

Periodically, review the whole situation as you go through the year and estimate what your tax liability for that year is going to be or ask your accountant to estimate it and make sure that what is going into the building society account is going to be adequate to deal with the tax situation which will arise, albeit not for a year or two.

Again, at the end of the year, look back and see over a couple of years what tax liability has built up and ensure that the building society account has enough to deal with it. If not, you have been overdrawing and must do something about it during the following year, both in terms of working harder and drawing out slightly less each month.

The need to build up a tax reserve of this kind is still important despite making a payment on account, especially when profits are rising. As they rise, so does the tax bill. It is easy to see large sums of money building up on office account and guessing the tax bill and committing the balance to other purposes only to find you have underestimated the tax. The sudden need to find an extra several thousand pounds can come as an unwelcome shock to the wallet.

The annual accounts examination

In order to comply with the Solicitors Act 1974, s.34 and the SRA Accounts Rules 2011, you will need to have your accounts examined by a qualified accountant during the period specified. A qualified accountant for these purposes is a Member of the Institute of Chartered Accountants of England, Ireland, Scotland or Wales, or of the Chartered Association of Certified Accountants. Section 34 of the Act (which is set out in **Appendix 9**) defines the period as covering not less than 12 months beginning at the expiry of the last preceding period for which an accountant's report has been delivered.

You will need to obtain advice from your accountant on how long your first accounting period should run. The accountant's report must be delivered to the Law Society within six months of the end of the accounting period that you have chosen. Your further accounting periods will normally be of 12 months, following on consecutively from the end of the first period, with further accountant's reports delivered within six months from the end of each. This rule is applied rigidly, catching a lot of solicitors, and even more accountants, who were unaware of when it first came into force. The delivery of the accountant's report was once considered something of a formality, and if it was a few days or even a few weeks overdue, provided there was nothing known about the firm which would give rise to undue alarm, the overdue report and a letter of apology was all that was necessary. Gone are those days. If you are so much as one day overdue, the provisions of the Solicitors Act 1974, s.12(i)(ee) will be vigorously applied against you. Even now there are accountants who do not understand the seriousness of being a day late, thinking that an apology and explanation that it is the accountant's fault will put things right. It will not.

The consequences of being late are not being able to apply for your practising certificate at the same time as everyone else – you will join the queue of those persons who have been out of practice for several years, in prison, struck off or made bankrupt. You will follow the same procedures laid down for them, which include obtaining references from at least two of your professional colleagues stating that they consider you are a fit and proper person to practise. In addition, you will have to pay an administration fee to the Law Society. That is the least of your worries compared with the considerable uncertainty which follows, as practising certificates arrive on everyone else's desk except yours and the time rapidly approaches when, to comply with the law, you will have to close down your practice until the certificate arrives.

I speak as one who has gone through this ignominious and worrying procedure due to my previous accountant's computer flagging the report as having been delivered by him to the Law Society when in fact it was still on his file. The Law Society has no discretion to waive this provision as it is laid down by Act of Parliament. The previous latitude given to solicitors arose out of a rather relaxed attitude towards the provisions of the Solicitors Act 1974 and the rules made under it, highlighted by subsequent litigation designed to bring this point to the Law

Society's notice and something which it is unlikely in the future to disregard.

The message is therefore very simple. Make sure that the examination of your accounts is put in hand in good time and that you highlight in your diary the final date for delivery of the accountant's report, i.e. six months after the end of your financial period. Press the accountants for the report well before that date, i.e. a number of months rather than weeks, and get them to send the report to you. Do not rely on a statement from them that they have sent it to the Law Society. Some accountants refuse to send the report to you and say their professional body requires that they send it direct. If needs be refer them to the Law Society, which will make it quite clear that they are to provide you with the report and it is for you to send it to the Law Society.

Your accountant's fees are likely to be slightly higher for the first year while they are finding out about your business and your financial affairs generally. You will have to give them details of all building society and bank accounts that you hold, not only in your own name privately but also for clients. You may, for example, have opened and operate a designated building society account on a client's behalf. Full details of all of these accounts will have to be passed to your accountants and it takes time for them to record the information, for the most part on computer. There may be one or two problems with the first year's accounts while any errors that you might have made are sorted out. The accountants should allow for this in any estimate that they give you. Since these set-up costs will not need to be repeated, you will be in a stronger position to argue fees with the accountants in the subsequent years. Hopefully, the business will have expanded, but the additional work the accountants will have to carry out in conducting the accounts examination and preparing a set of accounts for submission to HMRC will not be nearly so great as the amount of work involved in setting up the job originally. The choice of accountants is important. It is advisable to obtain a recommendation from another solicitor and to question the accountants on the number of solicitors' practices on behalf of which they carry out the annual accounts examination and to press them to obtain their clients' permission to talk to you. Solicitors tend to think that most accountants will have had experience of conducting the examination, but this is far from being the case.

It is essential to obtain a definite quotation from the firm concerned, not only for the first year but also for subsequent years. You will need to build an important item like this into your annual budget, and while there are plenty of examples of solicitors who will spring a nasty surprise in relation to their fees on their client, there are also plenty of examples of accountants who will do likewise. It may well be difficult for an accountant to quote for the first year for the reasons given above; this should not, however, preclude a quotation from being requested.

CHECKLISTS

Registering for VAT

- Obtain Form VAT1, complete it and send it to the local VAT office (obtain address from your accountant or another local trader).
- Pass details to printer for inclusion on invoice pads once VAT number is allocated or amend your bill template if producing your own.

Accounts examination

- Draw up shortlist of accountants.
- Invite them to attend your offices separately to talk about their services, inspect your accounting system and submit a written quotation to include:

  (a) accounts examination under the Solicitors Act 1974;
  (b) completion of report;
  (c) preparation and submission of a set of accounts to HMRC;
  (d) agreement with HMRC;
  (e) completion and submission of your tax return and, if appropriate, that of your spouse.

- Ask each firm for a reference from a firm of solicitors whose accounts examination they currently conduct.
- Take up references.
- Select firm and agree a start date no more than six weeks after your year end.
- Diarise a date one month later for chasing draft accounts if not submitted.
- Diarise a further date six weeks prior to final submission date of accountant's report to insist report produced immediately if not already submitted to you.
- Diarise final submission date, i.e. six months from year end.
- Send off report to Law Society prior to submission date.

9

Starting to trade

Publicity

So this is it – you have got your premises and you are in them, the phones are on, you have chosen the start date and the great day has arrived. Other than sitting behind your second-hand desk in your swivel chair waiting for the telephone to ring, is there anything else that you should be doing?

The first thing you should do is to get out your diary and make a note of the exact date on which you started to trade. It is remarkably easy months later to be unsure of the exact date on which your new firm was born. As you will probably want to celebrate its birth every year, possibly using it as an excuse for a party to invite clients and make them feel a part of the firm, it is important to know exactly when the occasion took place. It is also necessary to know the date for tax reasons.

Should you be sitting behind the desk waiting for the phone to ring at all? The first few months for any new business are an extremely difficult and uncertain time. You will probably be afraid to leave the office for fear that the telephone will ring and you will miss a client. It is particularly important in the first few months to reassure existing clients that you are still very much around and available. Especially with small firms, clients have the perception that given a couple of heavy cases you will be unable to cope with theirs – bereft of the substantial resources that you may have enjoyed at a larger firm, you will be submerged in other people's paperwork and their affairs will be neglected. You have to prove that this is not the case and you must therefore be totally available to your clients and fulfil their every need. Once this psychological barrier has been overcome, there will be no difficulty when a member of staff tells a client that you are unavailable for the moment and you will get back to them shortly, particularly when you have a good track record of a few months of the new firm's performance behind you. Clients will be quite happy to accept the situation and will not feel that this unavailability is the start of a deterioration in the service they have always enjoyed when you were with a larger firm. In the meantime, however, you have got to give them not simply a good service but an excellent one, so that, if anything, they feel that the start of the new firm on your part is a big step forward compared with the slightly less than adequate service they might have enjoyed previously with either your old firm (if they were clients of that practice) or any other firm they may have instructed.

Chapter 6 deals with advertising and the timing of the appearance of your advertisements in various types of media. If you are in time for annual directories such as the Yellow Pages and Thomson Local Directory, to some extent you will have taken care of the publicity side of things, but inevitably there is going to be a delay between the start of the firm and the appearance of advertisements in that type of directory. As discussed in **Chapter 6**, the gap can, to some extent, be filled by advertisements in local newspapers, but there are other ways of publicising the fact that you are in business. You will also have set up your website and any electronic advertising that you have decided upon.

Signage

Perhaps the most obvious form of advertising will be your firm's sign on the outside of the building telling potential and existing clients where you are. If you have decided to take a lease of premises that have a shop frontage, you will no doubt be arranging for a sign writer to put the traditional gold lettering 'Solicitors' sign in the window. You may want to opt for a brass plate with your name on it. Brass is quite expensive and needs to be regularly polished. It also will take a few weeks to be delivered. An alternative is the 'brass effect' plastic sign with a metal overlay, which still costs around £100 but can look surprisingly good. A silver effect version, which looks equally good, is also available. Many office stationery outlets can supply the plastic sign. A brass sign can give some clients the impression of being expensive and unapproachable. On the other hand, the plastic type with a metal overlay can give many people a more modern and friendly impression.

You will have to consider whether you need permission to put any sign up outside. If you have taken out a lease, the erection of such a plate may be controlled by the provisions of the lease. The terms of the lease may not cover the exterior of the building and the exterior may not form part of the demise. In either case, you may need the permission of the landlord to put up any signage, and this is something best negotiated at the outset when the landlord may be keen to have you sign a lease rather than as an afterthought when you are already installed in the premises.

The other consideration is planning law. The position is governed by the Town and Country Planning (Control of Advertisements) (England) Regulations 2007, SI 2007/783. These regulations permit the display of notices or signs advertising the fact that a person, partnership or company is carrying on a profession, business or trade at those premises. Advertisements fitting this description are given deemed planning consent without the need for a separate application to the planning authority. Your nameplate is, after all, an advertisement, since it advertises the fact that you are trading from the premises as a firm of solicitors.

The advertisement must not exceed 0.3 m in area (approximately 3.23 sq ft), and no character or symbol on the advertisement may be more than 0.75 m in height (2.46 ft) or 0.3 m (0.984 ft) in an area of special control. No part of the advertisement may be more than 4.6 m (15.08 ft) above ground level or 3.6 m (11.81 ft) in an area of special control. Only one such advertisement is permitted unless the premises have more than one entrance on different road frontages, in which case you may have one sign at each entrance, subject to a maximum of two.

Illumination is not permitted at all for solicitors and if you wanted such a sign it would need to be the subject of a separate planning application.

If the building which you occupy is a listed building, or if you are in a conservation area, different provisions may apply. In those circumstances, you would do well to check with your local planning officer before putting up the sign. It is unlikely that no form of signage will be permitted, but it may be rather less in terms of size and prominence than would be the case in an area not subject to such controls. If you have managed to enter into an office-sharing arrangement, you will need to have an arrangement with the people you are sharing the space with, and this in turn may need the agreement of their landlords. Again, this is something best dealt with at the outset rather than later.

At this stage, you should also give some thought to internal signage. If you are on the third floor, you will want a prominent sign downstairs directing clients up to your reception area.

Spreading the word

The other form of publicity is word of mouth. Tell anyone and everyone you can think of that you are setting up in practice. Tell your friends, neighbours, existing clients, and clients you have not spoken to for years; ask them to support you if they can – this is no time to be bashful, you are going to need every client you can get. You must also make yourself known in the locality. Contact all the bank and building society managers and arrange to see them. If you go into the newsagents, start a conversation about business generally and then, at a suitable point, introduce the fact that you have just opened up down the road and that if there is anything that you can help them with at any time you would be only too pleased to do so. You may have slight pangs of unprofessionalism and feel that you are being a bit like a door-to-door encyclopaedia salesman, but this is precisely what everyone else in business does. It is open to you to do the same so long as you do not infringe outcome 8.3 of the SRA Code of Conduct 2011 by cold calling (see **Chapter 18**). There is no need for the hard sell: simply tell people who you are, where you are and that you would welcome their business if they choose to instruct you. Do not forget to leave them a business card.

Informing clients

You may be leaving an existing practice either as an assistant solicitor or as a partner and quite clearly an obvious source of business for your new practice is the client base of that practice. Whether or not you can make use of this will depend on your exact status in the firm. If you are an assistant solicitor with a contract of employment there may well be a restraining clause preventing you from taking clients with you. If you operate in this area of the law, you may be able to take a view yourself on the precise effect of the clause and how enforceable it is. Be careful – the last thing you want to have when you are trying to wrestle with the problems of your new firm is a lawsuit from the old one. Unfortunately, it does happen. It is fairly common for people to put in restraining clauses which they know will probably not be upheld if challenged in the courts, but they take a deliberate decision to put in a fairly restrictive clause on the basis that the restrained employee is not going to want to take their organisation to court.

A rather superficial statement of the law is that such a clause will only be enforced by the courts if it is reasonably necessary to protect the interests of the employer and is not in unreasonable restraint of trade. If the courts decide that it is in unreasonable restraint of trade, the entire clause stands at risk of being struck out completely. There is a good deal of case law on the subject and if you think that your employers or partners are likely to be upset if you take certain clients with you, take some serious advice on the clause to the extent of going to counsel.

Further guidance on what ethically you can and cannot do used to be found in the Law Society's Principle 3.12 of *The Guide to the Professional Conduct of Solicitors 1999* (the Guide). Although no longer directly applicable since the advent of the SRA Code of Conduct 2011, you would do well to bear the guidance previously given in the Guide in mind to avoid accusations of sharp practice or unprofessional conduct if exception is taken to your approach to a client.

Once you are satisfied that you know what the position is, it would be a good idea to make a list of those clients who you think or know would follow you and to approach the partners and ask them if they would have any objection to you acting for those clients. You will probably find that most of the clients on your list are people that you have introduced to the firm anyway and you may be pleasantly surprised at the approach which the partners take. If the reaction is bad, however, you will clearly have to be rather careful in what you do. Keep strictly to the terms of the restraining clause unless you are certain that it will not be upheld by the courts. In the final analysis, the court is unlikely to prevent a client from giving you instructions where it is clear that the relationship with the former firm and the client has deteriorated through no fault of yours, other than the fact that you are offering a choice simply by setting up a new practice.

If you have been a partner in an existing firm, the situation may be very different. Again, you will have to look to the terms of the partnership deed, but in the absence of a lawful restraining clause there is nothing to stop you from circulating every single client of the firm with notification of your intention to set up in practice and to ask them whether they wish to have their files transferred to the new practice or to stay with the old one (see Principle 3.12 of the Guide). A useful precedent for this letter is contained in Annex 3F of the Guide, which is phrased as being written jointly by the continuing partners and the outgoing partner, but can be adapted if either side wishes to write unilaterally. However, if the firm is unwilling to follow the advice given in the Guide, you are in a rather difficult position. It may be helpful if the parties are able to talk to someone in the Solicitors Regulation Authority's Professional Ethics Department for clarification of the relevant principles. This may be enough to cause the parties to go along with the guidance, or you could perhaps confine yourself to ringing round people and passing the information that way. Where there has been an alteration to the composition of the firm, all clients who may be affected should be informed promptly. In addition, if the client's work would suffer from a restraining clause being enforced it would be proper to transfer the client's file despite the restraining clause.

In reality, there is no point in approaching clients who are wedded to the firm or to particular partners within it. It can, however, be surprising who follows you and who does not. People with whom you felt you had a close professional relationship will decide to stay with the present firm and others whom you had thought would never have followed you will go to considerable lengths to trace you if news of your departure has not reached them. You can often find that when you discuss this with them and say that you thought they were the client of another partner, they will come out with comments such as, 'Yes, he's great company in the pub but he's useless if you want to get anything done'. To have such people endorse your professional qualities in such a way can be heartening in the extreme at a time when you feel at your most isolated.

In so far as clients have made their choice and are coming with you, get your hands on the files. You do not want to have to wrangle with other people at a later stage over the actual transfer of the files to you. Get the files under your own control and get them billed up to date and explain to the client that the file can only be transferred once those costs have been cleared and the client has given instructions for the file to be transferred. When this has been dealt with, get the files ready to take home, in so far as this can be properly done without interfering with work on them.

The client's work must come first and any disagreement with the old firm should not be allowed to interfere with the proper conduct of the client's business. This is often easier said than done, but where a client has unequivocally decided to come with you, and has paid any outstanding bills, it would be difficult for someone to criticise you for trying to get hold of the file, since in doing so you are complying with general principles contained in the SRA Code of Conduct 2011 and the Chapter 1 outcomes that the client's interests must come first.

Obtaining new clients

You will find that in the first three or four months of opening there is a plethora of things to do. While there will undoubtedly be times when you are sitting doing nothing, for the most part you will be wishing that there were more hours in the day to get everything done. The initial shock waves of opening the new practice will have begun to subside and the telephones will have started to ring with comforting reassurance.

By this stage, you will have consolidated what business you have managed to take with you and you can start to attract new clients for the firm. You have introduced yourself to as many people as possible and put the word about that you have arrived in town and are ready to deal with whatever work comes your way. You now need to put in hand a series of marketing initiatives to make sure that you are taking the business to the clients as well as waiting for the clients to come to you.

If you have a lot of experience in business or have run a marketing campaign before, you may wish to start a major promotion of your practice right away. Running such a marketing programme is dealt with in greater detail in **Chapter 18**. Even if you feel it is not yet the right time for a full-scale marketing campaign, for which you may not, at this point, have sufficient time or money available, you still need to consolidate the ground you have gained. But the question is, how do you find new clients?

One answer is an inaugural party. This is simply an excuse to put on an enjoyable social engagement for as many people as possible with the intention of placing your name before as many potential clients as possible. The excuse can be a summer barbeque, bonfire night, an 'anniversary of one month and still in business' party, or anything else that seems appropriate. The cost of such a party is likely to be £200 or £300. If it results in a single conveyance, divorce or landlord-tenant dispute that you would not otherwise have had, it has paid for itself, and any clients that arrive as a result of your marketing initiative will be clients not only on a single occasion, but for a number of occasions in the future.

The business lunch

Nearly all the tax advantages of business lunches that existed in the past have been removed. This does not necessarily mean to say that they are a bad idea. Clients are still flattered, by and large, by a free afternoon out.

From the clients' point of view, they are able to convince themselves that they are acting in the best interests of their own organisation, which indeed they may be if they are able to replace a mediocre firm of solicitors with one such as yours that is able to do the job better. It also means that they are able to get to know a solicitor on a personal level and develop a relationship and rapport. All of these things are crucial not only from the solicitor's point of view, but also from the client's. If you are in business, you need a solicitor whom you can trust. There is a multitude to choose from and the business lunch provides the opportunity to make your mind up about someone. As a marketing tool, it still has its place.

Joining an organisation

The more societies, organisations and clubs you join the more people you will meet who are potential clients. They will be able to see you at first hand and decide what kind of individual you are. Join as many organisations as you can and be as active as time permits, and get the exposure to as many people as you can that a young business needs.

Citizens Advice Bureaux

The numerous, if shrinking, number of offices of the Citizens Advice Bureau (CAB) around the country fulfil a very important need within our society, and with the reduction in what used to be called legal aid their importance has perhaps never been greater. There are many people in society who are faced with problems that they simply cannot deal with and turn to the CAB for help and advice. Introduce yourself to the local CAB at an early stage and offer to provide it with such assistance as you can. Most CAB offices have an evening at which their clients attend by appointment to see a lawyer free of charge to deal with problems that the CAB personnel are not qualified to deal with. It is unlikely that this form of referral will result in a vast increase in your business, but it is precisely the kind of additional inflow of work that a new practice needs. In addition, there is no harm in letting people know, in appropriate places, that you are prepared to do such work. If you are prepared to devote such time as you can willingly to help those less fortunate in society, sooner or later the good works you have performed will reap their reward. People may respect you for the work that you do and be bonded to the firm that bit more as a result.

Talks and seminars

Many organisations will jump at the chance of having a lawyer attend for free to give a talk, especially if it is on a topical matter. The initiative must come from you. Find something on which you feel you can talk for half an hour (without making too much of a fool of yourself), put the talk together and then approach an appropriate organisation. The whole exercise will probably cost you two hours in terms of time in getting the talk together and presenting it. If that results in two hours' worth of chargeable time later on, it is an excellent investment. The probability is that it will result in more than that, and over the next five years you may find that your time and effort has been repaid many fold. It is not at all difficult to do. The biggest hurdle is the discipline required to take time out from the ordinary routine of daily practice to do the research and to fit the presentation into your daily schedule. From a marketing point of view, you take the floor as an expert in the particular field. Make sure that in the course of the talk people know who you are, where you are and what you can do for them. You should not go so far as to turn the whole thing into a gigantic sales pitch, but there is no point in giving up your time and effort if at the end of it people do not have the slightest idea who you are.

Newspaper column

Another marketing exercise you may consider carrying out is to contact your local newspaper and ask whether it would like you to write a legal column. You will be fortunate indeed if the newspaper will pay you anything for doing so, but it will give considerable publicity for you and your practice in the locality. As with seminars, you start off on the footing that you will be regarded by your readers as an authority on the law and as something of a minor celebrity. It is perhaps not so much the likely influx of clientele which is the value of writing a column as the increase in esteem in which you are held by your existing clients who get to know of it.

The existing client base

Within a few months of being in practice, you will have a clear idea about who your existing clients are. If you analyse those clients and the type of business they conduct, you will see that with their co-operation you will be able to reach a great many other people and those customers of your client's business will have considerable trust in what those clients say to them. This is a rather difficult and sensitive area, but with tact and diplomacy you may be able to persuade your existing clientele to intro-duce you to their clients. Many of your clients will themselves have set up on their own at some stage and may be only too acutely aware of the giant leap into the dark that this represents. If so, they may be very sympathetic to an approach in which you ask them to introduce you to their customer base. It is a rather slow process but can reap considerable rewards. If clients do allow you access to their own client base, it is even more impor-tant that the job you do for their clients is a good one.

If it is, your clients will rise in their own clientele's esteem. If you make a mess of it, your clients will feel betrayed and you stand to lose not only their clients but also the client who introduced you. Tread carefully, but if handled in the right way you could pick up some extremely valu-able clients by using this method of marketing.

Credit control and billing

Bills to clients were rightly described by a former senior partner of mine as the 'lifeblood of the firm'. The design and appearance of your invoice will be almost as important as that of your notepaper. Work should be billed, to quote the same former senior partner, 'while the tears of gratitude are fresh in the client's eyes'. Do not be bashful about putting in a bill – it should go in at the earliest opportunity. The clients who comment that you are rather fast at putting in the bill are those with whom you are likely to have a problem. It is certainly wrong to put in a bill prematurely, but once the actual work involved is completed, it should go in immediately. As well as the main office's bills delivered book, it is not a bad idea to make your own (as described earlier). It can be as informal as having a counsel's notebook divided into five columns with the following headings:

Client	Matter	Date bill delivered	Date bill paid	Profit costs
J Bloggs	Matrim. Procs	1/11/12	1/12/12	£500.00

In this way you have at your fingertips a complete summary of the entire billing of the firm. This may, depending on the stage of the evolution of the firm, consist of simply yourself, or you and one or two others, but no matter; you have the same up-to-the-minute information as a senior partner of a 20-partner, 80-fee earner firm with a multi-million pound turnover. The only difference is that such a senior partner needs a multi-million pound computer system serviced by a great many computer oper-ators to obtain that information whereas you have the same level of information at virtually no cost. You must ask yourself the question: who is managing whose business most efficiently? This is the advantage of being a principal in a small practice.

Giving credit

Many businesses inform the client on the invoice that they have 30 days or so in which to pay the account. This is an invitation to the client to take at least a month to pay the bill. Our invoices have always stated quite clearly on their face that they are payable immediately with the words 'this amount is due now'. In order to comply with Chapter 1 outcomes and in particular outcome 1.14, a suitable endorsement should appear on your bill such as:

> Sections 70, 71 and 72 of the Solicitors Act 1974 contain provisions enabling clients to have solicitors' bills assessed (i.e. checked by an officer of the court). Strict time limits apply. If you are dissatisfied with the bill please speak initially to whoever sent it and if they are unable to resolve the situation please speak to a partner. You also have the right to refer the matter to the Legal Ombudsman whose address can be obtained from the Solicitors Regulation Authority website or from our written complaints procedure, available on request. If this bill is not paid within one month interest at the High Court judgment debt rate is chargeable from the date of the invoice.

This enables the interest provisions in non-contentious matters to run and further serves as the necessary notice that is required to be delivered in a non-contentious matter before you can sue on a bill. Displayed in a reasonably prominent position on an account in this way, clients are unlikely to take umbrage. Commercial clients are used to seeing other people's standard conditions of sale and, if anything, the wording on the face of a bill is likely to convey to them a favourable commercial image by the solicitors rather than any kind of an aggressive stance. In any event, you cannot get away from the fact that in order to litigate against a client effectively if they fail to pay the bill in a non-contentious matter, you must serve a notice in the required form. By failing to serve that notice in the accompanying bill you are giving those clients who have determined not to pay the account an unnecessary extension of credit. Even though the notice is not required in respect of contentious work, it may indicate to the court that you have acted fairly in bringing the client's rights to his or her notice at the outset and so help you gain the moral high ground.

Make sure that the notice is on your copy of the bill as well as the client's copy. The district judge will need to be satisfied that the notice has been validly served and may not accept your bold assertions that you 'are sure it must have been on the top copy' as adequate proof of service if your file copy contains no such notice.

For those solicitors who are unfortunate enough to have to sue their own clients, a form of final letter and draft claim appear at **Appendices 5 and 6**.

Even the most basic computerised accounts system now provides for an aged debtors list. This will be in the form of a computer printout of those bills that are a month or more (depending on the program) in arrears with their accounts. Once a client has failed to pay after as short a time as a month, you should be chasing them immediately provided there is no cogent reason not to. At the very least, you should send a copy of the bill with a reminder endorsed on it that the account is outstanding. It is important to keep records as to what reminders have been sent out so that you can validly state at the required time that a client has had two or three reminders, as the case may be, and still failed to pay the account, constraining you to take stronger measures. There is nothing worse than a client correctly pointing out that he has not had the reminders, at least not as many reminders as you have said. It still does not put the client in the right but it shows that you are capable of making mistakes and makes you appear incompetent.

Apart from the aged debtors list, if you keep a personal bills delivered book and date stamp those bills that are paid, as I have suggested, you will quite readily see gaps appearing where bills are overdue even before the aged debtors list has arrived on your desk. Send out the chasing letters, keep on top of the debtors and where necessary sue those clients who it is clear are determined not to pay. Do not shy away from taking such action. If they are clients who cannot be bothered to pay for the work you have done, they are clients who are not worth keeping. If they are clients who are not paying because they do not have the money, the sooner you are on their tail the better, before the other creditors close in.

There will always be exceptions. There are clients who have fallen on hard times and who clearly do not have the money. You may be in a position to help them get through a very difficult time by not pressing them for payment and making it clear that you do not wish to add to their worries. These will be very much the exceptions. If you take the view that a client is verging on the point of bankruptcy and you are not going to get your money out of them, there is nothing to be gained by jumping on them along with the rest of their creditors. There may, however, be something to be gained by making a point of not pressing them, saying you will give them what help you can while they are going through a difficult time, keeping in regular touch with them and showing concern. People in that situation do have a habit of bouncing back at some stage in the future and they may need you to help set up a second time. Do not, however, make the mistake of rendering them additional legal services on any substantial scale and simply doubling the size of the unpaid bill.

If you have clearly made a mistake in the conduct of the client's affairs and it is for this reason that the client is disputing your bill, great care should be exercised in deciding whether to sue the client. Even if you do decide not to sue you have a duty to advise the client to seek independent legal advice if you think the circumstances would justify a claim against you (see outcome 1.16 of the SRA Code of Conduct 2011). If the client's claims are legitimate a defence and counterclaim will be filed, at which point you must notify your PI insurers of the claim if it is likely to exceed £500, unless your policy provides for a different figure. Your insurers may decide to take over conduct of the whole proceedings and in all probability the end result will be a compromise. If that compromise involves your insurers paying out money to the client, not only will you have failed to recover the fee but you will also have a higher premium to pay when you renew your PI cover. It does not mean that for every little mistake you make, you can allow the client unreasonably to refuse to pay the bill, but it does mean that great care must be exercised in deciding whether to issue a summons or whether it would be better to negotiate the best compromise you can and put the whole matter down to experience.

10

Holidays and staffing requirements

Solicitors Regulation Authority regulations

Complying with the requirements of the SRA Handbook and SRA Code of Conduct 2011 as regards the staffing of premises can present substantial problems for small practices. The preceding regulations and 2007 Code were designed to ensure that the standards of service and competence which the public is entitled to expect are maintained. It is fair to say that with fewer resources at their disposal smaller practices may be more tempted to cut corners as regards staff than larger practices.

Chapter 7 of the SRA Code of Conduct 2011 deals with the supervision and management of a solicitors' office. The earlier rules requiring you to make 'arrangements for the effective management of the firm as a whole' and to exercise appropriate supervision over all staff and ensure adequate supervision and direction of clients' matters have been replaced by more nebulous outcomes and the requirement to monitor the risks of non-compliance. Lest it be thought that this is a relaxation of the previous set up, be aware that it is in fact a more demanding regime. The whole ethos of outcomes-focused regulation (OFR) is that you no longer have a set of rules that would in effect provide you with a defence if something goes wrong. You cannot say that you complied to the letter with a given rule so it is not your fault if things went wrong. Under OFR if you failed to achieve the necessary outcome you are at fault no matter how hard you tried to achieve it. Further, you obviously failed to identify, monitor and manage the risk sufficiently and anticipate the situation because if you had it would not have happened.

Outcome 7.1 requires you to have a clear and effective governance structure and reporting lines. Outcome 7.2 requires you to have effective systems and controls in place to achieve and comply with all the principles, rules and outcomes and other requirements of the Handbook where applicable. Outcome 7.3 requires you to identify, monitor and manage risks in compliance with all the principles, rules and outcomes and other requirements of the Handbook where applicable and to take steps to address the issues identified. The remainder of the Chapter 7 outcomes continue in a similar vein, in essence requiring you to ensure that your practice is at all times properly and professionally managed, that the clients' affairs are efficiently and correctly dealt with and that the usual professional standards are maintained. Indicative behaviour 7.4 suggests that you might have achieved the outcomes if you have made arrangements for the continuation of your firm in the event of absences and emergencies, for example, holiday or sick leave, with the minimum of interruption to clients' business.

So, there are no specific do's or don'ts – just make sure it works. The earlier requirements of the 2007 Code to have someone who is qualified to supervise on the premises is not reproduced in the 2011 Code, but there is still an obligation to comply with rule 12 of the SRA Practice Framework Rules 2011 which sets out who the persons qualified to supervise are, and they are pretty much the same as under the old rule 5 of the 2007 Code.

The onus is shifted very much onto you. You run your practice how you think it should be run, but if there are problems and clients complain, you will have to show that the way in which you managed and supervised your practice at the time was not relevant to the complaint or problem. The way in which the practice was managed or supervised will come under scrutiny and it will be for you to show that your procedures and their execution were sufficient in the circumstances.

Supervisors and managers are entitled to take normal holidays and a breach of the 2011 Code does not necessarily occur just because they go on holiday. You must make sure that suitable arrangements are in place to ensure that any duties to clients and others are fully met. While you are away you still have a duty to conduct your clients' affairs properly and to continue to supply a proper professional service. If something goes wrong in your absence and one reason is that your management or supervision of the practice was inadequate, you will find yourself in trouble with the SRA. It all comes down to common sense. If things are hectic just before you go away and your staff are not sufficiently skilled or experienced to cope, you must get someone in who can handle matters, despite the expense. It is not fair to either your staff or clients to do otherwise. On the other hand, there is no point employing a locum to sit and do nothing for two weeks. (With luck, you'll be doing that!) You must balance the level of business with the experience and number of staff coping in your absence and the possibility of an emergency arising. Decide whether you can leave them to manage things in your absence, with perhaps a senior experienced employee in charge, or whether you need to hire a locum to manage and supervise.

If you are a sole practitioner and are intending to close down for two weeks you must make arrangements to ensure that clients' work will not suffer while you are away. This will involve getting things right up to date and putting in place contingency plans in case anything blows up during your absence, including temporary arrangements for another solicitor to be authorised to operate your client account in case a client should demand the return of funds you may be holding.

In some ways the new rules are more flexible than the old ones, so that if you shut the office for a few days you will not necessarily fall foul of the rules as there is no specific rule to prohibit it. If something does go wrong it will be a different story if you have not put something in place to deal with the unexpected. However, the rules do not allow you to open a branch office, put a trainee solicitor in charge of it and leave it to run itself. Neither do the rules allow you to have a trainee in the office at all times with the principal popping in and out on the odd occasion to supervise things. If that is the normal situation, you will be in trouble as soon as anything goes wrong, and arguably before that because you will not have sufficient systems in place to ensure compliance with the requirements of the Handbook. If, however, you have to be out of the office for the day on business or for court work, there is no need to hire a senior assistant simply in order to comply with the rules. It is a question of degree. If you are to be involved in a six-week trial which requires your constant attendance, you will be reaching the stage where it is becoming normal for you to be out of the office and the practice is being run by your trainee solicitor. In that situation, you will have to consider carefully whether you should take on additional qualified or experienced staff on a temporary basis. Failure to do so may lead to you being found in breach of the management requirements of Chapter 7 and the Practice Framework Rules. A good rule of thumb is to imagine that there is a terrible disaster with a client and you then have to explain yourself to the SRA. Explaining why you were out of the office for a couple of days without having made separate arrangements might not be too much of a problem, but you may feel that your excuses were rather thin if you had gone away for four or five weeks – albeit in connection with work rather than pleasure – and had left the practice in the hands of an inexperienced member of staff when something went terribly wrong. The difference between the OFR approach and the 2007 Code is that whilst you may have escaped a finding of a breach of the 2007 Code you will probably not do so under the SRA Handbook and your explanations will amount to mitigation rather than a defence. The whole point of OFR is to avoid the disaster happening in the first place, not apportioning blame after the event.

The locum

The traditional answer to prolonged absence from the office, whether it is for reasons of holiday or illness, has been the locum. Locums may wrongly be thought by some to be third-rate solicitors who are unable to hold down a full-time job. Undoubtedly, there are some locums who fit this description, but there are a good many very competent individuals who, for one reason or another, are unable or unwilling to work on a full-time basis. Go to a well-known agency and make sure you find out as much as possible about the person to whom you are about to entrust your practice. You need to know past history, knowledge and experience. Ensure that the locum has a sufficient level of competence and knowledge of the type of work that you carry out in your practice to be able to do a proper job in your absence. If you do not take these precautions, you may find that they cause a whole series of disasters and you return to a terrible mess. If you are able to obtain a recommendation from another firm as to a particular locum, so much the better. If possible, try and meet the locum to form your own views.

It is often possible to persuade a former employee in whom you have confidence to take a two-week busman's holiday in return for a suitably large bag of gold to look after your practice. You will have the reassurance of knowing that you are leaving the office in a safe pair of hands. The expense is partly financed by the fee-earning work which they will turn over in your absence and which would not otherwise have been done. They will need to clear this arrangement with their current employer first.

Sharing staff

Going away on holiday or being absent from the office for any other reason for a period of more than a few days will mean making arrangements to ensure that there are sufficient administrative staff as well as fee-earning staff. If your spouse works in the practice, you will be taking two key players out of the game at holiday times. People with children tend to go away during school holiday times and at half terms, so the call on temporary secretaries is at its greatest, and the quality of temporary secretary available is at its lowest. To a large extent, this cannot be helped. If you have been fortunate enough to share office space with others, you may at least in part be able to resolve the problem by making use of their staff. Obviously, you will have to be very diplomatic in your approach to your office colleagues, but you may well find that they are amenable to one or other members of their staff having one of your telephones on their desk, and this can relieve the pressure enormously. It is a most unpleasant feeling to be on the telephone yourself with two other telephones ringing and no one there to answer them.

Even if this only happens two or three times a day, the stress levels go through the ceiling. If, on these isolated occasions, there is a member of someone else's staff who can leap to the rescue to answer the telephone and take a short message, it makes an enormous difference.

Even if the people with whom you share office space are solicitors or other professionals, such as accountants, care must still be taken to ensure your client's confidentiality is maintained. Consider whether there is any chance of the other firm acting for clients on the other side to your own clients. If that is likely, you may have to think again about such an arrangement. Confidentiality must be preserved, whoever you share premises with.

Instead of asking them to come to your rescue when they are needed, or in addition to such an arrangement, you may be able to persuade fellow office workers to enter into a more formal arrangement whereby they put in a couple of hours of work for you either during their lunch hour, first thing in the morning or last thing at night. Again, it is absolutely critical that these arrangements are agreed in advance with senior management since it is their staff who are being used. In a great many instances there will be no need to call upon them, but the mere fact that they can be called upon if the workload gets too great for temporary or other staff in the office during the holiday period will be a considerable reassurance to them. With that kind of arrangement, it would be more appropriate to agree an hourly rate than simply provide a gratuity.

Shut up shop?

If you are about to go on holiday, why not simply close down for two weeks? This will avoid staff-sharing arrangements, the cost of a locum and the worry about what is happening while you are away. This solution has rather more to commend it than might at first be apparent. Indeed, many of our European counterparts do exactly that. They simply lock the front door and disappear for a couple of weeks. If you are lucky, you may just get voicemail.

This may well be a suitable solution during the first year when the level of business is probably going to be quite low. If you do opt for this solution, you must be mindful of your obligation to provide a proper pro-fessional service for your clients. If a problem crops up on something that was otherwise well under control before you left, you will have to answer for it not only to the client but also to the SRA at a later stage. Clearly, there is much that can be done by way of preventative surgery in antici-pating problems that may appear and in trying to head them off. You will nonetheless have to make some kind of contingency arrangement in case the worst happens, and to satisfy the requirements of Chapter 7 of the SRA Code of Conduct 2011. The most sensible thing you can do is to have an arrangement with a local practice so that if any real crisis erupts, the client can be referred on to that practice. If you explain your problems to a neighbouring practice and if you have managed to establish some kind of a rapport with someone within that practice, it is surprising how help-ful one's professional colleagues can be. There will undoubtedly come a time in the future when in some form or another you can repay them in the same professional way. Again, confidentiality must be protected and any question of conflict avoided.

You will have to make it clear to your clients that you will be away for two weeks and that other than coping with real emergencies – as opposed to those that are perceived by clients as emergencies – their matter will have to stand still for that time. If there is a problem with this, it is best to sort it out and, if at all possible, carry out the work they would wish you to be doing during the absence period before you go. The majority of clients are usually fairly understanding. They, too, take holidays and their work stands still for two weeks. You may also like to point out the reality to them that even in large firms, for the most part, anything other than something which gets to screaming pitch is left to pile up on the desk for two weeks. We all like to pretend that there are hundreds of people beavering away on our matters while we are away, but during the summer there are not enough people around and all routine items are left to accumulate. There is no reason why the same should not happen in a small firm. If, however, such a delay will amount to something more than a minor interruption to a client's business you will have to put something in place to comply with rule 5.01(k). This might be the locum solution or specifically handing over the file to a local colleague for two weeks and asking the client to deal with him or her whilst you are away. Bear in mind that if the colleague does a better job than you do, you might not have the client when you return!

If you are prepared to take a busman's holiday, today's IT solutions can make you almost as effective on the beach as you would be in the office. With smart phone technology, laptops and iPads you can talk to clients, draft documents and even exchange contracts whilst still in your beachwear. Whilst you will have a less relaxed holiday than might have been the case, at least your clients' interests are being served and you will have avoided the cost of an expensive locum. If clients are asked to restrict contact to urgent matters you may still get some quality time away and the batteries (yours, not the equipment's!) recharged.

The watchful eye solution

After the first year, it will probably not be practicable to close down the firm. You may have additional staff and unless you are going to insist that they take their holidays at the same time, you will have to pay them whether you are there or not. If you decide not to employ a locum because you feel that your staff are sensible and conscientious enough to be able to get on with work themselves, you will have to comply with Chapter 7 of the SRA Code of Conduct 2011 on management. Clearly, a locum could do this for you, but if you have ruled that out you may like to opt for the watchful eye solution. This involves your professional colleague in a neighbouring firm, who is suitably experienced, helping you out. If there is someone who is willing to take on the responsibility, you can brief them on any problems that are likely to occur. There are usually at least two or three files that will inevitably boil up to one degree or another, which the staff in situ will have to cope with while you are away. In addition, your professional colleague will have to agree to come into the office to ensure that all is running smoothly and be prepared to spend as much time there as necessary to ensure the smooth running of the firm and to deal with any problems. It is also a good idea to try to arrange for them to supervise the opening of your post.

If you are able to get everything up to date before you depart and if your staff are reasonably sensible and competent, that amount of time may not be very great. Staff often need a certain amount of guidance and direction and it is this steady hand on the tiller which your professional colleague can provide. It should not be necessary for him or her to actually do the work, but simply to be available to your staff to talk through problems which they encounter and for your colleague to make the decisions on it which you would make. He or she must also be there as a back-up in case a particularly nervous client is unhappy with the advice given by a less experienced member of staff and demands to speak to somebody with greater experience.

In practice, the supervision by your neighbouring colleague may only amount to half an hour a day unless a particular problem arises, but again, the rules make it clear that it is down to you to make it work. If you delegate this responsibility to someone else it will be your neck on the block if things go wrong.

The arrangements with your neighbouring colleague will probably involve you making temporary signing arrangements for your client account with your bank. You must realise that you are putting absolute trust in your professional colleague, who should be someone at partnership level in a neighbouring firm. It is also a good idea when making the signing arrangements with the bank to explain personally to the bank manager what is happening.

So far as the office account is concerned, cheques may have to be drawn for items such as searches. One solution is to leave half a dozen cheques drawn on office account and signed, but with the remaining details blank, and to endorse the cheque 'not to exceed £150'. This enables the staff to operate the office account in a very limited way and the extent to which they are able to dip into office account for the wrong reasons is limited. You may, however, prefer to draw cheques for specific purposes for use if needs be or, better still, to make temporary signing arrangements for your colleague across the road on the office account as well as the client account. Some firms are prepared to let staff pay for things with cheques on their office account and to settle up with you when you come back from holiday. Under no circumstances leave blank, signed client account cheques behind.

Holiday arrangements for some firms, and in particular sole practitioners, are never very easy, but holidays are important. If you fail to take them, you will become jaded and run down. It is important to get away, particularly during the first year. You will probably not realise quite what setting up has taken out of you until you go off on holiday and only after two or three days away will you begin to relax and feel an enormous weight disappearing off your shoulders. A recent scan of the obituary column in the Law Society's *Gazette* revealed that 24 per cent of the solicitors whose deaths were reported died before the age of 50. Do not rush to join them. Despite what you may feel to the contrary, the practice can and will survive without you for a week or two if you make sensible and practical arrangements beforehand. Take your holidays – you will have earned them.

11

Developing management skills

Many people who start their own businesses have little or no management experience – and solicitors are no exception. Management consists of organising and controlling things and/or people so as to produce the most efficient and hopefully the most profitable result. While a certain amount of knowledge and experience is needed to be able to manage properly, the most important ingredient of management for a solicitor is self-discipline. There are some people who are more organised than others, but most people can manage a business provided they make the time to do so.

If you have been a partner in a firm, you may have had the opportunity to manage part of the firm. In all but the smallest of firms, management is either spread across all of the partners, with individuals delegated to carry out functions such as finance and staff management, or else it is delegated to a small committee of perhaps three to five partners who will act as the firm's managers for a set period of anything between one and three years.

All partners in firms are theoretically managers – or at least they should be – but there are large numbers of partners who have little or no interest in the management of their own business and prefer to leave it to those who feel they have the aptitude, while they get on with what they feel is the important business of winning and servicing clients.

Ways to develop management skills

If you are starting a business with no previous experience of managing, how do you develop the necessary management skills to ensure that your business will be successful? There are four basic ways in which you can learn these skills.

Books

With the introduction of the CLS Quality Mark, and now Lexcel, in the last few years there has been an enormous emphasis placed on the right and wrong ways to manage a business. There have always been books around on the topic of management, and we are now rather spoilt for choice. I would recommend anyone thinking of starting a new firm to read at least one book on the subject.

The Lexcel practice management standard itself goes quite a long way towards ensuring that a practice is properly managed. My own view is that not all accreditation schemes are appropriate to all firms, and many are not really appropriate to sole practices, at least in their embryonic stages. However, a close eye should be kept on them as the firm develops and progresses, to ensure that anything that was not particularly appropriate at the outset, which has become relevant, is being implemented.

The Solicitors Regulation Authority has made the acquisition of management skills mandatory for anyone wishing to start their own practice. This is covered in detail in **Chapter 1**.

Seminars and courses

Much the same applies to seminars and courses as applies to books. With the growing interest in franchising arrangements and quality standards, there has been an upsurge in the number of courses dealing with management. If you are in the process of being made redundant and intend to set up your own firm as an answer to your future employment problems, you may have more time available to attend courses than would otherwise be the case. You may even be able to persuade your present employer to pay the cost of a course as a means of assuaging the guilt felt at making you redundant. At least as importantly, even if the employer will not pay for the course, you may be allowed to attend it on full pay. This is worth the course fee several times over. It is likely that once you have actually set up the practice you will find it difficult to take a day out to attend a management course until you have become reasonably well established. Life is just too busy to be able to take the time out even for half a day until you have reached the stage where you have a member of staff who can hold the fort while you are off on a course. As the practice grows beyond just you and a secretary, managing it effectively becomes ever more important. Different management skills are needed to manage a two- or three-partner practice in comparison with when you were on your own, and as you move into a six- or seven-partner firm the skills are different again. By the time you face these transitions, you should make the time available to attend a course so that you learn from other people's mistakes and benefit from their experiences.

Talking to people

An invaluable means of educating yourself on how to manage your practice is by talking to other people. They do not necessarily need to be other solicitors – they might be accountants or non-professional people. Talking to others about how they manage their business and, even better, watching them at first hand, can give you all kinds of new ideas. Such opportunities for discussion may present themselves at seminars or courses, at local Law

Society meetings, or on social occasions. If you share office space with other people, you have the perfect opportunity both to observe how other people manage their businesses and to discuss their way of going about things and your way. You may also have contacts within other firms. Talk to partners in different sized practices and you may find they are surprisingly willing to talk about how their practice is run and what their own thoughts are about the different ways of managing practices.

Experience

There are many things which you can pick up as you go along, and managing a practice is certainly one of them. If you are a sole practitioner, you have very little choice. You are going to be a manager and the only question is, are you going to be a good one or a bad one? Lack of management experience is certainly not something which should put you off trying to run your own practice or running it with one or more partners. The two key words are control and organisation. If you are in control of what you are doing because you take a close interest in what is happening and you make sufficient time to apply that knowledge to your business you will be able to organise things efficiently. By remaining in control you are more likely to realise, at an early stage, if some aspect of your business is not running smoothly and you will be able to rectify matters more easily. You will, of course, make mistakes. This does not mean to say that you are a bad manager. You only have to look at some major businesses that fail to see that the management has made mistakes. Sometimes these are avoidable and sometimes not. You will certainly improve your chances of success if you have the necessary degree of control, either on your own or collectively with partners, and if you have sufficient accurate information to organise your business in the most profitable and efficient way possible.

Three key management areas

To attempt to go into greater depth on how to acquire management skills would mean writing a complete book in itself, as indeed many other people have already done, but I will confine my comments to fairly superficial observations on three key areas.

Managing staff

The way in which you manage staff will be governed to some extent by employment protection legislation. If you behave badly towards staff, they may consider themselves constructively dismissed and sue you. This does not mean that fear of litigation should produce a situation where the 'tail wags the dog'. You are the boss and it is you who calls the shots.

Having said that, the trick is to let the staff know that without actually telling them in so many words. You should try to have staff carry out your instructions by persuasion and suggestion rather than by issuing orders. If staff offer a different solution to a problem from yours, it will in most cases be worth listening to what they have to say. Rather than stifling any comments or criticism that they may have, you may find that they are able to teach you something occasionally rather than the other way around. There will nevertheless come a point when a decision has to be taken and the contribution from the staff must cease and you make it clear that things are to be done in the way you have decided.

The Lexcel toolkit series is intended as a basic kit for firms from which to compile their own office manuals. The object of the office manual is to set out as extensively and as exhaustively as possible the firm's policies on how things should be done. If you decide to follow the Law Society's lead and produce such an office manual, it places you in the position of being able to provide staff with a copy of the toolkits as soon as their employment starts and, to the extent that they depart from the procedures laid down in these publications, they will have to justify their actions.

In a small office you will be working very closely with your staff. It is important that people get on with one another and that they have a good relationship with you as their principal. Certainly, over-familiarity can breed contempt, but there is nothing wrong with taking a personal interest in your staff and making them feel that your door is always open for them to discuss problems, whether of a professional or a personal nature. Equally, there will be times when it will be necessary for you to make it clear that you are cross with people's failings, but you should never find it necessary to embarrass or humiliate anyone, particularly in front of other people, nor should you be discourteous or rude.

Managing finances

There are many books written specifically on how to manage the financial affairs of a business. The basic message is that the figures must add up – they must *always* add up. The key is information. You must have good, accurate information as to what money is coming in, what money is going out and what the level of profit is. With a computerised system, this can be a fairly straightforward procedure. If you do not have a computerised system, you must either gather the information yourself as you go along or ensure that your bookkeeper provides you with the information. You must check it to ensure that it is accurate. You should insist on either manual or computerised reports at least once a month. This information should provide you with a detailed list of outgoings, which you will check against your budget figures to see how close to your budget you are keeping. If you are over budget you must either revise your budget and totally rethink all the figures or look for areas in which to make savings. For example, if by giving salary increases you have gone over your salaries budget, you must either increase your profits by working harder, accept that your profits will be lower because of your generosity to your staff or balance the deficit with the under-budget items so that the overall figure is still correct.

You must examine the figures carefully since there will be items, such as the PI contribution, which inflate figures if paid as a lump sum rather than by instalments – if you take three months' expenses to date and multiply by four to produce an annual total, a distortion will appear. If you have a six-monthly figure of income and outgoings, you are able to get a much clearer picture as to whether you are likely to achieve the objectives set out at the beginning of the year in your budget. However, adjustments at that time may come too late to have any real effect on the yearly figure. It is for this reason that you must take stock of the situation at least once a month.

If your profit costs figures for this month and last month have been disappointing, you must try to decide why this is and whether it is likely to continue. Is it time to cut back on staff? The important thing is that you make a decision, even if that decision is that you will do nothing for the time being. You cannot afford not to take a decision because you are afraid of doing so.

Time costing

Time costing is, and always will be, regarded as a chore by fee-earning staff and many principals. It comes as a standard part of many accounts packages and it is probably true to say that most practices cannot get very far today without introducing time costing at a fairly early stage. Time costing produces a substantial amount of information. As well as telling you who in the practice is working hardest (or who according to their time sheets is working hardest, which may be quite another matter), it tells you how they are organising their time so that you may spot where time is being inefficiently used and be in a position to correct this. It also tells you what type of work is being done and by which people, as well as the cost to the firm of doing the work, so you can price the rate at which you charge that work to the client. It will give an early warning signal of a fall off or increase in work and enable you to consider – sooner rather than later – whether any adjustments to staffing levels need to be made.

It is probably true to say that time costing can be safely dispensed with by a small trader for the first two or three years, depending on the speed at which the business grows. In a small office where you are probably literally able to see every one of your staff working, you are very likely to know who is doing what and how they are spending their time. If someone is spending a lot of time on personal telephone calls, you will probably be able to see and hear them doing so. The exception to this is emailing and web browsing. People glued to computer screens and keyboards can look very busy when in reality they are electronically chatting to their friends or doing their Internet shopping. I am afraid that the only way to tackle this is by intrusive supervision, i.e. have all your staff's emails copied automatically to your inbox (your IT expert can easily set this up for you) and check the browser history when staff have gone home. If you discover a problem send out a generic warning to everyone – not just the individual you think is abusing the system – and see whether their behaviour changes. If it does not you will have to collate your evidence and challenge them directly. At this stage you are likely to be working longer hours than anyone else and so you will be able to observe at first hand the exact time that people are starting work and leaving. As the sole person to whom they will be reporting, you will be able to see and judge the quality and extent of the work they produce. The acid test is of course the billing figures.

Once the number of fee earners exceeds three or four, they will be spread out geographically so that you are in a much weaker position to see how they spend their time and what work they produce. You may even have to introduce an intermediate tier of management in the form of a senior fee earner to whom a less experienced fee earner reports. Once you have reached this stage, you will need some form of time recording system. By the time you have grown to a two-partner firm with supporting fee earners, time costing will be a must.

Time recording systems will make the production of costs information for the client, now mandatory, very much simpler to produce. Similarly, the production of costs schedules for summary assessment for hearings lasting a day or less will be much more straightforward to draft when the information is readily available from a time recording system.

Choosing a system is very important. Since most systems come as an add on (and many would say an afterthought) to an accounts package, it is important to evaluate the time costing system and not simply to take it because it is offered as part of an accounts package which seems attractive in all other respects. The best means of selection is by recommendation from people who have that type of system and by discussing its merits with fellow professionals. For more guidance on choosing the right system see the section on accounts packages in **Chapter 7** and **Appendix 8**.

The introduction of such a system should be carried out very carefully. You should have meetings with staff to explain why and how the system is being introduced in order to secure their full co-operation. There is no point bringing it in if it is going to cause ill feeling and suspicion. It must be perceived as a step forward rather than a means of keeping tabs on the staff and making them account for every minute of the day. It must be seen as a means by which you can more effectively manage the firm, by detecting problems at an early stage and taking the necessary steps to resolve them. It will enable you to identify those areas of the firm that are not profitable or less profitable so that a management decision can be taken to make them more profitable or to avoid them altogether. Thus, the profitability of the firm will increase, which means better job security for staff.

Making time to manage

As discussed earlier, none of the information which you acquire through time costing or reports generated by accounting systems, nor any of the skills which you have developed, will be of any use whatsoever if you do not make the time to manage your business. How you do so is a matter for you. Most partnerships will have partners' meetings once a month. Committees may be appointed that will meet more or less frequently depending on their area of responsibility. Two-person partnerships can arrange an ad hoc get-together over coffee or lunch at some convenient moment during the day to discuss a particular item. A sole trader may use the arrival of a set of reports from the bookkeeper as a spur to getting out additional financial information and going through the figures to see to what extent he or she is or is not on target. You may decide to make a diary note to look at the figures and you may or may not keep to it. How you make the time to manage does not matter so long as you do. It is essential that you grasp the idea that it is every bit as important to look over the last three months' billing figures as it is to get out a set of particulars of claim on a client's case. There is no point spending 23 hours a day trying to produce profits for a business if the funds generated are not used sensibly and the effort is misdirected.

12

Regulatory bodies and legislation

Financial Services and Markets Act 2000

There are so many things to think about when you are setting up a new practice that you may make the mistake of giving little or no thought to the question of whether you need to apply for investment business authorisation under the Financial Services and Markets Act 2000. While it is true that if you choose not to apply for authorisation it is one less thing to have to worry about, this should be a conscious decision rather than something that happens by default. Authorisation is not something that is mandatory in order to conduct a solicitors' practice, so should you register or not?

Under the Financial Services and Markets Act 2000 most firms now performing only non-discrete investment business do not need authorisation. This is the reverse of the position before the Act. Then, many firms registered as a precaution to avoid inadvertently infringing the regulations and thus committing a criminal offence. Since 1 December 2001 only those firms wishing to provide mainstream investment business services have needed to opt into direct regulation by the Financial Services Authority (FSA). From that date the FSA became the only body with power to authorise firms to provide 'regulated activities'. The Law Society ceased on that date to have the power to grant such authorisation and became instead a designated professional body (DPB) whose members are allowed to provide certain regulated activities without having individual authorisation from the FSA. It is worth noting that since then the position of the Law Society has changed. The Solicitors Regulation Authority website (**www.sra.org.uk**) outlines the current position:

> the Law Society is a designated professional body for the purposes of the Financial Services and Markets Act 2000, but responsibility for regulation and complaints handling has been separated from the Law Society's representative functions. The Solicitors Regulation Authority is the independent regulatory authority body of the Law Society and the Legal Complaints service is the independent complaints handling body of the Law Society.

While there are some firms that have chosen to diversify into the areas of selling or arranging life policies or pensions or have decided to offer a share dealing service to their clients, the majority of firms of solicitors have decided not to do so. The problem has always been what to do with the odd transaction which crops up from time to time while you are dealing with something else for the client. This might be an estate where some of the assets are shares that the beneficiaries do not want and wish to sell. Because of the wide definitions in the earlier legislation of concepts like 'dealing' in investments, even filling out forms and sending documents to beneficiaries or executors for them to send off in order to sell or transfer the investments ran the risk of crossing the line and incurring the serious consequences entailed in breaking the rules. It remains a criminal offence to step outside what is permitted under the DPB regime and so it is important to understand what is allowed by being a member of such a body and what is not.

The rules which govern what solicitors are and are not allowed to do without obtaining full authorisation from the FSA are the SRA Financial Services (Scope) Rules 2001 (Scope Rules). The Scope Rules are designed to ensure that a solicitor carries on only regulated activities which 'arise out of or are complementary to' the provision by the solicitor of that service to that client. This concept is the cornerstone of the Scope Rules. If the transaction is ancillary to a service for a client that you are carrying out already, the chances are you do not need separate authorisation through the FSA. However, if it is the end in itself then you probably do need it. A client who asks you to sell a life policy as part of the divorce settlement will not be pushing you over the line into mainstream investment business necessitating authorisation from the FSA. The same client who says, 'By the way, while I'm here talking about the divorce, could you arrange a pension for me?' probably would.

The Scope Rules and the full information pack are published on the Solicitors Regulation Authority website (**www.sra.org.uk**). If you are in doubt about your position have a look at the Scope Rules and the advice given on the website before proceeding further.

Here are some guidelines to help you decide whether what you are thinking of doing runs the risk of breaking the Scope Rules, always assuming each activity is arising out of or complementary to a service you are already providing.

You do not need separate authorisation to:

- Introduce a client to someone who is authorised or exempt.
- Give generic advice, e.g. to advise on the difference between an endowment mortgage, a pension mortgage and a repayment mortgage.
- Advise on the disposal of a life policy, so long as you are competent to do so and consider all possible means of disposal.
- Arrange the disposal of a life policy.
- Give negative advice, i.e. advise the client not to buy or sell the investment.

- Buy or sell shares in a management or service company during the conveyance of a leasehold property.
- Arrange the sale or purchase of shares in the sale or acquisition of the day-to-day control of the affairs of a company.
- Give generic advice on shares, e.g. you might advise that shares in banks are a bad bet at present and a switch to government gilts might be better, always assuming you are competent to give such advice.
- Explain how a life policy or similar investment such as a pension works, provided you stop short of recommending the client to proceed with the investment.

Other tips

- If you are dealing with packaged products or shares offered to the public, especially where the transaction is buying and not selling, use an authorised person, i.e. a broker or independent financial adviser.
- Always be more cautious when buying.

You will need authorisation:

- If you want to set up a specific service for your clients or advertise such a service. ('We can provide the full probate service, including selling the estate's shares.')
- If you start to build up any level of business as opposed to the occasional one-off sale or purchase.
- If you generate serious levels of commission as a result of sales or purchases. Remember, the client must be informed of any commission, how much it is and that it belongs to them. Once disclosed to the client you are allowed to set it off against your fees or you can agree with the client that you will keep it, but this must be assessed on a case-by-case basis and not as part of your 'standard terms'. This means all commission – the £20 *de minimis* exception has gone. If you are going to be receiving regular commission for work, it is essential that you familiarise yourself fully with Chapter 1 of the SRA Code of Conduct 2011 and in particular outcome 1.15 and indicative behaviour 1.20.

Data Protection Act 1998

Computers have the ability to hold enormous amounts of information (data) and with the proliferation of computers it became apparent that a certain amount of control needed to be exercised over those people who stored data and the use to which it was put. The Data Protection Act 1998 came into force on 1 March 2000 and repealed the earlier 1984 Act, although some of the provisions of the earlier Act are retained and/or modified. The 1998 Act covers anyone processing personal data on or after 24 October 1998 for 'new purposes'.

The data referred to in the Data Protection Act 1984 was information stored on computers and it followed that, under the earlier regime, if you did not store any information on a computer you did not need to be licensed under the Act. Under the 1998 Act licensing is replaced by the duty to notify the Information Commissioner (what was the Data Protection Registrar) of the fact that you are processing data unless you are exempt from doing so. Data is given a wider meaning and now covers manual records as well as computer records. This is in line with the major changes brought about by the 1998 Act. Failure to notify when not exempt from doing so is a criminal offence.

Data controllers must comply with the provisions of the 1998 Act even if they are exempt from notification unless the processing of personal data is undertaken by an individual for personal, family or household affairs (including recreational purposes), in which case they are exempt from the notification provisions and most of the other provisions of the 1998 Act. This applies even if all you are doing is using your computer as a word processor to write letters and produce documents, as opposed to maintaining a database.

The Commissioner maintains a public register of data controllers. Each register entry includes the name and address of the data controller and a general description of the processing of personal data by the data controller. Individuals can consult the register to find out what processing of personal data is being carried out by a particular data controller. The Act requires every data controller who is processing personal data to notify unless they are exempt. 'Data controller' is defined as being the person who determines the purposes for which and the manner in which any personal data is or is not being processed. Those people who are exempt from notification are data controllers who only process personal data for any one or all of the following purposes:

- staff administration;
- advertising, marketing and public relations for their own business;
- accounts and records.

Accordingly, the likelihood is that few solicitors' practices will be exempt from notification unless they can identify an exemption relieving them of the burden of notifying. Given the wide definitions in the Act of 'processing' and 'personal data', it seems very unlikely that any solicitors' practice will be able to bring itself within one of the exemptions from notification. If you do need to notify the Information Commissioner, the notification period is one year and the renewal fee is £35. You can either obtain the notification form from the Information Commissioner from the address given or from the website at **www.ico.gov.uk**, where the form can be completed online – although you must also print off a hard copy to send with the notification fee.

Although manual records are now covered by the Data Protection Act 1998, there is no requirement to notify. The Information Commissioner's Office's advice on the requirement to notify if you were a legal practice that kept only paper manual records was somewhat confusing, but given that you are likely to be processing personal data on a computer in carrying out the client's work (unless you use only typewriters and not word processors) you will be caught anyway.

Anyone processing personal data – and this applies whether the data is manually processed or by means of a computer – must comply with the eight enforceable principles of good practice. These are that data must be:

- Fairly and lawfully processed.
- Processed for limited purposes.
- Adequate, relevant and not excessive.
- Accurate.
- Not kept longer than necessary.
- Processed in accordance with the data subjects' rights.
- Secure.
- Not transferred to countries without adequate protection.

Personal data covers both facts and opinions about the individual.

It is unlikely that solicitors will fall foul of any of the above principles if the practice is run along normal business-like, professional and ethical lines. It is second nature for solicitors to keep the information about their clients, and other matters to do with the practice, secure and accurate. Most solicitors are anxious to get rid of any such data at the earliest possible time but are prevented from disposing of it earlier than they would otherwise wish due to professional practice principles. These constrain them to keep files for, in most cases, six years and in other cases rather longer, as well as good practice principles and regulations requiring them to keep VAT and tax records for similarly lengthy periods. Clients are much less likely to contact solicitors to demand to see what data they have held about them and to complain about its accuracy than to make a similar enquiry to their bank after refusal of a loan.

While it is true to say that any solicitor who has a cavalier attitude to storage and usage of information acquired in the course of running a practice is likely to fall foul of the Data Protection Act, it is also likely that they will come up against more draconian sanctions when answering to the SRA and the Solicitors Disciplinary Tribunal (at the same time or earlier) than when they have to answer to the Information Commissioner or the courts for a breach of a provision of the Act. One might have hoped that the opportunity would have been taken to relieve the average solicitors' practice of the burden of complying with data protection regulation when bringing in a new Act. In fact the opposite has occurred and it has been made almost impossible for any practice to operate lawfully without notifying and paying an annual fee. While applicable to solicitors' practices, the Act is designed primarily to regulate those persons and organisations dealing with data that are not subject to the same kind of stringent controls on the handling of information and data as are solicitors' practices. It should not be forgotten, however, that breaches of the Act and failure to notify when required to do so are criminal offences.

Further information is available from the Information Commissioner (**www.ico.gov.uk**).

Solicitors Regulation Authority

Insurance

As a solicitor in another practice you will have been covered under the policy for that practice, but now you have founded a new practice you will have to arrange a new policy. The terms of that policy will be a matter for negotiation between you and your proposed insurers but it will depend very much on:

- The number of files you have taken with you and the gross fees you anticipate these files will generate.
- The amount of new business you expect to do in the first year.
- The amount of cover you wish to buy, subject, of course, to the minimum level set by the SRA (currently £2 million for each and every claim).
- The amount of any excess you wish to carry, again, subject to the limits applying.
- Your track record and that of your partner(s) and perhaps of your staff as regards negligence claims.

The Solicitors Act 1974, s.84(1) requires every solicitor who has in force or who has applied for a practising certificate to give notice to the Law Society of any change in place of business within 14 days of the change.

For the full text of the SRA Indemnity Insurance Rules, see the SRA Handbook (**www.sra.org.uk**).

The firm's name

As discussed in **Chapter 2**, Chapter 8 of the SRA Code of Conduct 2011 requires that publicity is not misleading or inaccurate (and this would include using the word 'solicitor(s)' in the name of the firm if none of the managers are solicitors). This is a substantial relaxation of the earlier position, which only allowed you to use a name which consisted of the name or names of one or more solicitors who were present or former principals 'together with, if desired, other conventional references to the firm and to such person'.

You would also be breaking the Code if you called yourself, 'The Hampstead Law Practice' if your office was located in Kilburn, just outside Hampstead, to give the name of the firm a more upmarket feel. Likewise, calling yourself, 'The Family Law Practice' in order to attract more family work when the bulk of your client base is conveyancing would also be a breach.

You can now use a more modern name such as 'Law 4 U' or 'The Legal Clinic', but it would be misleading to suggest the firm is bigger than it is, such as 'Bloggs and Partners' when Mr Bloggs is a sole practitioner.

For many, part of the attraction of setting up your own firm is to have your name in lights. If you are buying a practice, you may wish to retain the goodwill element associated with the name of the old practice.

Further information is given in the Law Society's practice note, 'Information on letterheads, emails and websites'. Do not forget Chapter 7 of the SRA Code of Conduct 2011 as regards the need to have effective systems and controls in place to achieve and comply with all the principles, rules and outcomes of the Handbook and rule 12 of the SRA Practice Framework Rules 2011 and the need to have someone who is 'qualified to supervise' and who can ensure compliance with the Chapter 7 outcomes, as explained in **Chapter 10**, and Chapter 1 outcomes on client care provision concerning costs information, complaints handling and information that must be given to the client as to who is dealing with their matter.

Legal Services Commission

If you are intending to carry out any legal aid work, you will also need to notify the Legal Services Commission (LSC) and apply for a franchise and a contract. If you are successful the LSC will allocate you a computer number to enable payment to be made for the work you carry out. First of all you will have to find out which LSC area covers the area in which you intend to trade and unless it is the same area in which you have previously traded, you will need to make a few telephone calls. The process for acceptance into the publicly funded scheme has been made increasingly demanding and laborious over the years and it is especially difficult for a new practice to satisfy the LSC's requirements without substantial investment in systems and staff. The likelihood is that unless you already have a thriving publicly funded practice which is dividing off you will find it very hard to gain acceptance.

Health and Safety Executive

The Health and Safety Executive operates as an arm of the local authority, generally from the local town hall. It has wide powers under a number of Acts, perhaps the most important ones are the Offices, Shops and Railway Premises Act 1963 and the Health and Safety at Work etc. Act 1974.

It is the Executive's task to ensure that employees are able to work in a safe environment. While it is probably fair to say that the Executive may be more concerned with an employee who is at risk of having a hand chopped off due to a missing guard on a piece of machinery in a factory, it is, nevertheless, keen to ensure that your trainee solicitor will not be electrocuted while making the tea using a kettle with defective wiring. It is extremely likely that within the first two years of operation you will receive a routine visit from a health and safety officer. They are fairly thorough and go to some lengths to ensure that even small failures are brought to your attention, without being overly oppressive about it.

Electricity at work

The Electricity at Work Regulations 1989, SI 1989/635 came into force on 1 April 1990. These place a duty on employers to assess the work activities which use electricity or which may be affected by it so that any foreseeable risks associated with electricity in the workplace are appreciated and the necessary steps taken to avoid danger or personal injury. In other words, the solicitor employer must look at how electricity is used throughout the office and at any dangers that may be posed and take all necessary steps to see that such danger is kept to a minimum. This might cover, for example, appreciating that a dictating machine plugged into a remote socket by means of an extension lead is a bad idea because someone may trip over the flex. The regulations may be another set that you are inclined to ignore when you are first setting up, but if you do, you had better hope that anyone you employ does not have an accident involving electricity since, if such an accident could have been prevented, there may be some very awkward questions to answer. Potential hazards will include a plug with the wrong size fuse in it which could overheat and start a fire. The only real way to make sure your position is protected is to have a survey carried out at some stage by a qualified electrician, who will produce a brief report of what appliances and installations have been inspected and problems that can be identified, or else the report can say that the inspection of the appliance and installation was satisfactory. You should be able to get a quote from a qualified electrician before such an inspection is carried out and it is unlikely to be more than £75.

First aid at work

The Health and Safety (First Aid) Regulations 1981, SI 1981/917 require every employer to make adequate first aid provision for all employees and to inform employees of the arrangements that exist. Operations that are considered low hazard, such as offices and shops, should have one trained first aider for every 50 employees. The regulations go on to provide for the display of notices informing employees of the first aid arrangements. Small establishments, i.e. of less than 50 employees, will not generally need a trained first aider, but someone must be appointed to take control in the event of an accident or injury and someone has to have responsibility for the first aid box.

First aid box

Every employer must provide at least one first aid box, clearly identified and marked, preferably by a white cross on a green background. The regulations provide detailed requirements for the contents of first aid boxes. Personally, I feel that unless your practice is in a remote area and you have a lot of employees, the regulations relating to first aid boxes are rather excessive, for example, six individually wrapped triangular bandages. There is no doubt that a well-stocked first aid box is an excellent idea, but if people are so badly injured that they must have their arm put in a sling immediately, my own choice would be to leave the injured person lying where they are and call an ambulance rather than try to strap up a dislocated or broken limb, especially if you are not trained in first aid. In any event first aid training as we knew it in the past, with splinting broken limbs and treating burns, has been replaced by emergency life support. As most injured persons can usually be reached by ambulance within half an hour, the emphasis now is on the 'first responder' keeping the injured person alive until the arrival of the paramedics rather than trying to treat the casualty themselves.

Reporting of accidents

The Reporting of Injuries, Diseases and Dangerous Occurrences Regulations 1985, SI 1985/2023, as amended, impose duties on employers to report to the Health and Safety Executive or the local authority certain accidents. These range from fatal accidents at one end, through to dangerous occurrences (such as explosions) down to accidents causing more than three days' incapacity. The regulations are fairly complicated, but by way of summary, a serious injury such as a fracture must be reported immediately by the quickest practical means, which would normally be telephone, to the relevant enforcing authority. If there is doubt as to whether the incident is reportable or which authority is the correct one to notify, you should ask the advice of the Health and Safety Executive. This must be followed up by a written report on Form F2508 to the enforcing authority within seven days of the accident. Accidents causing more than three days' incapacity from work must also be reported on the same form to the enforcing authority within seven days, but immediate telephone notification is unnecessary.

These kinds of incidents must be recorded in an accident book and retained for at least three years from the date the entry was made. Clearly, it is good practice to record any accident and to put as much detail down as possible in case there is a claim at a later stage or the Health and Safety Executive feels that it is a reportable accident, which should have been notified in writing or by telephone.

The health and safety officer

The health and safety officer will also be looking to see that you have the necessary employer's liability insurance and that your certificate of insurance is displayed. The statutory notice under the Offices, Shops and Railway Premises Act 1963 should also be in a place where it can easily be read by your employees in order to bring a summary of its provisions to their attention so that they know their rights under the legislation.

Department for Work and Pensions

The Department for Work and Pensions (DWP) was formed in June 2001 from parts of the Department of Social Security (DSS) and the Department for Education and Employment (DfEE). This is one area that may have escaped your notice completely. Perhaps surprisingly, the DWP appears to be one of the first regulatory bodies to demonstrate that it is aware of your existence and to pay you a visit. The DWP deals with a variety of matters which affect your business, the most important being the payment of both employees' and employers' contributions. If you have been a partner in general practice and are now setting up on your own, you may perhaps have been only vaguely aware that, in addition to income tax and NI contributions paid by employees, the employer has a substantial payment to make by way of employers' NI contributions. Over and above that, you will need to ensure that you are making sufficient contributions yourself as a self-employed person in order to obtain your full benefits in the event of sickness or retirement, and likewise if you employ your spouse in the business, you must make the necessary payments on their account also. An early visit by the DWP should correct any errors or misunderstanding which may have arisen before they get out of hand so that, if underpayments have been made, any liability that has to be satisfied to bring matters back into line is not too painful to meet. The pitfalls for NI contributions are very much the same as for income tax and VAT. The level of contribution will relate not only to the salary that is paid but also to any other benefits paid to the employee. If, therefore, you reimburse an employee for all or part of their home telephone bill or for fuel or repair costs in respect of a car used on the firm's business, it is treated as a benefit in kind and will result in an additional payment of employers' contribution. The rules are comparatively simple to operate once the correct procedures are in place. A routine rapidly develops and the DWP rightly takes the view that it is important that the right routine is in place at an early stage. If within the first three months of trading you have not had a visit from the DWP, it is not a bad idea to invite them to inspect your records.

National Insurance contributions

Employee Class 1 contributions

Anyone who works for an employer must pay Class 1 NI contributions. There is no exemption for casual, temporary or part-time employees except those who earn less than the lower earnings limit, at the time of writing (Winter 2011) £102 per week or £442 per month.

Employers are responsible for the payment of both their own and their employees' contributions but may deduct the employees' share from their pay. If someone is employed by their spouse's business, the situation is no different from any other employer/employee relationship.

HMRC encourages employers to pay NI contributions online and there is a very useful website at **www.hmrc.gov.uk/employers** which should answer any queries you have. I would also suggest obtaining the NI Contributions Tables so that you have a hard copy available at all times. These tables are renewed every tax year and can be requested from the employer orderline (telephone: 0845 7 646 646).

Class 2 Employer's own contributions

Any individual who has earnings from any business activity, trade, profession or vocation must pay a flat rate Class 2 contribution if he or she is self-employed. This is the case unless the self-employed individual is either under 16 or over 65 (women over 60 years) or below the small earnings limit for the current tax year. There are a number of other exceptions which we need not concern ourselves with, apart from possibly where the individual is sick for a complete contribution week. The flat rate contribution is currently £31.20 per quarter. Further information can also be obtained from the website mentioned above and **www.hmrc.gov.uk** or by phoning 0845 91 54655.

NI contributions are rather complicated and troublesome. If you have a cashier, or your spouse has taken on that role, it is important that they understand how the payments system works and that a workable system for collecting the contribution and making the payment along with, in the case of employees, PAYE payments is in place. Accountants are very familiar with the NI contributions system and if you have a problem which you cannot resolve with HMRC, an accountant will normally be able to sort it out for you and ensure that systems are in place to prevent problems occurring in the future.

Outcomes-focused regulation

Overview

On 6 October 2011 the Solicitors Code of Conduct 2007 was swept away by the SRA Handbook, and a new approach of outcomes-focused regulation (OFR) was introduced. Under OFR there are no rules and guidance – instead there are principles, outcomes and indicative behaviours. Under the 2007 Code of Conduct the SRA was a policeman rather than a supervisor, but under OFR it has now assumed a supervisory role. The 2007 Code ran to 200 pages. Every time something changed the Code had to be amended. Under OFR the onus is on the profession to deliver satisfactory outcomes to the consumer. The 200 pages of the 2007 Code have now been shrunk to 50. Solicitors are expected to think for themselves on how best to achieve a satisfactory outcome for their clients. They are expected to comply with broad principles rather than detailed rules.

There are 10 core principles, which in turn are divided into five sections:

- you and your client;
- you and your business;
- you and your regulator;
- you and others; and
- application, waivers and interpretation.

All solicitors will need to get to grips with mandatory outcomes and indicative behaviours. There are limited notes and no guidance at all! The good news is that if you were compliant with the 2007 Code you will very probably be compliant with the new Code.

Firms need to assess risk and to spot problems before they arise and take steps to head them off. Practices will need to ask themselves: 'What are the major risks we face and what steps have we taken to deal with them?'

The ten mandatory principles

You must:

1. uphold the rule of law and the proper administration of justice;
2. act with integrity;
3. not allow your independence to be compromised;
4. act in the best interests of each client;
5. provide a proper standard of service to your clients;
6. behave in a way that maintains the trust the public places in you and in the provision of legal services;
7. comply with your legal and regulatory obligations and deal with your regulators and ombudsmen in an open, timely and co-operative manner;
8. run your business or carry out your role in the business effectively and in accordance with proper governance and sound financial and risk management principles;
9. run your business or carry out your role in the business in a way that encourages equality of opportunity and respect for diversity; and
10. protect client money and assets.

The specified outcomes are mandatory. The indicative behaviours and notes are not but over time it is very likely that they will acquire that status. The likelihood is that the SRA will take the view that you should comply with the outcomes and the indicative behaviours or the onus will be on you to prove that you have not infringed the SRA Code of Conduct 2011.

Appointing a COLP and COLFA

All authorised firms will be required to have a compliance officer for legal practice (COLP) and a compliance officer for finance and administration (COFA). Firms need to make appointments to these positions by 31 July 2012 and the SRA will authorise them to carry out their roles from 31 October 2012. The COLP will be responsible for seeing that the firm complies with all of its regulatory obligations whilst the COFA's job will be to see that the firm meets the requirements of the SRA Accounts Rules. The SRA Authorisation Rules for Legal Services Bodies gives more information about how these roles should be carried out. In the case of ABS, individuals will have to be appointed to these roles once the SRA has granted the necessary licences to operate. No announcement has been made by the SRA on precisely how firms are to notify it of who will be taking on the roles of COLP and COFA. The requirements of compliance officers are set out in rule 8 of the SRA Authorisation Rules. The Law Society has published a practice note on compliance officers which also sets out the responsibilities of COLPs and COFAs.

COLPs and COFAs must record any failures of a practice to comply with authorisation and any breaches of statutory obligations, and they must make such records available to the SRA when requested to do so.

Any breaches of the rules must be reported by COLPs and COFAs to the SRA. 'Material' breaches must be reported to the SRA as soon as reasonably practicable. Non-material breaches will be included in the information report to the SRA as required under rule 8.7 of the Authorisation Rules. More information on what is 'material' can be found in the Law Society practice note on compliance officers.

It is important that COLPs and COFAs note that the SRA Code of Conduct 2011 covers not only those matters which might have been obvious under the old rules, such as accounting rule breaches, but also broader matters such as business management and financial stability. The COLP and COFA must be authorised persons and either managers or employees of an authorised body. An authorised person is, 'a person authorised by the SRA or another approved regulator to carry on a legal activity and for the purpose of these rules includes a solicitor, sole practitioner, a Registered European Lawyer (REL), an Exempt European lawyer (EEL), a registered Foreign Lawyer (RFL), an authorised body, an authorised non-SRA firm and a European corporate practice' (Part 1 of the Authorisation Rules).

The same person can carry out both roles providing they have the necessary skills to do so, but you cannot 'double up' with another practice so that someone from one practice is a COLP or a COFA for your practice as well as their own. Each authorised body must have an individual who is designated as its COLP and an individual who is designated as its COFA. The same responsibilities apply to COLPs and COFAs, whatever the size of practice. However, the SRA has emphasised that what needs to be covered by a firm's compliance plan will depend on factors such as the size and nature of the firm, its work and its areas of risk.

A COLP can be an individual who is a lawyer of England and Wales, a registered European lawyer (REL) or a European lawyer regulated by the Bar Standards Board, and who is authorised by an approved regulator. Anyone who is not a lawyer as defined above cannot hold either position. A COLP cannot pass his or her responsibilities on to someone else, but may be able to delegate some of the routine functions to other members of the firm.

Approval for the position of COLP or COFA applies only to that individual. If that individual then ceases to be the COLP or COFA, another individual will need to be selected and approved by the SRA. If for any reason, due to incapacity or otherwise, an authorised body ceases to have a COLP or COFA, it must immediately and in any event within seven days notify the SRA and appoint another COLP or COFA. It may be necessary to replace a COLP or COFA if they are likely to be unable for any reason, such as prolonged absence from the firm, to carry out the role for any lengthy period. In that event you should consult with the SRA to decide whether replacement is necessary in the particular circumstances.

Outcomes-focused regulation will take a little getting used to, if only because of the changes to the nomenclature and the introduction of a different ethos. You will no longer be faced with a problem and be able to turn to a rule book to see whether your proposed course of action is condoned or forbidden. Instead, you will have to look at the outcome that is expected under the new regime and work out for yourself how best to proceed.

Help is at hand in the form of *Outcomes-Focused Regulation, a Practical Guide* written by Andrew Hopper QC and Gregory Treverton-Jones QC and published by the Law Society. The excellent guide takes you through each chapter of OFR, compares it with the 2007 Code and tells you what is new. A summary of the main changes reproduced from the guide with the kind permission of the authors is set out in Table 12.1.

Table 12.1 SRA Code of Conduct 2011 changes

Chapter 1 – Client care	There is no longer any reference to contingency fees, and rule 9.01(4) of the 2007 Code, which outlawed arrangements with introducers in personal injury cases who charged contingency fees has been removed.
	There are new requirements concerning information to clients about complaints procedures.
	The rule on solicitors receiving commissions has been simplified, although as we explain, the illogicality of the old rules has not been removed (see 5.2.1 and 5.2.6). The £20 *de minimis* exception to the general rule about accounting to clients for commissions has been abolished.
Chapter 2 – Equality and diversity	There is a new emphasis upon 'encouraging' equality of opportunity and respect for diversity.
Chapter 3 – Conflicts of interests	Although it is not specifically stated in any of the outcomes, the SRA now takes the view that the circumstances in which there is no conflict of interest nor a significant risk of such a conflict between buyer and seller in conveyancing transactions are extremely limited, and it will become the exception, and not the rule, for solicitors to act for both parties in such transactions.
Chapter 4 – Confidentiality and disclosure	For the first time, there is specific reference to the importance of the protection of confidentiality by those to whom solicitors outsource work.
	The rules and guidance relevant to information barriers have been simplified.

Chapter 5 – Your client and the court	Little change but some alteration in phraseology which is helpful.
Chapter 6 – Your client and introductions to third parties	The referral provisions in Chapter 6 now apply to referrals between lawyers; previously, such referrals were exempted from the rules.
Chapter 7 – Management of your business	There is a substantial shift in emphasis in terms of the management of risk. Firms are required to identify, monitor and manage 'risks to compliance' and to take steps to address issues identified, and also to monitor risks to financial stability. A standard question in future might be: 'What are the major risks to compliance and the financial viability of your firm that you have identified, and what steps have you taken to address them?' Outsourcing has now become a specific regulatory issue.
Chapter 8 – Publicity	Letterheads must be changed again; the new requirement is that it should be announced that firms are: 'Authorised and regulated by the Solicitors Regulation Authority'. There are some new provisions appropriate for ABS providing both regulated and unregulated services.
Chapter 9 – Fee sharing and referrals	Much of the information that had to be provided to clients no longer has to be so provided, and the prescriptive set of rules in rule 9 of the 2007 Code is much simplified and reduced. Rule 9.01(4) of the 2007 Code, which outlawed arrangements with introducers in personal injury cases who charged contingency fees, has been swept away. The rule against fee sharing has been abolished. As noted above, the new Code applies to referrals between lawyers.
Chapter 10 – You and your regulator	There is now an unambiguous duty on a solicitor to self-report to the SRA where he or she has committed serious misconduct.
Chapter 11 – Relations with third parties	The rules concerning undertakings and multiple buyers have been simplified and reduced.
Chapter 12 – Separate businesses	There is simplification and reduction of the safeguards that had to be in place under the 2007 Code for solicitors undertaking a separate business.

Keeping going: how to manage the small practice

13

Periodic reviews

Where are you going?

You are by this stage established. You may still feel rather insecure and be wondering if you are going to be trading next month, but this is normal. Small practices naturally feel insecure for at least the first two or three years, and in many cases, much longer. Perhaps the most comforting factor is to look back and see that as a matter of history you have billed x thousand pounds each year since you started and there is no reason why you should bill substantially less than that for the following year, even if sometimes you wonder if you are going to bill anything at all for a given month. Insecurity of this type is perfectly normal. The fact remains that if you have managed to survive for that long you are established. All you have to do now is to keep going.

At this time, and at intervals of at least two to three years, you should ask yourself where the practice is going. Traditionally, business gurus will say that you should have a three-year and a five-year business plan, setting out targets that you feel are attainable with review dates to see to what extent you have failed or succeeded and what adjustments, if any, are needed to ensure that you stay on course or reach a revised target. Sole or small practices perhaps need not be quite so formal. The important thing is that you think about what you are doing rather than just drift.

Market focus

You may feel that having offered a general service to the public, possibly with a high percentage of legal aid work, and having attracted the attention of a number of company clients, it is time to focus on the latter. If you take this decision, it is vital that you do so in conjunction with a marketing plan – company clients will not simply beat a path to your door to secure your services, no matter how good you are. You will also need to ensure that you have the necessary degree of flexibility to be able to accommodate any significant increase in work. If you are already working 12 hours a day, you are unlikely to be able to cope with a demanding commercial client; on the other hand, you want to avoid having spare capacity and waiting for the clients to arrive. You must have in mind a plan for putting to one side a certain type of work and freeing staff of sufficient calibre and expertise in order to cope with the kind of work you are expecting to win. Your business plan will have to include costing out the wages of any additional staff you may need to take on. It may be difficult to develop your plans in detail, as you do not know how many clients you are going to win and what level of work they will bring with them, but this does not prevent you from pencilling in a few shapes even though you are unable to paint the whole canvas. If you have some sort of a plan, you can double or halve the size of it, as appropriate; if you have no plan at all, you have no material to work with.

Marketing plan

How you go about marketing your practice in order to move up market is a matter for you. The purpose of this chapter is not to tell you what your marketing plan should be, but rather to underline the fact that things will not happen unless you have a marketing plan worked out in order to put your business plan into practice. You may decide to write a newsletter to existing clients whose commercial or better quality work you are not presently handling. The plan may include a free preliminary legal advice hotline service. It may involve researching particular areas of law so that you are in a position to pass on your knowledge to others through seminars to which you may invite existing or potential clients whose work you seek to encourage and increase. You may need to publicise any and all of these areas by means of mail shots. You may decide to target certain individuals or certain businesses by means of a business lunch, a free 'legal health' check or a lecture to certain elements of their staff on a topic of interest. Consider your product carefully. What is it you are selling? What can you do for the client? Consider your message carefully. How can you convey to the client clearly and persuasively what it is you can do for him or her? Then decide how best you can get the message across, bearing in mind time, cost and effectiveness. How much will all this cost you, when are you best suited to put it all into practice and how will you cope with the work which results? Set out your timetable, preferably in writing, and if necessary put it all in your diary.

An analysis of where your profits are coming from and who your competitors are may serve to demonstrate that the work that is on the increase is not necessarily business or commercial work and may relate more to general high street-type work. Some practices, particularly those located in the more run-down areas of central London, have taken a positive decision to expand into what many other firms have regarded as less profitable work. They have identified certain areas as having a high immigrant and unemployed potential client base and have made themselves experts in immigration and welfare benefits law. They have sought to expand their criminal legal aid work and, having formed the view that their local competitors are not offering a service of particularly good quality, they have rapidly established themselves as the top providers of that type of work in the area. Such firms can move quickly ahead in profitability terms when other firms, geared to more commercial work, may be struggling – particularly in times of recession.

No one can really tell you in which direction you should go. These are business decisions which involve a certain amount of business acumen and a considerable amount of luck. With the right planning and the right amount of determination, coupled with sufficient funding, it is likely that you will succeed if you set yourself business objectives and plough your energies and your resources into them at a time when other people may well be sitting there waiting for the clients to come to them.

Image

If you decide to go for one particular type of work and this involves a considerable change in the nature of the practice, you must ask yourself if your image is right. This is really a rethink of the original decisions you took when you first started out. If you hope to attract more business clients, are they going to be impressed by the type of premises you are in? If you are seeking to increase your legally aided work, will the clients feel intimidated by the type of premises you are in? Should you be relocating to premises that are going to attract passing trade with a shop window so that you can appeal directly to passers-by? If you are looking for more commercial clients, should you be relocating closer to a commercial centre?

Niche practices

By this stage of the firm's development, it may become apparent to you that you have a particular expertise in a rather unusual aspect of law and the opportunity may present itself for you to increase your strength in that area and become what is known as a niche practice. Such practices can be extremely successful. You will need to assess exactly where your work is coming from and, as with any other marketing exercise, ensure that you are continually selling your product in that direction. This may take the form of referrals from other firms who, faced with a problem which is beyond their ordinary field of expertise, think of your practice as one to which they can safely and confidently refer their client, knowing that a competent service will be provided and that the client will return to them after the referral to fulfil their more usual legal service requirements.

There is always a danger with a niche practice that others may develop in your area of specialisation and beat you at your own game. If you have put all your eggs into one basket you may find yourself in difficulties. Niche practices generally succeed because the particular area chosen is so specialised that to develop a similar degree of specialisation and acquire the same level of concentrated knowledge would be prohibitively expensive and the market is not sufficiently large or the rewards sufficiently attractive to make it a worthwhile exercise. With a small practice whose overheads can be kept low, you will have a head start on the competition from larger firms and you are in a position to ensure that it is not worth their while competing.

Expand or stay as you are?

It should not be taken as axiomatic that expansion is synonymous with progress. It has traditionally been the case that most practitioners have felt that they are somehow failing if the firm is not getting bigger. While it is true to say that a firm should not stagnate by not knowing what it wants to do and making no plans to achieve it, do not make the mistake of thinking that expanding means success and cutting back is failure. Many firms have learnt this lesson the hard way in recent years. The economic successes of the 1980s were put into sharp contrast with the downturn in the economy and the recession of the late 1980s to the early 1990s. Those firms that had expanded with the economy without really thinking why it was happening and where it might be leading, found themselves in great difficulties when the recession began to take hold. The position became unusually dangerous because the recession took hold so gradually. There was no sudden falloff in work to cause alarm bells to ring and stir those responsible for managing firms into taking the necessary remedial action. It was felt by many people that it was a temporary state of affairs and that cutting back was an overreaction. By the time it was realised that the country was in the grip of a deep and severe recession, a great deal of damage had already been caused to many firms, particularly the larger firms, with the consequence that the economic surgery which then became necessary was all the more painful for all concerned.

Generally, larger firms can afford to make such mistakes more easily than medium-sized or small firms since they have the additional financial and other economic muscle to be able to survive such bruising experiences. Smaller firms, particularly sole practices, tend to experience an economic see-saw effect. When things go well, they can go extremely well and then when things go wrong they go very badly wrong. For the sole practitioner, it is either feast or famine. A sole practitioner's overheads may, for example, be £50,000 a year. If turnover is £100,000 a year, there is a gross profit of £50,000. If the firm has a particularly good year and the turnover goes up to £150,000 (which is quite a realistic proposition in any one year), the sole practitioner sees the firm's profits, and thus his or her own take-home pay, double in one year. If, on the other hand, the turnover drops to £75,000, the sole practitioner's rewards have been halved. He or she will only be taking home £25,000 that year instead of the £50,000 the previous year. There is no network of partners through which these economic ups and downs are filtered to smooth the effect out. The same is largely true of two-partner firms, although even at that stage the effect is less noticeable unless the partners have agreed that the profit share should be more or less equivalent to the work that they themselves have produced.

Can you afford not to expand?

Some people take the view that in the legal business you cannot afford to stand still. My view is that you can afford to stand still, provided you have taken a conscious decision to do so. If you have assessed the pros and cons of expansion and contraction – bearing in mind factors such as the rise in overheads, interest rates, the general economic outlook, the cost of staff and premises as your major expenses, and so on – and you feel that the size you are at is ideal for the current situation and what is likely to be the situation in the next 12 to 24 months, to stay precisely the same size you are at the moment is a perfectly proper and sensible decision to arrive at. It should not be seen as a shirking of responsibility or an overcautious approach. Many firms took this view during the worst period of the late 1980s recession and as a result weathered the storm far better than those who cut back drastically without properly considering why they were doing so or those who took no action until it was too late. It is those firms that emerged from recession perfectly poised to expand as the economy expanded and to take full advantage of the economic upturn. Their legal teams remained intact whereas others had to rebuild theirs. Do not be forced into decisions just because other firms are cutting back or, for that matter, are expanding. Make your own decisions based on accurate management information which you have ensured is available to you, and then continually review the position to confirm that your actions were correct.

Merger

The decision to merge one practice with another is perhaps one of the hardest to make. This applies both for multi-partner practices and sole practitioners.

Sole practitioners

For you as a sole practitioner, it is superficially very attractive to merge your practice with another sole practitioner. Being in sole practice can be something of a lonely life and the mantle of responsibility for the practice, its staff and its financial arrangements can weigh very heavily at times. There is the constant worry that disasters may be occurring while you are away through holiday or illness. If you have partners, these responsibilities are shared. There is also the worry as to what happens if you have a very bad year. A sudden downturn in a particular area of work vital to the practice can cause a severe body blow and the practice may have difficulty recovering. If there are partners operating in other areas of work, the continued generation of income from those partners provides a vital breathing space to enable areas of the firm which are becoming less profitable to be rearranged and the necessary corrective measures taken. With a merged practice, all overheads are shared and significant savings can be made. Unfortunately, though, life is not quite that simple.

Once sole practitioners commence talks on merger, serious obstacles are brought into focus. The most obvious one is perhaps lack of control. As a sole practitioner you and only you are the boss. As soon as there are two of you, you can no longer take decisions without consultation. Your total independence has immediately been lost. Fears creep in as to whether or not you will be compatible with your partner on personal, intellectual and professional levels. There is always the danger that as a result of poor health or lack of effort you will be saddled with an unwanted passenger. There is a natural inclination on the part of each sole practitioner eyeing up the other to wonder what will be in it for him or her if he or she amalgamates with the other sole practitioner.

For a merger to work, there must be considerable benefits to both sides over and above the ones discussed earlier. For example, one solicitor may have a client base which is not being properly serviced in a particular respect and the other solicitor can supply that service, having the necessary expertise and facilities. An obvious example is where a solicitor has a portfolio of company clients and services their conveyancing. The clients may have expressed a wish that this solicitor should also serve their litigation needs. Solicitor number two may be a skilled litigator but have no developed ability for conveyancing work. These two practices would have a better chance of succeeding as a merged practice since the merger itself opens up new opportunities which would not otherwise be available. The two partners will not compete against one another for the clients or for the work since they fulfil different functions. There are likely to be fewer problems of trust as the client is more likely to turn to the original solicitor for that area of work where the new partner is unable to service his or her needs. The original partner will probably feel more at ease since the danger of losing that client through a perceived need on the client's part to go to a firm that offers the full range of services instead of only some will have receded.

Takeovers

Perhaps surprisingly, some of the more successful mergers can be as a result of takeovers borne out of rather desperate circumstances as far as one practice is concerned. A practice may see itself floundering for a variety of reasons, be it a downturn in work, a substantial increase in overheads, the loss of an important client, and so on, and in desperation may turn to another firm to discuss merger. Merger is in these circumstances something of a euphemism since in reality the second firm will be taking over the first firm. The metamorphosis may be that much more successful since many of the usual fears which would hold back a merger under normal circumstances (whether you will get on with the new firm, whether they will take over your clients, how you will cope with the loss of independence and possible office politics) are all obscured by the more overpowering fear, namely that of imminent bankruptcy. The lack of bargaining position between the two parties means that negotiations for the terms on which the merger will take place proceed much more swiftly and with fewer difficulties.

Amalgamating with a struggling firm provides the means of taking a substantial step forward quite quickly. An entirely new client base is suddenly before you, providing new opportunities for generating more business. The target firm may have desirable premises, an extensive law library, and so on.

But the dangers involved are considerable. You must consider carefully why the firm became weak and ensure that any problems are corrected. Were the partners or staff incompetent? If so, was this on a professional or a managerial level? New partners who are bad managers can be educated, or persuaded to leave the management side of the practice to those with the necessary expertise. Partners who are professionally incompetent are much more dangerous. If that is how you view them it will be better to offer them salaried partnership or consultancy and to see the merger go off if they refuse.

The fee earner with a following

Potentially, one of the best ways to expand is to recruit a fee earner with a following of their own. You will need to be satisfied that he or she will be able to bill at least double what they are paid. At first sight, just covering the wages would seem attractive, but bear in mind the risk element of that extra work. Each matter is a potential negligence claim and if the firm is processing all that extra work and exposed to the extra risk there must be some financial reward for you at the end of the day. That increased turnover will also put up your overheads, especially professional indemnity (PI) insurance. There will need to be a margin for error.

People looking to relocate are in a difficult position. They may be unemployed or about to be. They may boast a larger following than they in fact have. If the figures add up where the following claimed is correct, but not if only half the following is real, you are taking a big risk.

You will need to interview the candidate thoroughly to ensure they do not have past negligence claims which will affect your PI premium and which suggest they are dangerous. Ask them to agree to let you obtain a printout of their PI claims from the Solicitors Indemnity Fund or an approved insurer, and to allow you to talk to their previous firm if that is feasible.

The candidate may be on the move because of being lazy, difficult to work with or incompetent, but if the client following is real, he or she is likely to have more virtues than vices. After he or she has started, watch carefully to ensure the client following and the billings materialise. If they do not, get rid of the new person before it is too late and without incurring redundancy or unfair dismissal claims. Check the sickness record and, if needs be, pay for a medical. Put in place a pay structure which means he or she only earns a substantial wage by hitting billing targets generated out of new work introduced.

Hiring such people carries considerable risks. If it works, it is the fastest way a small firm can generate substantial extra profits and broaden its base. Consider placing an advertisement and see what happens.

Loose associations

Because of the fear surrounding full merger, many people find the idea of a loose association stopping short of amalgamation more attractive. If partnership can be equated to marriage, loose associations can be equated to cohabitation. While such associations provide the opportunity to get to know a potential partner much better and to see how they operate at first hand, it tends to be the case that if the arrangement works well then people see no reason to change it; clearly, if it does not work well, people disengage from the arrangement and feel that they have had a lucky escape.

Sharing resources

There are considerable advantages to loose associations in terms of the sharing of expenses and assets as well as having a colleague whom you feel you can trust when you need someone to turn to for advice or help, but surprisingly few such arrangements lead to full mergers. It is possible to have a loose association which purports to be a full merger but in reality is not. The practice can be marketed as a merged practice and therefore a partnership with the accounts remaining separate for tax and profit-sharing purposes. In reality, therefore, what you have is two practices run under the same roof as more of a sharing of facilities than anything else. This has many dangers, the obvious one being the liability of each partner to third parties as they are held out as principals in the same practice. If the profit-sharing arrangements are separate, friction can arise where one practice becomes more profitable than the other, or one practice gets into difficulties and looks to the other for help. Since there is no proper partnership arrangement between the two partners, it would be unreasonable of the weaker partner to expect the stronger one to help out, either in terms of provision of services or finance, but there inevitably develops a false sense of injury on the part of the weaker partner and the situation can become acrimonious.

Such kinds of loose associations are best avoided. If you are going to have an association with another firm which is not thinly disguised as a partnership, you should make it abundantly clear from your notepaper that the practices are quite separate. If you are going to operate from the same building and have certain members of staff who in effect work for both firms, it should be clear so far as the member of staff is concerned exactly who the employer is so that if there are employment problems of unfair dismissal or redundancy the legal position is clear. It must also be clear to each member of staff to whom it is they answer, otherwise a rather chaotic state of affairs will arise with some members of staff having several managers, each issuing conflicting sets of instructions.

Upgrading and improving the systems

Now that you are established, your thoughts may turn to the question of whether the various systems you put in, i.e. computers, filing, storage, accounts, telephone, library, and so on, are sufficient or whether they should be upgraded. To some extent, these decisions must be taken in conjunction with the earlier decisions as to the direction the firm is going. If you have decided to become a niche practice, you will be attracting a specific type of client and your premises and supporting systems will need to be geared towards that type of client. This applies to everything from the furniture in the waiting room down to the contents of the library. If your practice is becoming far more specialist and less generalist, you may decide that money would be better spent on acquiring some expensive reference books on your particular specialist subject and that a more generalist precedent encyclopaedia to which you rarely refer can be sold to finance it.

Accounts

If you talk to people in the computer business, especially those in the computer supply business, they will on the whole advise you that after about five years of operation you will probably have to replace your present computer system with entirely new computer hardware and that you will probably be best advised to upgrade your software at the same time. Even if this advice is not partisan, it is not necessarily true. There are a good many computers which simply stop working after five years and you have no choice. They become expensive to repair and people are less willing to come out to provide the necessary technical assistance to keep them operating to their original specification. The mere fact that you paid only £650 for a computer software accounts package and £750 for a computer on which to run it does not mean to say that after three years you should throw it out and get a better one. When reviewing your computer needs, go back to the same drawing board you used when you decided to acquire your first computer. It is foolish to think that because you are paying £5,000 for state-of-the-art computer equipment, and another £3,000 for an accounts and time-recording package to go on it, you are going to have a better system. The same logic would mean that it is time to trade in your aging family estate car and buy a new Rolls Royce because expensive means better. Plainly, it does not. If what you are seeking to do is to convey the impression of success and wealth and appeal to certain influential and wealthy clients irrespective of the high servicing and running costs, the Rolls Royce is the right car. If, on the other hand, you need a vehicle that provides an efficient means of comfortable and reliable transportation with more moderate servicing and running costs, with a much lower capital investment, and with sufficient storage capacity to enable you to move an unwanted filing cabinet from the office to home, it is the estate car that you need.

Another consideration is whether you will need a system which is compatible with someone else's system. That someone else could be your spouse at home or a set of barristers' chambers which you use frequently. It is rarely a reason in itself for change, but is something to bear in mind in your choice of system.

A much more compelling reason for heavy investment in a new computer accounts system is the fact that the present system is having trouble handling the number of matters required because of the increase in the number of clients now using the firm. Another reason may be the need for several people to access the accounts information from several different locations and the inability of either the software or the computer system to accommodate that need. If there are no such pressing needs or corresponding failures on the accounts system to fulfil those needs, do not change the system just for the sake of change. Only do so if you can see that such needs will definitely arise within the next few months.

Storage

Similarly, if you are coping with your storage system well enough at the present time by storing your old files in the office or at home in the shed, continue with the same system. Periodically, we all receive mail shots from storage companies extolling the virtues of their air-conditioned storage space and trying to convince us that it is bad management practice to use expensive office space for the storage of files when the cost per square foot of storage space at their sites is much lower. This is entirely correct if you have a specific identifiable need for the space. There must be some sound economic reason why you should be incurring the additional over-heads of off-site storage, especially when this means that you will no longer have instant access to the files. As well as the cost of renting the storage space, do not overlook the fact that someone will have to travel to the storeroom, retrieve the file, bring it back and then reverse the exercise, all of which costs you money.

Telephones

If you took the decision to have expandable capacity on your telephone system when you first set up, it will probably be some time before there is a real need to change the present telephone system. The same rules apply. Can the present system cope and will it be able to cope in, say, the next 12 months? Can it be made to cope simply by the addition of extra incoming lines and telephone extensions? If so, why change? What you may wish to do at this stage is to consider the cost of buying your telephone system outright rather than renting it if that is what you have been doing up until now. I discovered – rather later in the day than I would have liked – that buying an identical system from a small independent supplier saved me £2,000 a year rather than continuing to rent from BT.

14

Cornerstones for future success

The six rules covered in this chapter will help your practice flourish.

Be nice

The relationship between a solicitor and client is something that merits considerable study. There are as many different types of relationships as there are solicitors and possible clients. To some, you are merely a means to an end. Business people need solicitors just as they need telephonists, managers, cleaners and receptionists. To them, you are just another of the hired help, another cog in the large machine. To other clients, you may be almost a hero figure, the clever and respected person who solved the most worrying and difficult problem they have ever had to come to terms with in their life – a sort of legal Harry Potter. To other clients, you may be a friend; a trusted confidant whose views are respected on a variety of issues of which the law is but one.

Many members of the public are still frightened of solicitors. Solicitors are not people with whom they come into contact on a regular basis unless they are business people who regularly use legal services. The average man or woman in the street uses a solicitor perhaps once or twice during their lifetime and sometimes not even that. To them, the solicitor is something of an unknown quantity. They will tend to regard the solicitor as someone who has trained for many years and is thus a very knowledgeable and clever individual who, because of his or her long years of training, charges extremely high fees.

This image has been built up over a number of years and to some extent has been enhanced by television and the media. The image is being broken down gradually, but there is still a long way to go. When clients set foot inside your offices for the first time, you must appreciate that they may have been steeling themselves for a number of days to pluck up the courage to come in and see you. For them it has been something of an achievement even managing to come through the door. If you are immediately able to put them at their ease and to show them that you are someone who is capable of being kind, gentle and understanding, as well as tough and strong when needs be, there may well be a sense of relief on their part that they have found someone with whom they can identify and with whom they can have a comfortable rapport. If you manage to achieve this in your first meeting with your client, you may have secured yourself a client for life. This bonding process happens with most professional people. Think how many doctors and dentists you have known and how many of them you have felt comfortable with. There must be a certain minimum level of understanding and trust between yourself and the professional before you make a mental decision that this is the person you are going to stay with and, provided that level is reached, you will be unlikely to change your professional adviser unless something happens to break that bond. You must, of course, supply the necessary level of skill and expertise to demonstrate that you can fulfil the client's needs, but clients will sometimes stay with a particular professional adviser even though the adviser has clearly made a serious error, simply because they appreciate that everyone is capable of making mistakes. It is this client bonding which will preclude the client from running off to a competitor at the first sign of a problem.

To achieve this relationship, you must be nice to the clients. Make them feel important and make it seem a pleasure each time you see them and each time you speak to them on the telephone. Be nice in your letters to them. Show them that you understand the difficulties they face and show them that you care. Keep your conversations with them as light as you can in the circumstances without trivialising their problems. Make them laugh if you can. By following this approach, you may even achieve a state of affairs where clients look forward to coming to see you. However, do not undo it all by leaving the client feeling they have been charged the full hourly rate for socialising. It is not just a question of using clients' first names and letting them use your first name at an early stage in the relationship. This can, indeed, be totally counterproductive and make it appear that you are being over-familiar with them – I have clients for whom I have acted for over 20 years and we are still not on first-name terms. Such matters are questions of style and individual taste rather than anything else. The use of first names and at what stage depends on what image you wish to project and the type of relationship you wish to promote. Make clients feel that they are part of your firm and that you want them to come back the next time there is the slightest problem. Even when clients are being rather tiresome and very demanding, you must still be nice to them. Without the clients, there is no firm. They are the ones who pay your wages and your overheads. The customer may not always be right. Indeed, the fact that he or she has ended up in something of a mess may mean that he or she is wrong more often than right, but the client is always important and should always be welcomed into your offices.

If you have a letter from a client which infuriates you, or he or she says something on the telephone to upset you, do not write a vitriolic letter telling the client just how ungrateful and obstinate he or she is. Leave it for at least a couple of days. As an alternative, write a draft and proofread it two days later. You will probably be shocked at the strength of your own feelings expressed in it. Are you glad now you did not send it the same day?

Ask yourself how you would feel if the letter was read out in court. Would it appear professional, or would you cringe as leading counsel reads it out in all its glory? Perhaps one or two changes might be as well after all.

Be the best

The profession is more competitive now than it has ever been. Successive governments and consumer groups have encouraged people to shop around for their legal services. They made it their aim to take away solicitors' monopolies of various areas of work and encourage competition between solicitors and were very successful. Before then, a large proportion of clients did not even ask what the cost of a conveyance was likely to be – many considered that to ask about a solicitor's charges or to ask for a quote was tantamount to an insult and was as good as saying that you did not trust the solicitor. Those days are long gone. People now will rarely instruct a solicitor in a conveyancing matter without having obtained at least two or three quotes. A large proportion of people will shop around until they get the lowest quote they can find. If you are to win work and keep it, you must not only be competitive on price but you must demonstrate that you are the best provider of legal services in the area and ideally better than any other supplier they could have chosen irrespective of area. Go the extra mile for clients and prospective clients.

Everything you do should have quality in mind. You and your staff must answer the telephone faster than any of your competitors. You must be friendlier and more professional than them. The speed of response to the client's problems must be rapid. The amount of effort you put in on the client's behalf must be higher than they expect. They must quickly form the view that your firm is very different from all the other firms they have come across. You must be the best. You will not achieve this by words alone. People will not be impressed by you telling them how good your firm is, at least not without specific proof. There is nothing wrong with a moment of self-indulgence with the client when you have completed a particularly good piece of work for them. Equally, there is nothing wrong with telling the client in advance what the philosophy of the firm is, particularly if they are questioning a price differential between your quote and someone else's:

> If price is the main factor, you may be able to get the work done more cheaply elsewhere, but we build into our price sufficient time to spend with you in making sure you understand what is happening on your matter and why.

You must live up to your promises. Clients will not easily forgive you for saying that you will do something if you then fail to deliver. Do not forget the requirements of outcome 1.13 of the SRA Code of Conduct 2011 – to provide costs information from the start of the job and to update it as you go along.

Be the fastest

A major criticism of lawyers is that they are slow. In most instances, solicitors today are not at all slow. They can move very quickly when required. It is hard work being the fastest, but that is how to succeed. There have been many occasions when a member of staff has said to me: 'This will be alright to go out tomorrow, won't it?' Almost invariably the reply is 'No – let's get it out tonight.' Staff can sometimes feel that you are being unreasonable in this way, but ultimately they tend to respect you for your ideals and enjoy being part of a successful team. There is, generally speaking, no good reason why something should have to wait until tomorrow if it can be done today. The work will be done faster, the firm will be more profitable, the client's problems will be resolved more quickly, the bill can go out earlier. Do not forget your staff's feelings in all of this. If they have worked hard to get something out on time, praise them for it. Being considerate to staff is conducive to a good office environment and thus to productivity.

When a potential client asks for a quote, offer to put it in writing and get it out that day. If he or she lives locally, deliver it by hand. That sends out the right message: 'We are efficient and we want your business!'

Keep planning

It is very easy for a firm to lose sight of where it is going. There is, after all, a great deal to be done during the working day. Planning is very much a matter of self-discipline. There must come a time when you stop taking any more phone calls and put things to one side while you sit down and think about the firm, what it is doing and where it is going.

Since your client's affairs come first, the obvious thing to do is to put off planning such things until the evening when the phones have stopped ringing and things are a little quieter. So long as you have sufficient self-discipline to do so, this is the ideal time. Unfortunately, all too often you decide to go home and think about the firm's future another day. If you do that often enough, the firm will not have a future.

Consider the following:

- Are we the right size?
- Do we need more staff?
- Do we have too many staff?
- Are they the right kind of staff?
- Should we be breaking into new areas?
- Do we need to buy new equipment?
- Are we targeting the right markets?
- Do we need a new marketing initiative, and if so, what?
- Is it time to refurbish the waiting room?
- What about our own rooms – is it time to brighten them up too?

- Are we making enough profit, and if not, what are we going to do about it?

It is no good thinking about these things superficially. You must go through the pros and cons and make some firm decisions. Having taken the decisions, you must put them into practice. If you make the time to do the planning, think things through and then take decisions but never act on them, the whole process will have been a total waste of very valuable time. Make the time, do the planning, take the decisions and then action them.

Keep monitoring

Small firms, by their nature, tend to worry a lot. We all wonder if we are going to be in business next month and the month after, particularly after a disappointing set of figures. It is usually when that happens that we get out the records and the reports that our systems have produced and start going through them to try to give ourselves some sense of security. There is nothing wrong with that except the timing. It is not only during the good months or the bad months that you need to keep checking to see where you are, but on a continual basis. There is no hard and fast rule of every month or every two months or whatever, simply at regular intervals. You must be the judge of how regular those intervals will be, but the situation needs to be seen in the context of a year and then to compare one year with another. In this way, you will be able to see what has happened to the firm and whether you are going in the right direction. You may be able to highlight particular problems and do something about them:

- Are the staffing costs too high?
- Is someone not pulling his or her weight?
- Is a particular kind of work not sufficiently profitable?
- Does someone take longer than everyone else to do the same job and need training?
- Is there a fee earner who is not pulling his or her weight? How should you handle the problem?
- Does another fee earner need an assistant?
- Are there too many people in general office or not enough?
- Do we need more secretaries?
- Do we need fewer secretaries and more computers?
- Has conveyancing work increased or decreased? What should we be doing about it?

Managing a firm is like driving a car. You can only afford to take your eye off the road for a few seconds at a time. You must constantly adjust here and there to ensure you are on course.

Keep marketing

Marketing should, even for a small firm – and some would say particularly for a small firm – be an almost constant operation. Advertisements in directories, etc., go some way to placing yourself and your firm in front of the public and potentially new clients on an almost constant basis, but all too often people think that once they have renewed their advertisement in the Yellow Pages, they have done their marketing for the year. Placing advertisements in the media is only one form of marketing. Some additional ways to market the practice are covered in **Chapter 19**, but the secret is to keep marketing. You should constantly be thinking about how you can win more clients. You should monitor the results of any marketing initiatives that you have at the present time. It is also a useful exercise to look back at new business and see where it came from and if there is a lesson to be learnt.

A few years ago I targeted a particular individual in a particular company. While it was very pleasant to renew an old acquaintance and we had an extremely pleasant lunch, I made no secret of the fact that I was looking for their work. I was in luck. The company was less than impressed by the solicitors it was using and that firm was a replacement for another firm with whom the company was dissatisfied. It tried me out on small debt collecting work and the first three rules discussed in this chapter were put into immediate operation. We were nice, we were better and we were faster. More debt collection work followed. One of them turned into a two-day county court trial with costs running into a number of thousands of pounds. Private client work for other members of the company followed. My business lunch took me out of the office for some three hours – time I had to make up for by working even later that day. The lunch itself cost a good deal less than an advertisement in the Yellow Pages, but it has resulted in business running into several thousands of pounds. Should I be having more business lunches and placing fewer advertisements? The answer is immaterial to the point being made. The point is: keep marketing. Your marketing plan may consist of several different types of marketing, but it is an ongoing, almost day-to-day affair, not a couple of ads placed and 'that's that out of the way'.

Do not forget that every communication with a client or potential client is a marketing opportunity. What you do and say on each occasion either enhances or detracts from the image the client has of your firm. Every time a member of staff answers the phone your firm is on trial.

15

Preventative medicine

What happens if I die?

It is all too easy to brush out of sight the problems that will be left behind when a sole practitioner dies with the fatuous comment that you will not be here to worry about it. There will be a good many other people who will be here to worry about it, including your immediate family and your clients. If you are a partner in a two- or three-partner firm, a considerable burden will fall upon the partners you leave behind.

Under the earlier regulatory regime contained in *The Guide to the Professional Conduct of Solicitors 1999* (the Guide), Principle 3.14 stated that a sole principal should make a will containing adequate provision for the running of the practice after his or her death. There was no direct equivalent to this provision under the Solicitors' Code of Conduct 2007 but the guidance notes to rule 5.01(1)(k) stated that a sole principal should make adequate provision for the running of the practice, in the event that the sole principal dies or becomes permanently disabled, by a person who is qualified to supervise. Whilst it is not entirely clear whether failure to demonstrate that such a system was in place before the emergency, for example death, is in itself a breach of the rule, the likelihood was that it would be regarded as such.

There is no specific requirement under the SRA Code of Conduct 2011 for a sole practitioner to have a will in place. However, the Chapter 1 outcomes require you to provide services in a manner which protects the clients' interests and to have the skill and resources to carry out their instructions and the Chapter 7 outcomes to have systems and controls in place to achieve and comply with all the principles, rules and outcomes of the SRA Handbook. It may be sufficient to trigger a breach of the Code if you have no will in place or other suitable arrangements to provide for the handling of your client's affairs if you die. In any event, it is common sense to do so to avoid the disastrous consequences created by those sole principals whose practices degenerate into chaos on the principal's death when no such arrangements are in place. It is unfair to clients and others involved in related transactions such as a conveyancing chain, as well as relatives and personal representatives of an estate where no proper provision has been put in place. The Guide formerly strongly advised that one of the executors of the will should be a solicitor and this again would be sensible, despite not being part of any regulatory requirement. It will be appreciated that, in most sole practices, the sole operator of the client account will be the principal, and on his or her death the client account is paralysed. It does not take much imagination to perceive the severe problems that would arise for clients in a busy conveyancing practice where clients were about to complete and the sole principal dies. Many hundreds of thousands of pounds of mortgagees' and clients' money could be locked up in client account for, at the very least, many days, if not actually weeks or months if there is no solicitor executor able to operate the account. An executor's authority to deal with the estate derives from the will itself, but not so an administrator of an intestate estate who, strictly speaking, has no power to act until such time as a grant of letters of administration has formally been given. Although not part of any formal rules or code, the advice given in the Guide is still very sound. The Guide acknowledges the situation outlined above but nevertheless goes on to say that in these circumstances prospective administrators are encouraged to nominate a manager for the practice before the grant is obtained. The Guide tacitly appears to accept that technically the administrators would be meddling in the estate if they take this action before obtaining a formal grant, but given the very unsatisfactory state of affairs that has arisen, it appears that the administrator's intervention before the formal grant is seen as the lesser of two evils. It is wrong of a sole principal to put their immediate family in such a difficult situation at a time when they are overcome with grief, when the very simple step of making an elementary will naming at least one executor who is a solicitor would have done so much to simplify matters. Better still, name a solicitor who is qualified to supervise, so that the practice's affairs can be managed in an orderly fashion whilst things are being sorted out.

The Guide goes on to set out the various other steps that can be taken, including those by the Law Society itself, to sort out the practice of a sole principal including, if needs be, an application to the court for a grant in favour of a nominee of the Law Society, which in most instances will be in connection with an intervention by the Law Society to enable the practice to be wound up. Given the fact that the ethos of OFR is to spot problems early on and stop them from turning into full-blown crises, sole practitioners and small practices should not be unduly surprised if the SRA at an inspection asks to see disaster plans dealing with the situation which might arise on the death of a sole practitioner or of a co-partner. You would be well advised to give these matters some thought now and commit them to writing. Indicative behaviour 7.4 refers expressly to making arrangements for the continuation of your firm in the event of absences and emergencies such as holidays or sick leave.

In most cases, the only practical solution will be to wind up the practice of a sole practitioner. It may well be that the practice has a sale value, but if it is to be sold, steps must be taken immediately to ensure that the practice continues to be properly run by the appointment of a manager to enable the business to be run as a going concern until a purchaser can be found. It is vital that the practice is put up for sale as quickly as possible after death, before the client base starts to drift away. Many legal staff recruitment agencies also arrange the sales of practices of both living and dead principals and, for that matter, will act as matchmakers for practices seeking merger. A copy of the relevant sections of the Guide is provided at **Appendix 12**, but bear in mind that we now operate under OFR and the Guide is only an example of what used to be best practice.

The deceased's family

An immediate consequence of the death of the principal will be that income from the practice by way of drawings ceases, at least in the short term, until a manager has been appointed. Every principal should ensure that sufficient insurance and pension arrangements are in place by the time of their death so that their spouses and families will be able to survive financially without them. It can be a salutory exercise to sit down and go through the family budget and then to see what funds would be available to satisfy the outgoings if you were dead. It is a reasonably straightforward, if a little time-consuming, exercise to work out what the proceeds of the various policies would be and to see whether there would be enough money to go round. If there is not, you may need to make extra provision by means of pension or life policies to make up any shortfall. You may find that your spouse is unwilling to discuss such matters, but it can also be a useful exercise to sit down together and try to think yourself through such a scenario. If your spouse is working part time or not working at all, how easy would it be to arrange childcare and at what cost? What kind of an income would be produced if your spouse then worked full time? Would a sale of the family home be inevitable or advisable? While it may be painful and a little demoralising to discuss such matters, these facts will need to be faced one day and a little pre-planning may go a very long way.

The reverse situation should not be ignored. For the sole principal to try to run a practice after their spouse's death, and possibly look after a young family at the same time, will be a very heavy burden. Making sure that the loss of one's spouse is counterbalanced to some extent by insurance and/or pension arrangements is just as important if the survivor is the sole practitioner. It is all too easy to fall into the trap of making sure that the sole principal is covered in insurance and then to find that he or she is the one who survives and it is the other half of the team who is struck down, and there is little or no insurance cover.

Why not leave a complete set of instructions? It will probably take no more than about two hours to set out precisely what your spouse should do on your death so far as the practice is concerned. You can cater for everything from drafting your own specimen letter announcing your death to your clients to which trusted members of your profession or other close friends your spouse can turn to for help and advice. You can go as far as dictating the strategy for the sale of the practice if you wish. You could nominate a particular agency through which the practice should be marketed and say that you would like efforts to be made for, say, a period of six weeks for a buyer to be found, but that if no buyer is found within that time then a further letter, also dictated by you, should be sent to all the clients advising them that the firms that had assisted you with the running of the practice in the past would be your choice of solicitor for them now, but that, of course, it is entirely up to those clients who they choose as their new solicitor. Your nearest and dearest may not be disposed to follow your blueprint for the disposal of your practice, but at least it will give them a few ideas and suggestions as to what to do at a time when they may be devoid of any ideas themselves.

Two or more partner firms

The blow of losing a partner in a two- or three-partner firm can be crushing. The importance of a particular individual to a firm is never more appreciated than when they are no longer there.

Clients will need reassurance that the work carried out by that partner will still be dealt with competently. There may be obligations to the family of the deceased partner under the terms of a partnership agreement. The outflow of funds to comply with such obligations may leave the remaining partner or partners short of the necessary financial resources to take on an assistant solicitor or principal from elsewhere of sufficient calibre to replace the deceased partner. The answer to this problem lies in insurance. It is vital that small practices insure their partners. The premiums can be paid by the practice as an expense. If the partner retires without the policy operating, the capital value of the policy can belong to the partner, if this is what is agreed by the rest of the partners. The firm may decide that the sum paid out on the maturity of the policy is in part payment of that partner's capital account. If proper insurance arrangements are made, the surviving partner or partners are free to spend what would have been that partner's draw in recruiting a senior solicitor to take his or her place. Such a replacement may well have hopes of partnership at an early stage themselves and so care must be taken in choosing the successor. Any immediate problems can be catered for by means of a senior locum. If you have consultants working two or three days a week, this may be the time to try to persuade them, with a suitable financial inducement, to come out of retirement for a short time in order to fill the gap. If they can see that it is a real emergency and that it is a one-off opportunity for them to make some cash, you may find that they are only too pleased to help out.

How to be ill and still trade

The way in which you tackle the problem of illness will depend to a large extent on what type of illness afflicts you and how long it is likely to take you to recover. It will also depend on how many staff you have. Planning for illness is every bit as much a part of managing a practice as any other aspect. Indicative behaviour 7.4 of the SRA Code of Conduct 2011 draws attention to the need to ensure that arrangements are in place for the continuation of the practice in the event of absences and emergencies for holidays or sick leave with the minimum interruption to the clients' business. Although merely an indicative behaviour and therefore not binding, it looks suspiciously like a rule and failure to make proper arrangements is likely to cause the SRA to take the view that outcome 7.2 has not been achieved. The important thing is to have a contingency plan. At least for the immediate future the one person unable to take decisions will be you, or you must assume, so you must take a worst case position. If it turns out that you are well enough to give instructions as to how to cope, so much the better. However, you may be in hospital unconscious as a result of a road traffic accident or you may have had a stroke. In this situation you have got to assume that you will be out of commission for at least two or three months. If not actually undergoing treatment, you will need considerable time to recuperate afterwards. There is no alternative in this situation but to conscript an experienced practitioner.

The ideal person would be a consultant from another firm with whom you may have a good relationship. They will need to comply with the provisions of rule 12 of the SRA Practice Framework Rules 2011, which in effect repeats rule 5 of the 2007 Code of Conduct regarding the definition of persons qualified to supervise. They should also be capable of fulfilling the functions of the COLP and the COFA unless one or other post is occupied by another person who will be in the office whilst you are away. The relationship may be because the firm is local to you or you have a contact in another firm and they have someone who may have been a partner and is now working two or three days a week. That firm may be prepared to release their consultant for a period of two to three months so that a safe pair of hands is running your practice while you are incapacitated. A proper commercial fee must be arranged with the firm concerned. It will probably be large enough to absorb the work which the consultant would have undertaken. The consultant will have sufficient knowledge and expertise to be able to cope with the situation and will also have the necessary support systems, such as access to partners of their own firm, to discuss particular problems which may be beyond them.

The effect on the clients should not be underestimated. If they hear that their solicitor has had a stroke and will be away from the practice for an indeterminate period of time, something akin to panic will set in and they will need the reassurance of having someone who is obviously experienced and confident in charge, quite apart from the requirements of Chapter 7 of the SRA Code of Conduct 2011 and rule 12 of the SRA Practice Framework Rules 2011, which also requires that proper arrangements are in place. Whether the Law Society or SRA are likely to impose disciplinary proceedings on a solicitor recovering from a stroke for having failed to make proper arrangements for the practice while he or she was ill is not really the point. You owe it to your clients and to your staff to ensure that proper arrangements are in place and you cannot make those arrangements from a hospital bed – they must be thought about in advance and a contingency plan made.

If you are unable to make arrangements for the loan of someone's consultant you, or more probably someone trying to cope in your absence, will very likely be forced into engaging a locum. A locum will be a fairly expensive way of answering the problem, but there are no cheap ways. Again, the locum will need to be someone who is qualified to supervise in order to comply with the Practice Framework Rules. It is unrealistic to expect a friend in another practice to split his or her time between running your practice and his or her own. It will be impossible to do both properly and, while it may be possible to carry out some emergency surgery within your practice to keep things afloat, he or she will always put their own practice before yours. It will also mean that half the time that clients wish to speak to a senior solicitor they will be unable to do so. Whether it is true or not, people will rapidly take the view that their affairs are being neglected. You do not want to return from your convalescence to find your practice has evaporated and the years of hard work in building the practice have been wasted.

The firm's client base is a pot of money. It makes financial sense to hire the staff needed to do the work so that clients' matters are properly processed, completed matters are billed and the clients are happy and will place their work with you next time. Spend the money, get in the extra staff and get the job done.

Lasting power of attorney

People tend to think that only the elderly need to consider making a lasting power of attorney. A lasting power of attorney must be executed before the onset of mental incapacity. Such mental difficulties are not the sole prerogative of the elderly and can strike even the young. In the way that death will paralyse a solicitor's client account if there is no one else able to operate it, the same will also be true for a solicitor who becomes mentally incapable of dealing with the practice. By executing a lasting power of attorney while they have all their faculties, sole practitioners should ensure that there is someone in a position to manage their practice in a professional way either until it can be sold or until it can be run down in an orderly fashion. There may be premises to be sold, and there will be considerable difficulties for the sale if the solicitor concerned does not have the mental capacity to dispose of a lease. This may require an application to the Court of Protection in the absence of a power of attorney, with the consequential delays and additional expense. Much criticism has been made of the complexity and expense of lasting powers compared with the relative simplicity and low cost of the earlier enduring powers, but at present it is the only type of power available for this type of emergency and will be better than having nothing in place.

How to cope with burglaries and fires

Next to illness, death and bankruptcy, probably the biggest fears for small practices are burglaries and, worse still, fires. Insurance policies for small businesses will often cover many of the immediate financial consequences. Policies may pay for the reinstatement of the premises and the loss of equipment, furniture, and books, etc. Depending on the kind of policy, there may be cover for loss of profits while the business is being reinstated. What it cannot properly cover is the disruption to the business and the inability to conduct the clients' affairs properly. It will also not cover satisfactorily the loss of precedent libraries and so on unless very specialised insurance cover is obtained. The answer to the latter point is duplication. You will need to have a disaster plan in place to comply with the requirements of Chapter 7 of the SRA Code of Conduct 2011 and to deal with the concerns of indicative behaviour 7.4.

The key to a practice is its financial structure. By duplicating the financial information, you will have a complete client list and full details of all financial transactions for each client, including how much client money you are holding and how much money they owe you. If you are running a time-recording system as part of your accounts package, you will also be in a position to know how much unbilled work has been carried out for each client. Many clients may sympathise with your predicament and may agree to such work being billed at that point in order to ease your cash flow problems.

A huge amount of information is contained within clients' financial ledgers. For example, if you need to obtain a copy of a statement of case or a divorce petition that has been issued and you do not know the action or case number, the court may have problems locating the matter. If, however, you can tell them when it was issued, the court may be able to provide you with a duplicate. The issue fee will be shown on the client's ledger. Having located that document you will have immediately located all other related documents filed with the court and ascertained the name and address of the opposing solicitors. A letter to them will undoubtedly result in a complete copy of the inter-solicitor correspondence and discovered documents and also your own client's name and address! Within a fairly short space of time, you will be able to duplicate most if not all of what was on the original file either from the court, the opposing solicitors or your own client. Without the original financial information from the client ledger, you may well be dependent on the client or the opposing solicitors contacting you. This may take a number of weeks, and letters may go astray if you have to relocate from one office to another in the case of a serious fire.

The one important set of information and documentation – that you will not be able to reproduce from the client or from the court or from opposing solicitors – will be the financial information relating to your client. If you are able to make any progress at all from these sources, it will be painfully slow and will be incomplete. It will be an enormous task to try to get all the figures to add up. This heartache can be saved simply by backing up your computer information on at least a weekly basis and taking the information home. Memory sticks are ideal for this purpose. Strangely, many secretaries and accounts clerks appear very reluctant to do this. They are quite used to backing up information on a memory stick and leaving it in the office but show great resistance to the idea that they should either take a disk or memory stick home or make an additional copy to keep at home. It is also common for people to agree to take an extra copy of the accounts home in this way but to then unilaterally stop doing it. You may have what little satisfaction there is in saying 'I told you so' when disaster strikes, but it will be of small comfort and of no practical use whatsoever. You must insist that the information is backed up and removed from the office so that the information, more or less up to date, can be reproduced in the event that the original information is destroyed by fire or is stolen.

Also, many websites enable you to use spare capacity or you can buy additional capacity that will enable you to store a back-up copy of the accounts on a hidden section of your website. Even better, there are inexpensive computer programs which will automatically create a back-up every time the computer is switched off and will back the accounts up onto the website. This does not do away with the need to take your own back-up copy in the usual way as servers and websites crash from time to time or the back-up system may malfunction.

The software and data removed from site should include the program for the accounts package itself. Do not forget that your duty to your clients to keep their information confidential extends to financial information and applies just as much to information stored at home as elsewhere. Suitable safeguards should be put in place at home to ensure your clients' affairs remain secret.

You should also remove from site a back-up of your major precedent library. All original disks of commercially purchased software should be kept away from the office. As you create your own precedents or store drafts on disk to await a client's approval of, say, an affidavit or a will, these should also be backed up onto a memory stick or a portable external hard drive and taken home. Alternatively, the automatic backing up of accounts data to the web can be used, although because of the extra space this will involve it is very likely you will need to rent extra space from your Internet service provider.

The amount of information that can be stored on memory sticks or external hard drives can be enormous. The task of making copies and of taking them away from the office is minute compared with the quantity of information that you have put out of harm's way. It does not make any kind of sense to do otherwise. Again, back-up copies are confidential material and suitable safeguards to ensure they stay that way must be put in place.

In the last five years, we have had about four or five burglaries. On each occasion the only thing that was taken was cash and postage stamps. Fortunately, we never keep more than £100 of cash on the premises at any time. Having grown tired of losing the £30 or £40 that happened to be in the cash tin every time the offenders struck, we now take the petty cash home with us out of office hours. Other solicitors in the area have not been quite so fortunate and have had expensive computers and fax machines stolen. It is tempting to think that you have nothing worth taking but, apart from anything else, burglars can cause considerable destruction once they have gained access. The usual crime prevention rules apply. Do everything you can to keep them out. You will not have gone too far into the future before you will need to carry out a thorough review of your security arrangements. This may entail putting in a burglar alarm system and possibly a video camera, placed fairly obviously where potential thieves will see it but where they cannot attack it. A visit from the crime prevention officer of your local police station is always worthwhile, and can be extremely enlightening, pointing out hazards and entry points that you had never considered.

While the loss of a computer in itself can be mitigated by your insurance arrangements, a burglar may have carried off all the information stored on your hard disk or removed and stolen the computer's chip. If you are not backing your information up at regular intervals onto memory sticks and removing them from site, or backing the data up onto your website, the burglar may well have inadvertently stolen many hours of your and your typist's work, which will have to be repeated. Consider buying specialist locks from computer suppliers for clamping the computer to a desk or a device which means the chip cannot be removed from the machine without a key or great difficulty.

Many sole practitioners will have some sort of office capacity at home as well as in their office, assuming that they do not work entirely from home. As well as providing the ability to work from home out of hours or when the need to get the client's work done in a hurry requires it, this also means that you have additional computer hardware, telephone and dictating facilities should those in the office be lost due to a fire or stolen. If you have the necessary computer information on your duplicate set of disks, the recovery period is much shorter. You will be able to write to your clients, courts, other solicitors and so on virtually immediately to tell them what has happened and to enlist their help in reproducing any files that have been lost. It is almost worth having a second base for this reason alone, but I suspect most people will have the facility anyway for the reasons given. If not, there is nothing for it but to rush out and buy another computer, reload your software and data and get going again.

16

How to structure the firm

Partner/staff ratios

In this context, the staff discussed are fee-earning staff. All fee-earning staff and partners will need adequate support in terms of secretaries, receptionists, outdoor clerks, messengers, and so on, and it is important to put in place and maintain a correct balance between having sufficient support staff for the fee earners and having people sitting around idly. Most small firms will not be able to afford the services of a practice manager and the management of the firm will be split between the partners until such time as the practice grows to at least five or six equity partners, unless you wish to engage the services of a retired solicitor who has good management skills on a part-time basis. A good practice manager will cost £40,000–£50,000 a year, and small practices cannot afford such an expensive luxury. The money is better spent on a good assistant solicitor if that sort of cash is available.

I have known some quite prestigious, if rather old-fashioned, firms in the City and the West End which give the appearance of being medium-sized to large in terms of being 10–15 partners strong, which in fact hide a dark secret. All partners on the notepaper are equity partners and they have no assistant solicitors. Worse still, all partners are more or less the same age, except perhaps for one or two. Such a partner/staff ratio is akin to a hand grenade with the pin out of it. It is only a matter of time before the firm supernovas and probably ceases to exist. All partners are likely to want to retire at about the same time or will become ill as they become older and their health deteriorates. All partners will want to have their capital out of the firm at about the same time. A great many of the important players in the client base are of a similar age to the partners who attend to their business needs and are also likely to retire within a year or two of the solicitor concerned. It is only a question of time before two-thirds of the partners will have retired, their contacts within the client companies will also retire and will probably be replaced by younger men and women who have little or no association or loyalty with anyone else within the firm and will have little trouble in persuading other people within their companies to go to other solicitors. The remaining partners will find themselves very few in number, with a sudden and massive fall off in work, several partners clamouring for repayment of their capital at the same time and the overheads of the firm continuing unabated.

Such problems are the result of bad management and planning. Those charged with the management of the firm should have one eye to their own successors as well as keeping several other eyes looking into the future. Those younger assistants who have demonstrated a talent both for legal work, and winning and retaining clients should be seen as the assets of the firm that they are and should be wedded to the firm by means of partnership. Such gaps in the structure should be openly recognised and suitable calibre replacements should be sought so that there is a good spread of talent coming through with individuals being groomed for partnership.

Supervision

Until such time as fee earners get to the stage where they can work with virtually no supervision, by which time they should normally be serious contenders for partnership, they will need supervising to a greater or lesser extent. Partners have their own workload and there is a limit to the extent to which they can supervise. No partner should be expected to supervise the work of more than three fee earners. More than that and it will be impossible to render a proper service to the partner's own client base while checking properly through work which the other fee earners are producing. Such partners may also have administrative jobs within the firm, which will also take up their time. There comes a limit when even the ablest and most hard-working partners can no longer cope.

It is possible to delegate all or part of the supervision of a fee earner to a senior assistant solicitor, but again, such a senior assistant, if able and required to supervise others, will be on the brink of partnership anyway. Having in place arrangements for the effective management of the firm is required by Chapter 7, outcomes 7.1 and 2 of the SRA Code of Conduct 2011, and outcome 7.6 requires that you properly supervise and train staff in order to maintain a level of competence appropriate to their work and level of responsibility.

Salaried partners

Salaried partnership is something of a mixed blessing. The salaried partner is, from a legal point of view, held out to the world as a partner of a firm and is thus ostensibly liable for the firm's debts. It is extremely rare for firms to show salaried partners in that capacity on the notepaper – to an outsider, no distinction is drawn between salaried partners and equity partners. Indeed, some firms may go to great lengths to conceal such information, both from clients and from other firms of solicitors. In fact, salaried partners are employees just like other employees. They will have a contract of employment and be liable to be dismissed. Things may be different once ABS have bedded in. Historically, salaried partners do not share in the profits of the firm unless there is a bonus scheme in operation but do benefit by the fact that they draw a salary every month irrespective of the firm's fortunes. This is not always true: in some cases due to the exigencies of recession, staff in all types of businesses can be asked to take a cut in pay to help the firm survive. Salaried partners, in many instances, go along with such proposals rather than see the firm try to make savings in other ways, such as by making some staff redundant and running the risk that they may be the one to draw the short straw. During a recession, it is common not only for partners to be expected to take either no draw for a month or half their usual draw, but also to inject additional capital into the firm. Accordingly, not only have they not been paid, but they have sustained a loss for all the hard effort they have put into the firm for that month, or in some cases, over a period of several months. This is not normally the fate of the salaried partner.

Salaried partnership is seen as a stepping stone to full partnership. As a small practice, should you be making people salaried partners? There is a school of thought that says that salaried partnership is something of a deception. It is a means of keeping quiet a member of staff who is fairly useful, but not so useful that you wish to be saddled with him or her for the rest of your professional life, and while they may perform a useful function, you do not see them as deserving of a substantial slice of the profits. It is dishonest to use salaried partnership as a means of retaining a member of staff who is important to the firm but whom you do not regard as having the qualities necessary ever to become a full partner, unless you tell such an individual frankly that you are prepared to make them a salaried partner and to give them the status of partnership but that you are most unlikely ever to offer them full equity partnership.

Such news may come as a considerable disappointment but can perhaps be softened by pointing out the advantages enjoyed by salaried partners (as outlined above). You may make it perfectly plain to them that you have no wish to see them leave the firm but you feel it only right and proper to tell them how you feel about the situation. You may also point out that it is difficult to form a view about how someone will perform at partnership level in advance and that they may yet develop qualities and talents which have hitherto escaped you and that no such decision is irreversible, but they should be under no illusion as to what your present views are. So long as this is said and meant sincerely, it is perfectly fair and reasonable to put forward such views. People do behave differently when brought into partnership, even at salaried partnership level, and you should be prepared to change your opinions of people if the situation warrants such a change of heart.

Consultants

Consultants are usually former partners and often have a valuable part to play in a firm. They may have spent 20 or 30 years with a practice and, as well as having a wealth of experience and knowledge, have a considerable client following. The sudden loss of a partner can have a detrimental effect on the client base. By offering a partner a consultancy with the firm, a transitional phase is provided which enables the client base to be passed on to the succeeding partners and strengthens the bonds that have already been made. Clients gain considerable reassurance from knowing that, although not perhaps quite so available as before, and with a much lower profile, there will still be a familiar and trusted face dealing with at least part of their affairs. This reassurance is invaluable until such time as partners have gained the confidence of the consultant's clients and, as well as providing a settling-in period for the succeeding partners, it gives a 'bowing out' period in which the consultant can slowly withdraw from full-time practice, perhaps dropping down to four days a week, three, two and ultimately retiring completely, as agreed with the continuing partners.

Retaining consultants

There is also considerable goodwill attached to most consultants and the respect attached to a consultant's name will continue to reflect upon the firm while that name still appears on the notepaper, albeit a little lower down and under a different heading.

Unlike salaried partners, consultants are not held out as principals. There is a clear distinction to be made between partners of any kind and consultants. Nevertheless, often they are employees and can be dismissed or if they are self-employed their contractual arrangements can be terminated. Most consultants will have a consultancy agreement, which is a form of contract of employment. A specimen consultancy agreement appears in **Appendix 2**.

When a firm is purchased by new partners, it is a very common arrangement for the vendor to negotiate a consultancy with the new firm as part of the overall package. Equally, on mergers, the stronger of the two merging practices will probably not wish to retain all those persons in the weaker firm who were partners and who may not have the enthusiasm and drive that their younger counterparts possess. As senior members of the practice, it may be that they have been drawing substantial proportions of the profits which may not be proportionate to the effort expended in the practice. This in itself may be the reason why the weaker firm has found itself in a position where it makes good economic sense to merge with a stronger practice. In these conditions, a consultancy with the merged firm is often the answer. Some consultancies can go on for years. The normal term of a consultancy agreement is three years, but you may wish to extend it to five years, depending on your perception of the consultant's value to the firm. It is generally a bad idea for any fixed-term contract to last any longer than five years, although there is no reason why it should not then become a rolling agreement so that it continues from year to year until terminated by a notice provision by either side, normally of either six months or one year. Most consultants will not wish to go on forever and after many years of loyal service to a firm they are entitled to enjoy their retirement. There are, however, some consultants who will not recognise that the time has come for them to hang up their briefcase and a notice provision may need to be operated. Such considerations will undoubtedly form part of a firm's overall business plan. In most instances, after three years of diminishing chargeable hours spent with the firm, the continuing partners will have absorbed the goodwill element of the consultant's client base and will probably be looking to bring the arrangement to an end. There will always be those exceptional people who will continue to be a considerable asset to the firm beyond that period of time, but these people will be rare. If the arrangement with the consultant is that they are self-employed, care must be taken with the contractual arrangements as HMRC may consider them to be employees if the arrangements continue for any great length of time. Not only is this relevant from an income tax point of view but it also has a bearing on NI contributions – who should be paying them and at what rate?

Partnership agreements

I wonder how many solicitors have actually made a will? As solicitors, our thoughts will inevitably at some stage turn towards the question of a partnership agreement once we have partners. Is there any need? The Partnership Act 1890 was once described by one House of Lords' member as a 'model piece of legislation'. The mere fact that the partnership agreement is still the one that was passed in 1890 and has not been amended out of sight like so many other pieces of legislation is a good indicator of the fact that, like many products of the Victorian era, it was made to last. The Act can always be excluded by agreement, either in whole or in part but, where partnership agreements do not provide an answer, the Act is usually there to step in to fill the gap. The question therefore arises: is there any need for a partnership agreement at all between solicitors? In general, the only time when you need to refer to a partnership agreement is when things are going wrong. If everybody behaves reasonably and sensibly, solutions automatically emerge. It is only when people start to behave dishonourably or unreasonably that there is any need to look to the terms of any contract, including that of a partnership agreement.

Like any other contract, if you are going to bother to have one it is crucial that it works. You must agree on the fundamental points, such as profit share, dissolution, expulsion and interest on capital introduced. Having agreed on the salient points, you should then commit them to writing in such a way as to leave no room for doubt and no room for manoeuvre for those seeking to avoid the terms which they had previously agreed. If your agreement has been properly drawn up, it should mean that you will not finish up in court. The only occasions when people go to court are when they think they have a chance. If the agreement is in unambiguous terms and is properly drafted, it should leave no room for doubt as to who will win or who will lose, no matter how reasonable or otherwise the agreement may be. If the agreement provides an answer in clear, unequivocal terms, there is no point going to court because the court will only reach the obvious conclusion.

No partnership agreement at all is better than a badly drafted one, but a properly drafted agreement is always the preferred option. If the agreement is badly drafted, it will be capable of several different interpretations and each party will fancy their chances before a court. Such an agreement is a blueprint for a lawsuit. A suggested form of partnership agreement appears in **Appendix 1**. In the light of the foregoing observations, I would like to disclaim any responsibility if anyone enters into such form of agreement but nevertheless ends up in court. The suggested form of partnership agreement is intended as a starting point and may need modification depending on your particular circumstances. You may need to instruct another firm of solicitors to draw up your deed or to modify the suggested one. As you can see, the only thing that I am better at drafting than partnership agreements is exclusion clauses!

17

Managing growth

If all has gone according to plan, you may be sitting in your office one day and suddenly realise that you are no longer the firm. From the day that you set up in practice until this moment, you have been indispensable. The entire practice has revolved around you and without you there would have been no practice. The clients came purely because of you, your name, the advertisements you placed and the way you had managed the firm. Suddenly, it dawns upon you that this is no longer the case. Clients are giving the firm instructions because of the helpful way in which your assistant dealt with them previously. You may have a trainee solicitor who attends CAB evening surgeries and has developed a client following. You begin to realise that if your assistant solicitor left next week they are quite likely to take half a dozen clients with them. The firm is no longer just you – it is a separate entity and has almost taken on a persona of its own. You might even be able to go away on holiday for two weeks and be fairly certain that the firm will still exist when you return!

Rewards, benefits and risks

Is getting bigger necessarily a good thing? Not necessarily. The larger the practice the more things there are to go wrong as well as right. When you were on your own the closest thing to office politics or staff management was when you asked a family member to answer the telephone for you for an hour whilst you picked the kids up from school and they were not too keen. Now you have to consider the form of contracts of employment, disciplinary procedures and the like. It is a whole new world. The numbers get bigger. The overheads are so much more and the stakes so much higher. As you expand the potential rewards get bigger, but then so do the potential losses if it all goes wrong.

When you reach the stage where you are having to consider whether to expand and you decide to give it a go, it is time for a few changes. The first of these changes is the psychological adjustment needed to be able to view this new state of affairs as a positive development which takes pressure off you, as opposed to having lost something, since, strangely, this can be the case. There is almost a desire to take a few steps backwards because of the feeling that the firm is getting out of control. It is no longer just a question of getting the work done at what is often breakneck speed and keeping the clients happy. Members of staff have grown in importance and their loss could be a severe setback to the firm.

For a solicitor who has never been in a position of management within a firm before, the problems of a growing business can seem quite overpowering at times. Where does the line of sympathy and understanding towards members of staff end and strong management and a firm hand begin? Only the experience of different kinds of situations and making mistakes can teach you the finer points of how to handle staff. One thing you should always keep at the back of your mind is that staff are always replaceable. It is undoubtedly the case that some staff feel that they are irreplaceable and often some principals begin to feel the same about them. There is no such thing as an indispensable member of staff. Your staff are there to make your life easier.

When the point is reached where they cease to do that, they must be given their marching orders. It may be painful psychologically and financially, but when staff become a burden for whatever reason, it is time for a change. It may perhaps be a little unkind to say that within a matter of a few months it will be almost as if they had never been there, and the firm will continue on without them no matter how unlikely that may seem at the time.

Staff morale

Part of the essence of managing a firm well is to be able to cater for the idiosyncrasies of individual members of staff to maintain stability. Rapid turnover of staff is bad for morale and is bad for the service that is delivered to the clients. Continuity of staff helps to develop a happy family atmosphere which also rubs off onto the clients.

Next to the clients themselves, the greatest asset of the firm (apart from you!) is the staff. Choose your staff carefully and do not be rushed into taking someone on because there is a gap to fill and you are tired of interviewing. Having said that, with a small practice often you cannot compete with the salaries of larger and more established practices and you sometimes do have to compromise between the calibre of staff you would like to have and the calibre of staff you can afford. Nevertheless, there are minimum levels to be set and you should be looking for honesty and integrity above all else, together with commitment and personality. Sheer ability is probably the least of the qualities needed for the individual to fit in well with your practice. Their educational and professional qualifications will, hopefully, ensure a certain minimum level of ability. The fact that the individual does not have grade As and first class honours at each level does not mean to say that they would not do well within your practice. Indeed, if someone is particularly well qualified, they may be taking your job as a stop gap before moving on to bigger and better things at the first opportunity. Someone with their sights set a little lower may prove a more loyal and committed member of staff. In my view, it is more often the case than not that the better-qualified applicants do not necessarily make the better fee earner. They may be so wrapped up in the theoretical side of their work that they take their eye off the need to get the work done and bill it.

Put yourself in the client's shoes. Would you like this fee earner to be handling your matter? Do they inspire confidence and make you feel that you will be properly looked after? If this receptionist were talking to you on the telephone would it make you want to place your business with the firm?

Training

Having found what you consider to be the right kind of applicant for your position, they will need to be given some training by you, if only in the way that the firm operates and its general ethos. After spending the time necessary to settle the applicant in and to have them working productively, you will then need to work at ensuring that they stay for a long time. You may need to be more thoughtful and considerate than had been the case in earlier days. You need to be sensitive to the way in which staff interact with one another. Petty squabbles, particularly in a relatively small office, can soon appear and may get out of hand. You may need a firm but thoughtful hand in resolving them. At the same time, you must always ensure that the tail never wags the dog. There can be discussion and points of view exchanged, but at the end of the day there is only so far you can allow the member of staff's views to go before it is time to say that this is the way it will be, simply because that is what you have decided.

Monitoring systems

The days may be gone when you could sit in your office and physically see and hear everything that was going on around you. You may have moved premises or taken on extra space. Although you should still be seeing all the incoming and outgoing post and be able to keep a careful eye on things in that way, inevitably your grip on the firm will be considerably less by now than it had been when you first started. Now is the time to put in place proper and effective monitoring systems.

The Law Society's Lexcel quality standard contains helpful advice on how to put these systems in place. One should not be too dogmatic about these things. Some systems that are appropriate for some practices will not be appropriate for others. Much depends on size and the volume of work as well as considerations such as the physical location of supervisors, fee earners and support staff. The important thing is that there comes a time when you take a long, hard look at the degree of control you have over what is happening and what you need to put in place to ensure that any loss of control is regained. The Lexcel standard and toolkit publications can go a long way to putting forward suggestions to achieve this. Here are just a few suggestions to get you thinking.

Centralised diary

By issuing an instruction to all members of staff that they will not only diarise court hearings, time limits, deadlines and even, if necessary, appointments with clients and conferences with counsel in their own diaries but also in a centralised diary (probably one for each department would be sufficient), you will benefit in two ways. First, you can ensure that appointments and time limits are not missed. This produces an added benefit if someone is away ill unexpectedly. Second, it gives an extremely good idea of how busy everyone is. The regularity with which the entries are made will show how meticulous a particular individual is. By keeping a close eye on the centralised diary, it may rapidly become apparent that certain people are somewhat less than enthusiastic about what they see as unnecessary bureaucracy. This will immediately identify them to you as people on whom you will need to keep a close eye. If they are going to cut this kind of corner, they may be of a mind to cut other corners. Your level of supervision over such people will necessarily increase.

Perhaps a further bonus of the centralised diary is that it gives a good idea of how busy the department is. The fewer entries in the diary, the more cause for concern and the earlier you will be able to detect a fall off in business and start to look for causes and solutions.

Time reports

Due to the pressures on a small practice in the early years, the time recording side of an accounts package may have been ignored. It is only worth operating a time recording system if it is going to be used as a proper management tool. If an accounts department or a secretary produces time reports that sit on your desk for a number of weeks until filed away after a cursory glance, it is a waste of good paper. The time will come when your practice becomes sufficiently large that even if you have been able to ignore time costing up until that point, you will no longer be able to run your practice satisfactorily without it.

As well as telling you how much you should be charging for the work you carry out in order to make a profit and persuading cost judges that they ought to allow your bill in full, time recording also tells you who has too much work within the department, who has too little and who is working profitably. A downturn in work can be identified at an early stage, as can an increase. Work in progress can be accurately monitored, which can assist with cash-flow forecasting. The type of work which is unprofitable can be spotted and either phased out or reduced, and those areas which are profitable can be targeted for special attention to capitalise on, so as to maximise the available profits. If your software program produces an unbilled time report, you can chase those people who are bad at getting out their bills.

Weekly meetings

Whether you have staff or department meetings once a week, once a fortnight or once a month does not really matter too much. You are presumably operating an open door policy so that people who have problems before scheduled meetings can come to you with them for guidance. A weekly, fortnightly or monthly meeting (possibly even a combination) can help to formulate policies of one kind or another. Such meetings should be kept as brief as possible. Tying up several fee earners for an hour or two is extremely costly in lost billable time. Conscientious members of staff will regard attendance at such meetings as a chore unless it is clear that they are benefiting the department as a whole. You may be able to keep your meetings as short as 15 minutes. People should be invited to contribute to an agenda before the meeting. They should be chaired by someone who will keep the meeting moving so that there is no prolonged discussion on matters that only affect one person and are not relevant to the whole department. Such matters can be discussed individually, either with you or with someone who is responsible for the department, outside the larger meeting.

Remember to take steps to reduce the burden on those who have too much work. As well as being more likely to make costly mistakes, their morale will fall and they may look for a job elsewhere. Even just talking to them about their workload tells them you are concerned about them and that you value what they do.

File lists

The software program on your computer may be capable of producing a list of files that each fee earner has under their control. If not, fee earners concerned should be required to produce such lists, which should be updated at least monthly. It may be that the matter ledger listing system of a time recording program can fulfil this function, but if you are not running a computerised time recording system or the system you have is incapable of producing such a list, a separate manual list may have to be produced. While the numbers of files under an individual's control may not give an entirely accurate picture of how busy that person is, it is nevertheless quite a good guide. In any event, by discussing file lists with fee earners, you will soon get an idea of which files are weighty matters and which have remained dormant for some time and you will be able to take this into account when assessing who has spare capacity and who is not pulling their weight.

Sickness and holiday book

Someone fulfilling an administrative function within the firm, i.e. not a fee earner, should be tasked with keeping a sickness and holiday book. The firm may be small enough that an individual's physical absence from the office can easily be noticed. If only half a dozen of you work there, it will be fairly obvious when someone does not work. However, you may be at the stage where this no longer applies, in which case you will need some kind of reporting system so that any person's absence can be notified to the individual responsible for keeping the records. A periodic review of the statistics gathered in this way can be quite revealing. Absences are a drain on even large firms, and with a small firm are quite intolerable. You will need to tread carefully for purposes of unfair dismissal, and terminal and mental illness are classed as disabilities under the Equality Act 2010. It is especially important to monitor the performance of those persons with less than one year's service as terminating their employment is much easier since it does not carry the same risks so far as unfair dismissal and redundancy are concerned. Bear in mind also that part-time and temporary workers have the same rights as full-time workers, although to qualify for various employment rights employees must have served a minimum period of continuous employment with their employer. Agency workers have the same rights as directly employed workers after 12 weeks.

Holiday request slips

If your staff have increased in number, it is very easy to lose track completely of who is going on holiday and when. The answer is the holiday request slip. Do not allow staff to catch you when you are only half thinking about what they are saying and ask if they can have next Tuesday off. Make it a universal rule that anyone who wishes to have even half a day's holiday must complete a holiday request slip which comes to you or their head of department, and once the slip has been dealt with, one copy of it goes back to the employee and the other copy goes to the person responsible for collecting the data centrally. An additional advantage is that if people start arguing over whether or not they have used up the whole of their holiday entitlement for the year, you can go back to the raw data. It may well be that they have genuinely forgotten about a half day or day here or there. If you do not have the data to fall back on, it will be difficult to refuse the member of staff's request for time off and you may find you have granted them more holiday than had been agreed upon. An example of a holiday request slip can be found at **Appendix 13**. This form carries a full record of what the holiday entitlement is and how much has been used. You will still need to transfer the data to the sickness and holiday book.

Photocopying slips

Should you charge for photocopying? Courts have made it clear that photocopying should not be added as a separate item to a solicitor's bill and should be treated as part of the normal overheads of the office unless the number of copies produced is exceptional. One is tempted to say that such pronouncements from the Court of Appeal demonstrate perfectly how easy it is to spend other people's money for them, and before making such pronouncements, the Court of Appeal ought to try its hand at running a solicitor's office for a week or two. Nevertheless, there is a point to be made, namely that it is bad practice to charge people £5 or £10 on the bill for photocopying charges. If you are going to charge for photocopying you need to have a system of recording the number of copies taken in place. It may seem like a rather pedantic point, but insisting on each member of staff completing a photocopying slip before taking copies can save the firm a great deal of money. You may have made arrangements for a member of general staff to do the copying on behalf of the fee earners. Even if you have not and individuals do their own photocopying, they should still complete a slip and anyone seen copying who has not made out the appropriate slip should be taken to task. The number of copies should be recorded on the slip, which is placed on the correspondence tag of each file so that when a bill is prepared the number of copies made can be totalled. You will probably find that, by enforcing a fairly strict regime for the completion of photocopying slips and their placement on the correspondence tag, over the course of a year's work on the file the amount of copies produced is substantial. If the copying charges thus collated result in a charge to the client of £25 or £30, in my view it is perfectly proper to add those on to the bill as a separate item. Clients rarely challenge such items where it is clear that it is not part of a general sundries item. Furthermore, if either the client or the court on a detailed assessment challenges the figure, it does mean that you are in a position to justify it by stating precisely how many copies have been made, and producing the slips for examination, if requested.

Monthly billing targets

Virtually all commercial organisations, including professionals such as accountants and surveyors, have monthly billing targets. Members of staff are left in no doubt that they are expected to achieve a certain level of billing each month and will be required to provide some compelling reasons if they fail to achieve that target. To the extent that this is not universal practice among solicitors, we are the exception. There are all kinds of reasons given as to why this cannot be achieved – for example, a lot of work may have been carried out but the job is not complete and it cannot be billed until it is complete, or that there is a long-running case which has not come to trial yet, and so on. The fact remains that profit costs are the life blood of the firm. Without the costs coming in, the firm will slide gently into oblivion. There is nothing wrong in a solicitor's practice with the supervisor assessing what level of costs a fee earner should produce and applying pressure each month to see that they keep to the billing figure. If it proves that the targets are unattainable, they will need to be adjusted. The fact that it is not as easy to set billing targets for solicitors and their staff as it might be for a car salesman does not mean to say that it should not be attempted.

Bonus incentives

Staff bonuses can go hand in hand with monthly billing targets. This can be a bonus for a department which achieves a certain figure, or an individual or possibly both. Allowances will have to be made for work which is less profitable or for fee earners who are also expected to carry out certain administrative tasks. One must be careful with bonuses since there may be accusations of unfairness where one individual's targets are perceived to be easier than others. If targets are set too low and easily reached and then raised to more realistic levels, you will be accused of moving the goal posts, which, of course, is exactly what you are doing. If you feel that this kind of performance-related pay has dangers attached to it, you may prefer to have a bonus system in relation to new work introduced. Members of staff will quite naturally point work in the direction of the firm where appropriate, but the fact that they may receive a bonus for work they have introduced may make them press that little bit harder once there is a suggestion from a friend or relation that there is legal work in the offing. It is important to make a record when such work is introduced so that there can be no doubt as to whether the work qualifies for a bonus, and it should be paid as a percentage of profit costs once the bill has actually been paid.

Career paths

You will need to bear in mind each member of staff's hopes and aspirations for their progression through the firm. Trainee solicitors will be thinking about whether to remain with the firm on qualification, even if you are not. If they are retained by the firm on qualification, their thoughts will at some stage turn to the question of partnership. Inexperienced office juniors will not wish to stay as office juniors for the whole of their lives. Some will be more ambitious than others, but few people will see standing in front of the photocopier eight hours a day as a fulfilling vocation. If you do not anticipate their future needs, the first you may learn of their dissatisfaction is when a month's notice of their intention to leave the firm arrives on your desk. Many people's attitude is that, as and when the office junior leaves, a new one is simply employed. This overlooks the fact that the individual concerned is someone you know. You have had the opportunity to observe them over the time they have been with the firm. You have been able to assess their qualities and their limitations. If you have planned ahead, you may have been able to see a way in which you can use their services better and groom them to fulfil an emerging need that is developing within the firm. If you fail to map out career paths for your members of staff, there will be a lack of continuity within the firm and you may be paying substantially more in recruitment fees and advertising than need be the case.

Staff parties

Some firms view expenditure on staff parties, or for that matter on anything to do with staff welfare, as money down the drain. In my view, they are an extremely cheap and effective means of promoting unity within a firm. They are best held at the end of the week and should be arranged by the staff themselves with a set level of contribution from the firm and the opportunity for members of staff to contribute themselves by bringing a bottle or a plate of sandwiches or whatever. There is no reason why they should not be held on a regular basis, such as every two or three months, and should be attended for at least an hour or so by a partner. Gatherings of this nature do an enormous amount to show that employees' services are valued and to break down barriers between principals and employees and among employees. It should also be made clear in advance that staff are expected to behave sensibly at such functions and that overindulgence with drink will not be held to be an excuse for bad behaviour. Reminders should be given that staff should make arrangements before the party starts for getting home as the firm views a conviction for drinking and driving with the utmost seriousness and it might lead to dismissal, depending on the circumstances. Make sure a paragraph to this effect is included in the office manual. It should also be made clear that staff are expected to clear up after such functions and that the debris will not be left for the cleaning staff to deal with.

Office manual

If you do not have an office manual by this stage, perhaps now might be the time to put one together. It is a requirement of the SRA Code of Conduct 2011 that you have a clear and effective governance structure and reporting lines (outcome 7.1) and effective systems and controls in place to achieve and comply with all the principles, rules and outcomes and other requirements of the Handbook where relevant. An office manual is a good place in which to locate your evidence of compliance. Simply having a manual with all these points in it is not enough. You will need to demonstrate that the information is brought to the notice of new staff and that monitoring and checking procedures are in place to ensure that staff actually comply with and operate the systems laid down in the manual.

Apart from anything else, it may be useful when dealing with any unfair dismissal applications which may come your way. If office procedures and policies are clearly set out in an office manual and an employee repeatedly goes against what is laid down, it may stand you in good stead for dealing with an unfair dismissal application brought by a disgruntled former employee. The manual itself may provide you with an aide-memoire for the installation of such systems that are not already in operation. The Lexcel Office Procedures Manual was intended to form the basis of an inhouse manual, and is a starting point, although more specific and up-to-date precedents can be found in the Lexcel toolkits. These publications are supplied with Word files on disk, which saves hours of typing.

Complaints procedure

It used to be mandatory to have a written complaints procedure (see rule 2.05 of the Solicitors' Code of Conduct 2007). Whilst no longer obligatory, Chapter 1 of the SRA Code of Conduct 2011 and indicative behaviour 1.22 suggest that not having one is a dangerous course to take. In any event it will be difficult in practice to comply with outcomes 1.9 and 1.11 without one. The office manual is the perfect place for this – in fact you may focus on issues such as this which may have not been dealt with adequately elsewhere. The Law Society has issued a practice note on complaints management and the Lexcel Client Care Toolkit contains a complaints policy which you can amend as appropriate and incorporate into your office manual. As a sole practitioner, while you can adjudicate on those complaints made against other fee earners in your firm, you will have to make other arrangements for dealing with complaints made against you – have a reciprocal arrangement with another sole practitioner or a partner or senior fee earner in a local firm. Make sure it is not an open-ended arrangement; you do not want to find that you are spending hours dealing with someone else's endless stream of complaints for free while you are lucky enough to be complaint free.

A change of funding

It is a fact of economic life that as a firm expands its requirement for working capital accelerates. The more staff you have, the bigger your wages bill, the more PAYE to be paid at the end of each month, the higher the stationery and telephone costs, the more search and court fees, etc., there are to be paid.

While your practice is small and your working capital requirements comparatively modest, you may be able to fund this yourself. This becomes progressively more difficult as the firm expands. It is for this reason that most businesses, and that includes most firms of solicitors of any size, ultimately have to rely on banks for the funding of their working capital.

As discussed in **Chapter 3**, overreliance upon banks can prove costly. They have a nasty tendency to want their money back when you can least afford to repay it. In addition, you are at the mercy of the bank rate, so that if the banks suddenly decide to quadruple the interest rate, the cost of borrowing goes through the roof.

Another nasty habit that banks have is of suddenly requiring either additional security to be provided by the principals of the business or a substantial injection of capital from the partners' own resources. Principals of businesses, solicitors included, are often prone to wax lyrical about how sound their business is and while there may be short-term difficulties, the long-term outlook is very promising. It can be at this point that bankers will in effect tell the principals to 'put their money where their mouth is'. If the principals want the continued support of their bankers, they must find some cash to put in themselves so that they are not only playing with the bank's money but also with their own life savings. If you have no life savings to play with, this can prove something of a problem.

Nevertheless, it may be that you have no choice. Unless you single-handedly – i.e. both you and your partners – are going to finance the firm from your own capital resources (which may mean not being able to enjoy the fruits of your labours quite so much), you will have little choice but to find some of the capital needed by the firm from bank borrowing.

Getting the balance right

At one time the teaching was that anyone who financed the working capital primarily out of their own resources was a mug. Many of the recipients of that advice are now living under assumed names in different parts of South America. My own view is that for firms of three or four partners and 10–20 members of staff, a 50/50 relationship is probably about right. In other words, if your total working capital can be split equally between bank funding and contributions by partners, this is a reasonable compromise. Alternatively, you may prefer to err on the side of caution and to ascertain two figures: the first being the absolute minimum amount of working capital with which the firm could operate, and the second a more realistic working capital figure. If the partners contribute the first figure and then borrow the difference to make up the second figure, you should have a fairly safe operation. If the bank suddenly decides to withdraw its support, the firm can keep going without making any drastic changes. It may need to operate even more efficiently by taking a firmer line on credit control, increasing its output and making a few cutbacks, but it is not suddenly going to have to dispense with half of its labour force and move to smaller premises.

One policy decision which will have to be taken is as to whether the funds contributed by partners will carry interest. This is something of an old chestnut and can be quite a contentious issue. My own feeling is that probably the better course is not to have interest on capital, which serves as a great encouragement to have an equalisation of capital between partners. If you do pay interest on partners' capital, you generally find that certain partners who have been with the firm longer amass substantial capital accounts and a large slice of the firm's profits go in paying a healthy rate of interest on to the capital accounts of the partners concerned. This can cause widespread dissension between the younger partners and longer-serving partners. It may lead to a feeling that younger partners are spending most of their professional lives paying out to the senior partners – who have lost much of their sharpness and drive and are contributing far less in real terms to the firm than the younger partners, who are doing all the work and seeing very few of the rewards.

If partners are not being paid interest on their capital, the capital accounts will rise much more slowly or not at all, depending on the policy adopted in relation to the retention of profits within the firm. There will then be greater pressure for younger partners to put more money into the firm and for the older partners to take the money out. All in all, this makes for a much healthier working environment and prevents a potentially dangerous and explosive situation from building up, i.e. the younger partners tempted to rebel against what they see as a wholly inequitable system, whereby those who contribute the most take out the least.

18

Recruiting and retaining staff and avoiding problems

There is no right or wrong time to hire additional staff. Generally speaking, the preferred course is to wait until the particular area of work is under pressure and if it looks as though that situation is going to continue then recruit at that stage. This does mean that whilst the recruitment process is underway you or someone else for whom you are recruiting an assistant will be working at the kind of level that is unsustainable in the long term. The alternative is to try to plan ahead and to recruit when work appears to be picking up in a particular area. The problem with that is that such increases may be short lived and if you have taken on extra staff you may find you have an expensive passenger. If you wait until things are getting fairly frantic before recruiting you then have to find even more hours in the day to spend interviewing. Further, competent people are rarely able to join the practice immediately and you will have to wait for them to serve a period of notice with a current employer before they become available. This can sometimes be as long as three months and there is always the risk that after you have waited during the notice period there is a change of plan. Prospective employees may have a change of mind, particularly if their current employer realises their worth and makes a much better offer, or a better offer from elsewhere comes along. The fact is that the recruitment process is very often an unavoidably painful one.

Discrimination

The recruitment process can be made even more painful by generating a claim for compensation by a job applicant or by an employee who at some stage feels that they have been discriminated against in the workplace. The areas in which discrimination may lead to a claim against an employer have been added to at what, for the employer at least, would seem to be an alarming rate over the past few years. There are now nine 'protected characteristics' under the Equality Act 2010, which cannot be used as a reason to treat people unfairly: age, disability, gender reassignment, marriage and civil partnership, pregnancy and maternity, race, religion or belief, sex and sexual orientation. Those seeking anything more than a brief overview of the situation should consult the Law Society's

Employment Law Handbook, 5th edn (2011) by Henry Scrope, Daniel Barnett and Keira Gore. However, in this section observations will be made in relation to sex, race, age and disability discrimination.

Whilst some employers might feel that the law has turned so strongly in favour of employees that they are faced with potential claims at every twist and turn, it should be borne in mind that the legislation has been prompted by a lack of sensitivity and common sense on the part of employers in the past. Turning down a job applicant with a comment that you do not want to employ them because they are too old or female, and the like, is insensitive, insulting and illegal. There may be employers who would like to reject an applicant for precisely that reason, although no reason or a different reason may be given. As those employers who insist on discriminating have been driven to greater subtlety in their methods, so the risks have increased for those reasonable employers who have declined to employ an applicant for a perfectly legitimate reason but whose motive the applicant distrusts. It is, therefore, vital to be aware of the hazards and to take steps to minimise them wherever possible. The position has been further underlined by Principle 9 and Chapter 2 of the SRA Code of Conduct 2011 requiring firms to encourage equality of opportunity and respect for diversity. Also note that firms were previously required to have a written policy of diversity under rule 6 of the 2007 Code. Your written policy should now be amended where necessary to comply with indicative behaviour 2.1. You will need to examine the Chapter 2 outcomes and indicative behaviours in detail to ensure that your policies and procedures are OFR compliant.

Sex and racial discrimination

As with most forms of discrimination it is possible to discriminate both directly and indirectly. Victimisation and harassment are other forms of discrimination.

A person is liable for unlawful discrimination if he or she discriminates against others (either directly or indirectly):

- in the arrangements he makes for the purposes of determining who should be offered employment;
- in the terms in which he offers that employment;
- by refusing or deliberately omitting to offer them that employment;
- in the way the employer affords access to the opportunities for promotion, transfer or training or to any benefit, facilities or services, or by refusing or deliberately omitting to afford access to them;
- by subjecting them to detriment; or
- by dismissing them or by subjecting them to harassment.

Effectively, this has an impact in all areas of employment, including recruitment, terms and conditions, pay and benefits, status, training, promotion and transfer opportunities, right through to redundancy and dismissal. If different job applicants or different employees are treated in a different way in any of the areas listed above because of either their sex or their race the employer will have unlawfully discriminated. Direct discrimination is fairly straightforward. Indirect discrimination is a rather more subtle concept and is unlawful whether or not it is done on purpose. For example, a requirement that only persons living within a two-mile radius of the place of employment need apply might amount to indirect discrimination if it could be shown that persons living within the capture area were predominantly white, even if the motive was purely to avoid disruption to the business caused by possible travel problems during the winter months.

Bear in mind that it is also possible to discriminate against an applicant or current employee if they are treated less favourably because they have brought proceedings in the past or given evidence in such proceedings against another employer. This is viewed as victimisation. There is no qualifying period for someone to bring a sex or race discrimination claim, hence the right of a mere job applicant not just an employee to bring a claim. Also, an illegal contract of employment will not prevent an employee from bringing a sex discrimination claim.

In the case of indirect discrimination, and since October 2010 discrimination arising from disability, an employer may seek to justify the action by means of the defence of objective justification, i.e. that the provision, criteria or practice is objectively justified by a legitimate aim and the means of achieving that aim are appropriate and necessary. The defence is not available for direct discrimination.

It is not only in relation to your own acts that you may be found liable for discrimination, but also those of an employee, as you will be vicariously liable for any act of discrimination on the part of those whom you employ. It is, however, a defence in both sex and race discrimination cases for the employer to show that it took all reasonable steps to prevent the employee from doing discriminatory acts. In order to have a reasonable chance of such a defence succeeding, you will normally have had to demonstrate that you have proper equal opportunities policies and other procedures in place and that they are regularly and accurately monitored to show that they are working. You cannot make a half-hearted attempt to put such policies in place and then hope for the best. You will have to take full steps to ensure that they are actually working in practice if such a defence is to stand any chance of succeeding.

Disability discrimination

The Equality Act 2010 makes it unlawful for an employer to treat a disabled person less favourably at work or when providing goods, facilities and services, renting or buying property or in education. The rules apply not only to employees but also to job applicants and the self-employed who contract personally to provide services. The Act also requires employers to make reasonable adjustments to working conditions in order to assist in overcoming the practical effects of disability, unless there is objective justification for not taking such steps. It is also unlawful to victimise employees because they have tried to enforce their rights, or tried to assist someone else in enforcing rights under the Act. If the complainant establishes facts from which it may be presumed that discrimination has taken place, it falls to the employer to prove that there has been no discrimination. In deciding whether someone has been less favourably treated, a comparison is drawn with someone who is not disabled but whose abilities are the same or not materially different from the abilities of the disabled person.

In order to bring the claim the claimant must be disabled. The Act defines such a person as someone with a physical or mental impairment which has a substantial and long-term adverse effect on his or her ability to carry out normal day-to-day activities. If the person was disabled for the purposes of the Act at the time the discrimination took place it is no defence for an employer or potential employer if the complainant subsequently recovers.

In order for a particular condition to amount to a disability for the purpose of the Act four conditions must be met. There must be an impairment which has a substantial effect which is long term and which adversely affects ability to carry out normal day-to-day activities. A substantial adverse effect is a negative effect that is more than trivial, and the effect is long-term if it has lasted or is expected to last for more than 12 months. People with HIV, cancer or multiple sclerosis are protected by the Act from the point of diagnosis.

The following conditions have been held to be impairment under various types of legislation:

- asthma;
- autism;
- blindness;
- chronic fatigue syndrome;
- diabetes;
- dwarfism;
- dyslexia;
- epilepsy;
- general learning difficulties;
- obesity;
- obstructive sleep apnoea;
- panic attacks;
- rheumatoid arthritis; and
- schizophrenia.

Reasonable adjustments

You will be expected to make reasonable adjustments both in relation to employers and clients and other persons visiting the premises. This could involve changing an employee's working hours, providing an adapted piece of equipment to help him or her to do the job, or for visitors, putting in a ramp. You must also take care to avoid questions on an application form or in an interview about health or disability unless it is simply for monitoring purposes or to assess what reasonable adjustments may need to be made. Whether or not it is reasonable to expect an employer to make an adjustment to premises will depend on several factors. These include the size of the undertaking, the cost involved and the degree to which not making the adjustment would disadvantage the disabled person compared with people who are not disabled.

The concept of indirect discrimination applies in the same way with disability discrimination and there is a defence of objective justification. The employer has to show its action is a 'proportionate means of achieving a legitimate aim' (Equality Act 2010, s.15 and s.19).

You are not expected to employ someone who is incapable of doing the job. It is no defence in disability discrimination to show that an employer was not aware of discriminatory acts carried out by its employees in the course of their employment. The only defence is the one set out above, i.e. that the employer had taken such steps as were reasonably practicable to prevent the employee carrying out the discriminatory acts.

Age discrimination

Since the implementation of the Employer Equality (Age) Regulations 2006, SI 2006/1031 it has been unlawful to discriminate against or harass on the ground of age and the Equality Act 2010 now applies in this regard. As with other forms of discrimination, both direct and indirect discrimination must be considered. Whilst there will be many instances of discrimination against the older generation, claims are not confined to that age group. Thus it is just as much an act of discrimination to say that only applicants above the age of 40 need apply (so being discriminatory towards those aged under 40) as it is to say that no one over the age of 40 may apply.

Direct discrimination will occur when a person is treated less favourably on the grounds of that person's age or apparent age than another person was treated or would have been treated (actual or hypothetical) in circumstances which were the same or hardly any different.

Indirect discrimination will occur where an employer applies a provision, criterion or practice equally to everyone which puts or would put people in the applicant's particular age group at a particular disadvantage. Once again, the employer can use the defence of objective justification but needs to show a proportionate means of achieving a legitimate aim.

For example, physically demanding work could have an upper age limit for health and safety reasons. As there is now no official statutory retirement age (although there is a state pension age), the objective justification defence would need to apply to compulsory retirement.

Summary

There is no getting away from the fact that discrimination in all its many forms is a minefield. We have dealt with only a few here and only in outline. It will be hard for even the most conscientious and well-meaning employer to put in place practices and procedures that are likely to be claim-proof. Smaller businesses in particular are unlikely to be able to afford the kind of professional help in putting effective practices in place. The best thing is to ensure that recruitment and interviewing are handled as carefully and sensitively as is possible, and to be as fair and even handed as one can be with all potential applicants. Once staff have been recruited, an ever-watchful eye should be kept to ensure that members of the firm are treated equally and that anything which smacks even vaguely of discrimination is dealt with swiftly. A culture of non-toleration of harassment, bullying or any other form of discrimination or victimisation should be encouraged and fostered, and any murmurings of discontent treated seriously and quickly with tolerance and understanding.

Written material in handbooks and elsewhere should also make clear that such behaviour will not be tolerated. Clear paths should be laid down and promulgated to ensure that any persons feeling that they are being subjected to such unfair treatment have a direct line to managers, who will be expected to resolve such matters.

It is fair to say that well-run practices are less likely to encounter such problems than poorly run practices. Employees of various categories, be it of age, gender, sexuality, religion or disability, who are part of a well-run firm and who are happy in the workplace are less likely to reach for a discrimination questionnaire or a claim form at the first sign of trouble. By contrast, for someone who is being overworked and who feels that their efforts are not properly appreciated in a chaotic work environment, an unpleasant remark by a colleague or a manager may be the final straw and in reality the ensuing claim may be more the visible symptom of what was a much wider problem.

Maternity leave and maternity pay

All female employees are entitled to a full year's maternity leave (consisting of six months' ordinary leave and six months' additional leave) irrespective of how long you have employed them. You could, therefore, find yourself in the situation where a week after recruiting a new female member of staff you are informed that she is going on maternity leave.

The amount of maternity pay is dependent on the number of weeks of continuous employment with you. Ordinarily, the employee is entitled to statutory maternity pay if she has worked 26 weeks continuously into the 15th week before her baby is due (see below).

Note also that it is a criminal offence for an employer to allow an employee to work during the two-week period from the day on which she gives birth. This period is counted as part of the 26 weeks' ordinary maternity leave. Note also that in addition to any maternity leave to which the employee may be entitled she is also entitled to her statutory minimum annual holiday.

Note also that she must not be subjected to any detriment by the employer because she is pregnant or because she took maternity leave. If she is subjected to any such detriment it may be penalised by compensation before a tribunal. Also, if a female employee is dismissed for a reason related to her pregnancy or because she attempted to take maternity leave, the dismissal is automatically unfair and may be discriminatory.

Employees who return after ordinary maternity leave should be offered their old job back or the employer may face claims of unfair dismissal or discrimination. After the additional leave period the employee has the right to return to a suitable and appropriate job on the same terms and conditions as her old job.

Remember to notify the employee on maternity leave of the end date of that leave. If you take on new staff to cover the gap whilst the employee is taking leave you should inform them in writing when you take them on that they are being employed to act as cover for a member of staff on maternity leave and that it is very likely that they will be dismissed once that employee returns. This should then make that dismissal a fair dismissal on the basis that it constitutes 'some other substantial reason' under the Employment Rights Act 1996.

Pay entitlement

Unless the contract of employment gives the employee the right to continue to receive her normal pay or a proportion of it, she will be entitled to statutory maternity pay (SMP) for 39 weeks. SMP is a state benefit but it is paid by the firm, which then recovers the majority of it by way of deductions from NI and PAYE when making the usual monthly payments to the state. Smaller employers are able to recover the whole of the payment and an additional handling charge of 4.5 per cent. You may also be able to obtain permission to make the deduction in advance if you cannot afford to make the benefit payment when it falls due.

The first six weeks of SMP amounts to 90 per cent of the average weekly earnings in the eight weeks immediately before the qualifying week. Thereafter it drops to £128.73 (figures correct as of December 2011) per week provided this is not more than 90 per cent of the previous earnings. The regulations are complex and clearly if you find yourself in this position you will need to contact your tax and benefits office to obtain the full details. An employee must have been in continuous employment with the same employer for at least 26 weeks into the 15th week before her baby is due in order to qualify for SMP and earning an average of £102 per week, the current lower level of NI earnings limit.

Paternity leave

Entitlement to paternity leave is currently substantially less than a female employee's entitlement to maternity leave. When originally introduced the leave was unpaid but that has now changed. To qualify the employee must have been continuously employed for at least 26 weeks ending either with the 15th week before the expected week of birth, be the father of the child or the mother's husband or partner and have, or expects to have, responsibility for the upbringing of the child. The latter provision would not be satisfied if, for example, the biological father was no longer living with the mother and the parties were estranged, with the mother refusing contact.

As with maternity leave the father is not automatically entitled to contractual pay but instead is entitled to statutory paternity pay provided he earns more than the NI lower earnings limit.

The amount payable is the lesser of £128.73 per week (figures correct as of December 2011) or 90 per cent of the employee's normal weekly earnings. The contract of employment may, of course, contain more generous provisions.

The period of leave is either one week's leave or two consecutive weeks' leave. The employee must give the employer notice of his intention to take paternity leave before the 15th week before the expected week of the birth of the baby or as soon as reasonably practical. The notice must specify the week that it is anticipated the child will be born, the period of leave and the date on which the father is to begin his leave. This date cannot be before the baby is born and must be taken within 56 days of the birth.

Additional paternity leave and pay

An expectant father may be entitled to additional paternity leave of up to 26 weeks. If the mother has returned to work leave can be taken between 20 weeks and one year after the child is born. To qualify:

(a) the purpose of the leave must be to care for the child; and
(b) the mother must have been entitled either to statutory maternity leave, statutory maternity pay or various similar benefits; and
(c) must have resumed working so that the benefit has stopped.

To qualify for additional statutory paternity pay the employee must:

(a) be an employee(!); and
(b) earn at least the NI lower earnings limit; and
(c) the mother must have started working again and her benefits ceased.

The benefit is only payable during the mother's 39-week maternity allowance or statutory maternity pay period. For full details see **www.direct.gov.uk/en/parents/moneyandworkentitlements**.

As with maternity leave, subjecting the employee to any detriment as a result of his taking, or attempting to take, paternity leave may be punished by an award of damages before a tribunal. Also in the same way any dismissal for any reason relating to paternity leave is automatically unfair. Similar provisions relating to possible redundancy during the leave period also apply.

Sick pay

Employees are entitled to have their rights to pay during illness set out in a contract of employment or statement of particulars. Rights given by contract may, of course, be more generous than those provided by the general law, and if they are then that will prevail. By statute employees are entitled to statutory sick pay (SSP) from their employer for a period of up to 28 weeks in any period of three years. Some employees below the lower earnings limit (at the time of writing (December 2011) £102.00 per week) are excluded but most employees will be covered. The rate is £81.60 per week (figures correct as of December 2011) after the first three days of absence through illness. After seven days off work the employer can demand the production of a medical certificate. The employer must issue a Form SSP1(T) after 23 weeks of sickness notifying the employee when SSP will be ending. If the employee is still too ill to work they may claim incapacity benefit.

There is no SSP payable during the first three days of absence through sickness but, of course, the contract may provide for normal pay during that period.

For further information see the government website (**www.dwp. gov.uk**).

Holiday entitlement and holiday pay

As with sick pay, contracts of employment should deal expressly with holiday pay and entitlement and the contractual arrangements are often more generous than the minimum statutory requirements. The Working Time Regulations 1998, SI 1998/1833 gave workers the right to four weeks' paid annual holiday. This has now been increased to 5.6 weeks' minimum paid annual leave so that an employee working a five-day week is entitled to 28 days' paid leave in each year. Part-time workers have a proportionate entitlement so that someone working four days a week is entitled to 22.4 days' paid annual holiday (5.6 x the usual number of days worked each week). However, the employer can include bank holidays and public holidays within the holiday entitlement unless the contract of employment stipulates otherwise, or such a term can be implied.

The holiday entitlement must be taken during the holiday year, which is normally stipulated in the contract of employment. If the employee does not take the annual leave during the holiday year there is no entitlement to payment in lieu except on termination of the employment. The Working Time Regulations 1998 do not prohibit employers from specifying when leave can or cannot be taken or the number of days at a time. Accordingly it is open to you to insist that part of the annual leave entitlement is taken during the annual Christmas shutdown.

There is no right to time off or extra pay for working bank holidays unless the contract provides otherwise or it can be implied. The employee's right to paid holiday continues despite time off for maternity or paternity leave.

The regulations only apply to employees, so you will be free to work as long and as hard as you like and take no holiday, but I would not recommend it if you wish to remain sane!

Disciplinary and grievance procedures

Statutory dismissal and disciplinary procedures and statutory grievance procedures were abolished in April 2009. At the same time the Arbitration and Conciliation Service (ACAS) Code on Disciplinary and Grievance Procedures was promulgated. Though not having the force of law, employers and employees are expected to follow the procedures set out and an unreasonable failure on the part of the employer to do so gives a tribunal the power to increase the award by up to 25 per cent and to decrease the award to an employee who similarly has failed to follow the code.

The basics of the code are:

- Have a written set of rules and procedures and inform employees of where they can be found.
- Tribunals will take account of the employer's size and resources when deciding on relevant action and it may not be practicable for all employers to take all the steps set out in the code.
- Issues should be raised and dealt with promptly.
- Employers should act consistently.
- Employers should carry out investigations to establish the facts.

- Employers should inform employees of the basics of the problem and give them an opportunity to put their case.
- Employees should be allowed to be accompanied at any formal meetings.
- Employers should have an appeals procedure.

The code of conduct can be found at **www.acas.org.uk**. It is written in clear, comprehensible language.

The government is set to bring in sweeping changes to this area of law in the spring/summer of 2012. As from April 2011 the qualifying period for an employee to be able to bring a claim for unfair dismissal is increased to two years and fees are to be charged to the employee on the commencement of the claim, which will no doubt deter some unmeritorious claims. It is proposed that all claims shall be lodged through ACAS so that mediation can be attempted.

An idea of compensated no fault dismissals has also been floated for small businesses. All firms will need to keep a close eye on this rapidly changing area of the law.

The above summary is an outline of the procedures to be followed so that you as an employer, possibly for the first time, are aware of their existence and the areas that they cover. In the event that you find yourself faced with the prospect of having to discipline a member of staff or to consider a dismissal, you need to tread extremely carefully and either do your research in depth or take professional advice yourself if employment law is not one of your fields of expertise. The *Law Society's Precedent Library for the General Practitioner*, 2nd edn (2009) written by myself contains specimen letters to assist with complying with the procedures. Helpful information and guidance on a wide range of topics including written statements and contracts, holiday entitlement, redundancy, maternity and paternity leave, and pay and working hours can be found on a document website: **www.businesslink.gov.uk/employingpeople**. It also contains downloadable written statements of employment and a redundancy pay calculator and, best of all, it is free of charge!

19

Marketing your practice

Planning a marketing campaign

The hardest thing about a marketing campaign is getting around to planning it. The smaller the firm, the more difficult it is. Trying to cope with the clients' work, managing the practice, recruiting staff and the thousand and one things that have to be done during the normal working week is difficult enough, without also having to make time to plan and execute a marketing campaign. It is something that everybody agrees is a good idea and should be done, but can always be put off until next week. As a result, it tends to be something that we finally get around to when business is slack.

Marketing should be done more or less continuously. Once one marketing campaign is over or the returns appear to be diminishing, the next campaign should start to take shape on the drawing board.

Targeting

The best way to approach a marketing campaign is to treat yourself as just another salesperson, with your product being your legal services. Solicitors are simply purveyors of legal services. What is your product and to whom are you trying to sell it? You will see instantly that instead of having one range of products, you have several. This may cause you to split your marketing campaign into several parts. It may also result in different individuals within the firm having responsibility for different marketing campaigns, each concentrating on their own area of expertise. So the first question is, are you selling the whole firm or just certain aspects of it?

Let us suppose that you perceive there is a demand in the marketplace for employment law expertise. Your firm may lack this expertise, but it is always possible to develop it. You read everything you can on employment law and you attend a few courses – basic, general ones at first, moving on to more specialised, in-depth ones as your knowledge increases. Then you start looking for the work. Having acquired a degree of expertise, you can now start your marketing campaign. Your product is your expertise, knowledge and ability in employment matters. If you have covered the ground comprehensively you are now able to offer clients advice on such matters as unfair dismissal, sexual and racial discrimination in the workplace, redundancy, the construction, interpretation and drafting of employment contracts and dealing with hearings before employment tribunals. Having identified your product, you now need to target your potential clients. The first place to start is your existing client base. Which clients are likely to need help and advice in those areas in which you have a degree of expertise? A list of targets among the existing client base will then be drawn up.

Who else could you sell to? There may be local businesses for whom you are not presently acting but that may have an unfulfilled need in these areas or may be dissatisfied with their current advisers and already be half looking for someone more suitable to fulfil that need. More names for the list. It is important to ensure that the person within the organisation you will be contacting is in a buying position. It is no good taking the sales manager of a company out to lunch if all decisions relating to legal matters are taken by the managing director. You may have to do a little phoning around and talk to one or two telephonists or secretaries in order to identify who it is that makes these decisions.

A word of warning: Chapter 8, outcome 8.3 of the SRA Code of Conduct 2011 prohibits unsolicited visits or telephone calls to 'members of the public'. Current or former clients, existing or potential professional connections, a commercial organisation or public body are unlikely to be considered to be within this definition. The relevant rule is reproduced in **Appendix 11**.

Timing

With a product such as legal services, timing the start of a campaign is not crucial in most instances. The campaign can be started at any time unless, of course, you are approaching a time when most of the people you will need to speak to will be away, such as a holiday period. Timing is nevertheless important from the point of view of setting yourself a timetable for each phase. Consider the following:

- How long will it take you to go through your existing client base and prepare lists of names and addresses?
- How long will it take to do the same with local businesses?
- How long will it take you to phone around to find out who makes the decision on which firm of solicitors to use for which work?
- How long will it take to carry out the campaign itself?
- How long will it take to analyse the results so that you know how successful you have been and what lessons are to be learnt for the future?

All of this should be mapped out in advance so that the campaign is properly co-ordinated and is actually executed. The easiest way is to write the whole thing out and then to make diary entries for the beginning and end of each phase, with possibly a mid-point date as a reminder. The person responsible to carry out each task, who will oversee things and chase the progress of each phase, must be clearly identified. There must be no instances of 'I thought you were doing that'.

Executing

Strangely enough, this is probably the part where most people fall down. Having done much of the work in terms of targeting and mapping out the timing, when it comes to execution there is a psychological barrier that needs to be broken down. It is possibly because solicitors as a breed are rather shy and conservative; pushing ourselves forward and telling people how good we are does not come easily. We do, after all, have little or no training in it, unless (like me) you had a few years in selling before coming into the profession. We are not natural salesmen and it was only the severe trading difficulties of modern recessions that caused us to develop the skills. Recessions come and go but as a result the world of commerce generally now operates at a faster pace.

Make no mistake, gone are the days when we can sit back with the brass plate on the wall and wait for the clients to form an orderly queue outside our doors. We must go out and find them and convert them into clients. The simple message, therefore, on the question of executing the marketing plan is 'get on with it'. You will have your timetable drawn up – stick to it. You may have to commit the unholiest of sins and put off the clients' work until tomorrow while you spend today, or at least part of it, on your marketing exercise. There will probably have to be several such sins committed over the next few weeks. Like robbing banks, the first one is the most difficult and then it gets easier with every succeeding one!

Analysing

Although probably not as hard as executing, analysing is still something which people are a little reluctant to carry out. A careful analysis of cost, time and the resultant benefits of your marketing plan is very important, as is comparing one type of campaign with another. Only by this careful analysis will mistakes be recognised and those methods which are successful pursued and the less successful ones screened out.

A spin-off benefit of analysing the campaign results is the recognition of the fact that marketing works and has tangible benefits. The measurement of the precise level of success is the sharpest spur to planning and executing a further campaign at a later date. When, possibly some months later, you are trying to find the necessary energy to plan another marketing campaign, you can look back at how many new clients the last campaign produced and the level of additional profit. Suddenly you find the incentive to stay in the office that bit longer to pencil out your next campaign.

Ten suggested marketing tools

1. Mail shots

Mail shots are both time consuming and expensive but the development of word processing software and mail merge features has made them faster and cheaper. You can also do this by email. It is particularly important to ensure that the mail shots are going to the right target audience. Mail shots of no interest at all to the recipient will go straight into the bin with hardly a glance, and your time and money will have been wasted. The message must at least be read. This means that the message must be attractive and get to the point early on, and will at least prompt the recipient into a buying decision. If the recipient gets as far as reading right the way through the mail shot and then pauses to consider whether to take up the offer or not, the exercise has at least had limited success. If enough of the recipients fall into this category, a small percentage will decide to act on the mail shot, and an even smaller percentage will go as far as engaging you to do something for them. Again, the letter or email must be addressed to the person able to take the buying decision. The mail shot may be a prelude to some further action, the most likely thing being a follow up telephone call to see whether the recipient is interested in taking things further, but this will only be permissible if the call is to a current or former client or to another solicitor, or to an existing or potential professional connection. Rule 7.03 of the Solicitors' Code of Conduct 2007 allowed telephone calls to people in these categories but not otherwise. The relevant provision is now under outcome 8.3 of the SRA Code of Conduct 2011 (see **Appendix 11**). The letter may be designed to set up a meeting and the mail shot may state that you will be telephoning to see what level of interest there is in such a meeting.

There have been some very innovative mail shots recently by solicitors marketing to other solicitors. These have included initiatives such as offering specialist advice in areas such as employment law, welfare law and the like, in an attempt to sell the products that they have produced in preparing for a legal aid franchise and which will avoid solicitors having to duplicate the effort that they themselves have put in. I have also received mail shots from solicitors who buy and sell land in other countries. They have recognised that they have an area of expertise which the average solicitor is unlikely to possess, but may well be asked for advice on the subject by clients. Unable to satisfy the clients' needs themselves, there is a good chance that they will pass the client on to the firm with that expertise, and the mail shot in that event has worked.

2. Talks and seminars

You may be fortunate enough to be able to supplement your earnings in general practice by being invited to lecture or give talks by professional providers of legal education. Undoubtedly, such public appearances enhance the reputation of lecturers and their firm. There is, however, no need to wait to be asked. There is nothing to stop you from contacting a large organisation and offering to come along and give a talk on a subject which may be of interest to them. This can be anything from a talk to the local rugby club on civil and criminal liability following a claim arising out of injuries that they may cause during a game, to a talk to a group of doctors and nurses at the local hospital on the possible dangers of administering first aid to the victims of road traffic accidents who subsequently allege negligence.

You will be regarded by your audience as an expert on these matters simply by reason of standing in front of them for 20 minutes and addressing a subject they know little about. You must, therefore, make sure that you have a reasonable knowledge of your subject and have done your homework in advance. You will need to know a little more than precisely what is in the notes in front of you as there will be questions from your audience at the end of your talk. Inane waffling in an attempt to avoid admitting that you have no idea of the answer rarely impresses. Do not allow the fact that you are not an expert put you off giving such talks. You are imparting a good deal of knowledge to people which they will find useful if you have hit upon the right subject and have tried to make it interesting.

Remember, the whole point of the exercise is marketing. There is no point in walking away from a talk leaving your audience in the dark as to who you are and where they can contact you. There is always the ceremonial distribution of business cards, but why not produce a handout such as a summary of the talk, a specimen statement of claim, a list of judicial authorities or whatever, making sure that the firm's name and address are suitably displayed? The one thing that talks and seminars do is to bring you into contact with fresh potential clients in a very favourable scenario. You are there as someone who knows their stuff when it comes to legal work and they have the opportunity of seeing you perform first hand. At least as importantly, they have the opportunity to talk to a real solicitor and to see what kind of person you are, all at no expense. If you have impressed on both fronts (and there is no reason why you should not, given that you have had the opportunity to do as much preparation as you want before placing yourself there), some of your audience may come to you when they need legal services. They may be interested in services unrelated to your speech, but if it is good fee-paying work, that does not matter.

A spin-off benefit is that the preparation and delivery of such talks counts as part of your CPD hours.

3. Free advice surgeries

A marketing initiative that is always popular with the general public is a free advice surgery. Generally speaking, this will have to be carried out during the evening or at a weekend. The reasons for this are that, first, you may be too busy during the day and such matters should not really be taking precedence over other clients' work and second, clients attending such advice surgeries will find it far easier to come along after work or at the weekends. Such sessions can be rather expensive in terms of resources so it is important that they are not counterproductive. If people come in expecting free advice and are then made to wait for an hour, they will not be very impressed with the practice; on the contrary, they will go away feeling rather disappointed. If people are to be seen promptly, the individual advice sessions must necessarily be kept short, no more than 15 minutes maximum, and you will need at least two legal advisers conducting the interviews. You may be able to persuade people to give up their time to carry out these advice sessions without any form of additional payment. They may find the concept of pro bono work in their own time socially fulfilling and may also feel they are making a real contribution to the firm's progress and ultimately their own job security.

Beware of blackmailing staff into feeling they must take part in these exercises if they are to have a future with the firm. The wish to take part must come from the heart and not out of fear.

In addition, you may well find that you need to have at least one other person to act as a receptionist and provider of cups of tea. There is nothing like a free cup of tea for promoting an image of friendliness.

Such advice sessions are not intended to be an instant solution to people's problems and it is important that their expectations are not raised to think otherwise. In 10 or 15 minutes you can assess whether the client has a problem that lawyers can help solve, and if they are not eligible for legal aid, whether it is worth their while committing resources in the form of lawyers in an attempt to solve the problem. Once again, it provides the opportunity for interaction between the solicitor and a client. It is from such situations that long-term solicitor/client relationships can arise. You will need to give some thought on how to publicise the event and the publicity should include a description of what is offered (e.g. 15 minutes' free advice) so that people do not come expecting you to devote the whole evening to them.

4. Citizens Advice Bureau

The CAB provides a very valuable outlet for many people's worries and frustrations. Inevitably, the advice which a proportion of CAB clients need is of a legal nature. The CAB is scrupulously non-partisan. It will not recommend any particular firm, but it can advise its clients of the names and addresses of local firms and who to speak to within those firms. It can also tell clients of the particular areas in which the firms operate and of any specialisms. A high proportion of CAB clients can only pursue solutions to their problems with the assistance of legal aid, and many of them may qualify for this. If your practice accepts legal aid work and you have the necessary franchises and contracts, you should constantly ensure that your lines of communication with the CAB are good so that it is aware of the type of work you do and any changes within your practice. It will often run legal advice sessions in the evenings for clients who clearly need legal advice and you may be invited to attend. Having obtained an initial view from you, the client may wish to engage you to deal with the problem since the barrier between solicitor and potential client has been broken down, and the fear of coming to the solicitor's office will not be so intense.

5. The business lunch

There was a time when the business lunch was the main form of marketing, particularly when the costs of such entrepreneurial dinners were tax deductible. Sadly, this is no longer the case. The strange thing is that if you take a member of staff out to lunch, it is tax deductible under the heading of 'staff welfare'. However, taking a potential client out to lunch in the hope of increasing business, which ultimately will increase the amount of taxes that you pay, is not tax deductible. Perhaps the thinking is that the business lunch is still such a useful marketing tool that it would survive despite the removal of tax relief. The business lunch is useful, both for breaking new ground and also as a means of consolidating existing ground.

The business lunch should not be treated as a gastronomical bribe. People who are in a buying position are not so stupid as to feel obligated to use your services simply because you have spent a lot of money in wreaking havoc with the elaborate menu of a high-class restaurant. While there may be the odd naive individual, on the whole such people are businessmen first and *bon viveurs* second. By all means make it abundantly clear that the object of the lunch is to acquire their business, but the occasion should be seen as an opportunity to ascertain from the potential client what their prospective needs are and to tell them how you may be in a position to fulfil those needs at least as efficiently if not more efficiently, and more cost-effectively (never use the word cheap) than is currently the case.

Before the lunch, you must go back to basics and decide precisely what image you wish to project, and this must be borne in mind throughout the lunch. There is no point in selling yourself as a cheap (oops, I mean cost-effective) practice if what the client is primarily after is quality and speed of service. You should be concentrating on the fact that because you are hungry for work you will try that much harder to conduct the client's business while maintaining high standards and providing a quality service. The fact that you may happen to be less expensive than their existing provider of legal services can then be seen as an added bonus rather than that being the whole point of changing firms. Indeed, it may be the case that you are no less expensive than the competitor. The chances are that if prospective clients are coming to see you, they may be less than content with their current firm and keeping an eye open for a suitable replacement.

When changing firms, there is always a fear area which must be overcome. The person taking the decision may be putting themselves out on a limb. If you are appointed and your performance is less than adequate then your appointer will not call again. The safe thing, therefore, is for them not to appoint you unless the level of dissatisfaction with their existing provider of legal services is very high. You need to reassure the prospective clients that your commitment to the work will be unstinting and that you will not betray the confidence that they place in you by giving you the instructions. The key is to persuade them to instruct you in minor matters, while not necessarily terminating the instructions to the other firm. This will give you the opportunity to demonstrate the level of service that you can provide. If you are given such an opportunity, it is desperately important that you do not waste it. You should equally be aware of overkill. The idea is to impress, not to play the part of a fawning sycophant for whom the client's every wish is your command. You must win the client's respect by providing a cost-efficient and, above all, professional service.

The lunch itself should not consist of one long sales pitch, which will have the result of boring the client to death. Neither should the time be spent purely in idle chitchat without getting the message across. There is a delicate balance between the two extremes. As with all other types of marketing, the lunch must be with someone who is in a buying position. There is no point in taking a junior executive to lunch if it is a superior who is in a position to say yes or no to the appointment of your firm as their solicitors. The junior executive may come away thinking you are wonderful and start singing your praises to their boss only to be dismissed at a stroke with, 'Oh, no – we always use Bloggs and Co'. No matter how well you sell yourself to the junior executive, no one will ever sell your firm as well as you will, so you must ensure that you are talking to the boss, not the junior.

Above all else, beware of drinking too much and making a fool of yourself. If at all in doubt, do not drink alcohol during the meal. You may run the risk of being accused of not entering into the spirit of things, but that is a far better crime to be accused of than making an idiot of yourself because you have misjudged your ability to handle drink. It will also mean that you will be in no fit state to work during the rest of the afternoon. If it takes you two hours to sober up, it has increased the cost of a lunch from £80 to £380 due to lost chargeable hours.

Beware of clients who ask you out to lunch. While it is flattering to the ego, almost certainly the purpose of the lunch is to obtain free legal advice. From the clients' point of view, this provides an opportunity to pick your brains for some two hours for £60 instead of £400, half of which the client spends on themselves! There is no reason why you should not go along with the idea, but be under no illusions as to what most people have in mind when they invite a solicitor out to lunch, unless perhaps it is to say thank you for a particularly good piece of work you have done for them.

6. Joining organisations

The more organisations of which you are a member, the more people with whom you will come into contact. Each person that you meet is a potential client. If they know you on a social or professional level, there may come a time when they have a requirement for legal services, or possibly a friend who does, and you may be in line for a recommendation. The classic organisation is the golf club. I would never suggest to anyone that they join such an organisation purely for business purposes, but it is a fact of life that an enormous amount of business is carried out on the country's golf courses. There are hundreds of organisations you can join, either sports clubs or those connected with social activities of other kinds, such as the local chamber of commerce, parent/teacher associations and committees of one kind or another. With each organisation that you join, you will meet new people, make new contacts and provide the opportunity for such people to become clients. The opportunity may present itself for you to join a charitable organisation. I have always considered it repugnant that people should join such organisations with anything other than the welfare of others in mind. People who do otherwise, in my experience, are rapidly recognised for what they are. On the other hand, someone who gives of their time freely for the benefit of their fellow men may find that their efforts are rewarded, not only in terms of the thanks from those whom they may have helped but with the respect of other like-minded individuals, and with that respect may come the opportunity to serve them in a professional way as well as in a purely altruistic way.

7. Banks, building societies and accountants

These organisations all have one thing in common: they are considered respectable and trustworthy. As a result, if a bank or building society manager suggests to clients that they use your firm of solicitors, the recommendation goes a long way to securing them as your client. In some cases, the recommendation is not made for purely unselfish reasons. Rightly or wrongly, banks and building societies often recommend people to use those firms of solicitors with whom they have an existing connection, namely the large sums of money that the solicitors have deposited with them. This arrangement whereby the solicitor helps the bank or building society and they help the solicitors is euphemistically known as reciprocal business. There is nothing wrong with reciprocal business so long as it is all done for the right reasons. If you offer a poor service to persons referred by banks or building societies, they will not recommend you to their customers no matter how much money you might deposit with them. As commercial organisations that have been brought up in an atmosphere of competition and selling, they are generally happy for you to sell to them, and indeed may respect those firms who try to sell to them over those who do not bother. Accordingly, such organisations should be a feature of your marketing campaign. It may be that the business lunch is a suitable approach but, equally, a busy bank manager may not want to give up two or three hours and may be just as happy with a 20-minute interview at the office so that you can get to know them, explain the kind of work that you do and give them the opportunity to make up their own mind as to whether they feel you are the kind of solicitor to whom they can confidently recommend their customers.

Banks and building societies

It is quite surprising how often bank and building society managers will say that they do not really know or have any kind of a relationship with solicitors in the locality and how they welcome the opportunity to enjoy such a rapport. The senior personnel of such organisations do have a rather unfortunate habit of moving around quite a lot. It is not unusual to find that the manager with whom you have spent two years cultivating a relationship suddenly moves to a branch miles away and you have to start all over again with someone new. Providing you are aware of what is happening and continue your marketing campaign, you can carry on where you left off, albeit a little further down the field. What can happen is that the contacts are neglected until it suddenly dawns upon you that you have had no referrals for five or six months and you then discover that not only has your contact taken over as the manager of the local branch in Port Stanley, Falkland Islands, but that the replacement has just been seen having lunch with the senior partner of the firm down the road. Local managers have lost a lot of their power in recent years as banks and building societies have regionalised their administrative systems, but there is still a worthwhile connection to be made. They still have important contacts and friends to whom they can recommend you.

Accountants

Not only do accountants have a reputation of honesty and professionalism, they are also regarded as having the ear of their business clients, and their advice in business matters is not to be disregarded lightly. Solicitors in days gone by were regarded in at least as much standing, if not more, and it is a sad indictment of our profession that we have allowed ourselves to be usurped by fellow professionals. The Law Society is doing much in terms of improving the image of solicitors through marketing initiatives and promoting Lexcel as a means of raising the standards of the profession, but there is a lot of lost ground to make up. Accountants fit into the same category for these purposes as banks and building societies, namely they welcome the opportunity to be able, with confidence, to place a client in a safe pair of hands. They see this as simply another part of the total service that they are able to offer their business clients. If you can win the trust and confidence of a firm of accountants with the result that they feel able to recommend their clients to use your services, you will have secured a valuable source of referrals.

As fellow professionals, accountants approach business and the management of their own firms in the same way as solicitors, except that by and large they do it rather better. They know all about marketing techniques, seminars, mail shots and the rest, and you are unlikely to impress by the business lunch approach. A totally direct and open form of marketing may be far more successful. You may have more success by suggesting a meeting where you can discuss the ways your two firms could co-operate for their mutual benefit. Again, you will have to win their respect and vice versa. It would be wrong of you to refer your clients to them when they need the services of an accountant if you were not convinced that the firm was competent and it would be in the client's best interests to use them. By the same token, the accountants will need to be satisfied that you are the right firm for their clients. These relationships are not easy to build up, but if you succeed they can work very successfully to everyone's benefit, not least the client's.

Estate agents and mortgage brokers

Many firms of agents and brokers will already have strong links with local firms or even be obliged by their head office to recommend a particular firm if they are part of a chain. Nevertheless, those able to choose whom they recommend may not be entirely happy with their existing contacts and may be persuaded to pass customers in your direction. They have a vested interest in a transaction going through promptly and efficiently and if that is not happening it may be time for a change. Many agents expect a referral fee. We have never been prepared to pay a referral fee and the appropriateness of such arrangements is currently under governmental review. You must also be careful not to find yourself in the agent's or broker's pocket so that they are able to influence what advice you give to your client. You must make it clear from the outset that you will always advise a client to pull out of a deal if it is in their best interests to do so, even if it means the agent or broker loses out as a result.

8. Newsletters

A newsletter is an opportunity to place your firm and its image in front of both existing and potential clients. It will need to tell its audience of recent changes in the law and give examples of how those changes might affect the reader. Putting together a newsletter is a surprisingly time-consuming business. In addition to composing the newsletter itself, there is the compiling of the list of people to receive it. The advent of computer databases and software programs that can easily handle mailing lists represents an enormous step forward in bringing such marketing tools within the grasp of even the humblest of practices, but it is nevertheless a substantial undertaking. Even if you have a client database and the necessary software on your computer, the software may not be easily programmable to enable you to sift through it and select only certain clients. There is no point in sending a newsletter which deals primarily with commercial matters to a divorce client unless that client is also a business person. A comparatively easy method of achieving the same end is by buying the newsletter of a contract publisher which can be customised with your firm's own logo. Accountants have this particular marketing tool highly refined. They are able to produce a very polished product, which looks as if it has been personally produced by the firm in question, for a comparatively low cost. Ideally, each firm would like to produce its own newsletter so that it can take full credit for the content and govern precisely what is included in it, but it may be difficult to devote sufficient time to do this exercise justice on a regular basis and cope with everything else in the daily routine of practice.

If you do opt for a newsletter, it is sensible to include some kind of disclaimer. This should not be phrased in a way that gives the impression that you are not prepared to take responsibility for your own articles, but it should state that each situation is different and only general advice can be given in a newsletter. Any clients who feel that they have specific problems related to the item in the newsletter should seek professional advice rather than relying on the contents of the newsletter, the advice preferably being given by you, of course!

9. Newspaper column

If your local newspaper does not run a legal column, why not offer to write one? They might even pay you a modest £40 or so for it. A fortnightly column is more sustainable than a weekly one. It is amazing how the copy deadline will creep up on you before you know it. Once you have thought of an interesting and informative topic, it will take you about three-quarters of an hour to write. It must have direct relevance to the ordinary member of the public, or else people will not bother to read it. The article should state that you are a local solicitor and give a contact telephone number, but if it looks too much like an advertisement for your practice it will not be read in a favourable light and will be counterproductive. Something of the order of 'Mr Bloggs is a solicitor practising locally in Any Town. Should you wish to speak him, you can contact him on 020 8111 2233' is perfectly acceptable and does not detract from your professional image.

10. Entertainment

Used sensibly, entertainment can be a very powerful marketing tool. The bigger firms tend to go a little over the top with entertainment such as golf days, evenings at the theatre, the dinner dance, the box at Ascot and the corporate hospitality tent at Twickenham. If you are not careful, you will create a state of affairs where a client accepts an invitation to that type of event because he or she feels flattered and because it is free, only to find that it is rather more of an imposition on their time than first imagined and attendance is merely out of courtesy as it is too late to cancel. A ridiculous situation is then produced whereby they are attending only out of a sense of duty and to preserve good manners, and you are giving up the whole of a Saturday or most of a Sunday evening thinking how you would rather be at home with your family, while wondering how you are going to meet the expense of putting on the event and thinking how there must be an easier way of earning a living.

If you go in for this kind of marketing, the event must be thoroughly enjoyable, one which preferably does not take up too much time and is sufficiently expensive to flatter your guests without anyone feeling that you are trying to buy their custom. A simple cocktail party for two or three hours, either at your offices or at home, can prove quite an enjoyable occasion. People will have the chance to meet new contacts among your other guests and may feel honoured at the fact that you have included them on your guest list. The event does not take too long to organise and is not too costly. If people can drift in and out during the two- or three-hour session, it has not become a chore; they can drop in when it suits them without being tied to a deadline and can leave as soon as they wish. It is important that you make the flexibility of the evening clear to your guests, to take the pressure off them both in terms of having to attend and the length of time they need to spend there. It is important to select your guests with care. Including some people who are friends or acquaintances of others who have not been invited can lead to the latter feeling left out. If need be, have two such events and tell the second group that you have had to organise things that way in order to make the gatherings manageable. Take your lead from former President Clinton, who organised his celebratory election party by holding two such events so as not to offend some of his supporters while at the same time rewarding the others. By means of such methods, the President was, on this occasion, able to please all of the people for much of the time.

In the summer a barbeque can often be a popular event. Like the cocktail party, you can quite successfully declare open house and let people drop in for an hour or two between certain times. If you pick the right day and you have a garden big enough for activities such as table tennis, badminton and so on, it can prove to be a very successful day, at comparatively low cost and without an enormous amount of organisation.

Some firms with the necessary space available have been able to include their own games room for entertaining clients. Rather than inviting clients out for a full business lunch, they invite them over for beer and sandwiches at lunchtime coupled with a game of snooker or table tennis, an excellent idea if you have space available, even if you do have to let the client win every once in a while. Similarly, a bridge evening with clients and their other halves can prove enjoyable unless those concerned are likely to take the game too seriously.

How about a quiz evening? If your own staff are willing to make time available for a couple of hours in the evening to make up a team, perhaps with an additional client on their side here and there with other clients and their staff or friends making up two or three other teams, a very pleasant evening can be spent.

All of these types of event demonstrate that you understand the need to market your practice and are prepared to make time available to do so and will enable people to get to know you better, affording you the opportunity to make new contacts and reinforce the ties with those who are already clients of the practice.

A note on the Law Society's Conveyancing Quality Scheme

The Law Society's Conveyancing Quality Scheme (CQS) was launched in 2010 in order to provide a type of branding which the public and lending institutions could associate with safe, competent conveyancing to counter the branding power of larger organisations expected to enter the conveyancing market with the advent of ABSs. It goes against the grain for many solicitors to have to prove themselves to the public and lenders by joining such organisations when the title of solicitor should be a sufficient guarantee of safety and competence in itself. Is it getting to the stage that if you are not a member of the CQS scheme, the Association of Personal Injury Lawyers or Resolution you are not fit to practice conveyancing, personal injury litigation or family work? What is the point in having to take examinations in these areas if you are then considered with suspicion if you have not gone on to achieve acceptance by one of these accreditation bodies? Certainly in the area of residential conveyancing, it is likely that it will be lenders who will call the shots and with some already excluding panel membership to those without membership of CQS the decision will be made for you if any more large lenders follow suit, as appears likely at present. The upside is that insurers are likely to offer you more favourable terms for your PI cover if you are inside the scheme than if you are not.

For Law Society guidance on both the CQS and the Lexcel practice management standard, please see the appendix on Law Society accreditation schemes at the back of this book.

20

Exit strategies

Should you retire? So, you have reached the stage where the daily trip into the office and putting up with the clients' ever-increasing demands are getting that bit too much for you and you think it is maybe time to call it a day. We all know that retirement normally means a drastic reduction in income, but have you actually stopped to work out quite how much a drop it will be? You now need to go through a thorough accounting exercise. What pension plans do you have in place? Ask your pension provider(s) to send you quotations for what lump sum you can take and what the annual pension would be. Do you have any with-profits life policies? If so, get quotes for what they are likely to pay out. Add those figures to any other savings and any liabilities you may have so that you can work out what your net capital and income position will be, assuming that you will be investing the capital, or at least a large chunk of it. Hopefully that in turn will be producing further income. You will need to estimate what that additional income will be by looking at the various financial products on the market and seeing what a typical investment would yield. Whether they are working or not, you will need to do the same with your spouse, if you have one, whether they are retiring as well, because you will need to try to work out what your joint tax positions will be in order to calculate your overall net income. If you cannot be bothered to find out what the various tax free allowances are and you just want to do it back of envelope style, add all the income together and reduce the figure by 20 per cent unless your income is going to be huge and you are likely still to be a higher rate taxpayer despite the drop in income.

Next you need to work out your likely outgoings. You can get your regular standing orders from your bank statements and you will have to extract other regular outgoings from credit card statements and bills. The checklist at **Appendix 16** may assist you: it is taken from my book *Precedent Library for the General Practitioner*, 2nd edn (Law Society, 2009) from the matrimonial section, but it should cover most of the usual items.

In this way you will have calculated your net income and your likely net outgoings. Bear in mind that if you are paying into a pension plan and/or a life policy which will mature, those usually hefty outgoings each month will cease. The calculation should show you whether you will be able to keep your head above water. Ideally, you will be looking for a fairly healthy surplus each year to provide for holidays and the cost of replacing the car, the central heating boiler and the like. If you do not like the amount that you are left with, it may be that you are not in a position to retire, at least not just yet. You may, however, be able to go into semi-retirement by working, say, three days a week; otherwise it will mean a more drastic lifestyle change such as selling the house and downsizing.

When?

If after your calculations you decide that you can afford to retire the next question is when. You will need to have a target date in mind and this will need to be anything between three and five years ahead, depending on your personal circumstances. A partner deciding to retire has a major impact on any firm and also on the clients that that partner has been servicing. It is not something that can be arranged overnight, nor should it be.

Multi-partner firms

The partners normally best placed to be able to retire are those in firms which have several partners, provided they do not all want to retire at the same time. The partnership agreement will doubtless provide a procedure, and this is generally commenced by the service of a notice on the other partners and frequently it is a period of a year. By negotiation it may well be possible to arrange a shorter period, but it is not something that should be sprung on fellow partners and it may be wise to take some soundings amongst your other partners before doing anything. The biggest problem is likely to be the partners' capital account. In good times healthy balances may have built up and so the retiring partner may be owed quite a lot of money by the firm. The partnership agreement will normally provide for staggered lump sum payments over a period of several years. Unfortunately, not every partner is able to get their capital out. If the firm goes out of business before all the capital has been repaid the retiring partner may be left with the unenviable prospect of pursuing his fellow partners, who themselves are now probably impecunious. It may be that the retiring partner owes the continuing partners money. Much will depend on the terms of the partnership agreement and whether it covers situations such as an overdraft for which all partners are responsible. A further complication may the lease of the premises occupied by the partnership. A retiring partner may be a lessee and if so it would be wise to investigate the possibility with the landlord of a deed of variation substituting another partner. If there are several other continuing partners who will remain on the lease, the landlord may have no great objection. Better still would be for the retiring partner to be replaced by someone else who is being promoted to equity partner and who has agreed to go on the lease in the retiring partner's place.

One- and two-partner firms

Generally, the smaller the practice the more difficult it is to retire. In a three-partner practice where the continuing partners are still comparatively young, the proposed departure of the retiring partner may come as welcome news. However, if all partners are roughly the same age it could prompt a chaotic situation where the thought of one partner retiring causes panic and the other two want to go at the same time because they do not want to be left holding what seems to be a poisoned chalice if the practice is struggling. As will be seen below, the least attractive way of retiring is via a cessation of the business. Again, if there is a partnership deed in place it will need to be examined carefully to see precisely what procedure is laid down if a partner wishes to retire. In a two-partner practice things are even more difficult unless there is someone readily available to come into the partnership in place of the retiring partner. If it is otherwise, it will be seen as one partner leaving the other partner in the lurch, causing them to continue on as a sole practitioner. Given the suspicion with which many sole practices are regarded by financial institutions and by PI insurers, the prospect of one partner leaving the other may be perceived as something akin to betrayal. This in turn may lead to the second partner attempting to retire before the first one does so that they get left holding the baby. For these reasons the matter should be raised sooner rather than later so that careful thought and planning can go into the precise procedure to be adopted, with both partners planning their exit strategy to fit in with each other.

There are four basic pathways for a sole practitioner or small firm to bring about the retirement of a partner.

Close down

As discussed before, this is the least attractive solution. Unfortunately, as a profession we have managed to get ourselves into a situation where in effect a massive fine is levied for committing the highly serious offence of daring to shut up shop. If there is no successor practice the cessation of the business automatically causes the existing PI insurer to put in place six years' worth of run-off cover. Neither the retiring partner(s) nor the insurers have any choice. Insurers will typically charge three times the annual premium for providing the run-off cover. Premiums, of course, vary widely depending on the level of business conducted, the claims history of the firm and the type of work conducted, but even a firm with a relatively modest annual turnover and with a good claims history can find itself landed with a premium of £60,000 for run-off cover that it has no choice but to provide. This is a nightmarish situation and one that the general public cannot begin to understand. Whoever heard of a restaurant owner or a plumber having to pay out such a huge sum of money just because they want to stop work and close down when they are too old to carry on? Before you start thinking that this warms the heart of the PI insurer, you should know that PI insurers absolutely hate providing the cover as they are being forced to provide six years' worth of cover in return for premiums for only three of those six years. Indeed, if they think you may be about to retire they may refuse to quote you for next year's cover in case they get stuck with the run off. The other two major considerations are redundancy payments to any staff you may have and the remaining liability on the lease of your premises. Unless you have a very understanding and rather foolish landlord or someone else coming in to take over the remaining term of the lease you are probably going to have to coincide your retirement with the end or very nearly the end of the term of the lease.

Bear in mind that there are certain regulatory points to consider if you opt for the close down solution. The Law Society has published a practice note of 4 January 2012 on closing down your practice, highlighting the issues and underlining the need to comply with the mandatory provisions of OFR and the SRA Code of Conduct 2011, and in particular outcome 10.13, which states: 'Once you are aware that your firm will cease to practise, you effect the orderly and transparent wind-down of activities, including informing the SRA before the firm closes.'

Grow your own

It is possible to plan a succession to the firm if you are able to recruit and retain good qualified staff. The difficulty is that you have no way of knowing whether they will see themselves as future partners or be willing to take on such a responsibility, particularly if you are not there to guide them in the future. Even if they express a wish to do so it may be a very different story when it comes to the crunch. It is quite astonishing how people will back away from such a proposition despite the fact that you can make out a very convincing case on the figures that it will increase their income substantially and that as masters of their own fate their job security will be greatly enhanced. To many people there is nothing like having the security of a regular pay cheque at the end of the month, no matter how badly the firm is doing, despite your pointing out to them that any such perceived security is illusory. If the firm is indeed doing badly, it is only a question of time before they will be made redundant. Staff always think that it will always happen to someone else and not to them. They cannot see that by stepping in as an owner of the business they are much more likely to create a secure future for themselves. If you have managed to cultivate people of the right calibre and mindset, there is then the question of the terms on which the practice is handed over. You could try to secure a premium from them to buy their way into partnership with a view to you leaving it soon thereafter, but it is very likely that you will end up giving the practice to them for free. It will not take long before they realise that there is an uncomfortable run-off cover premium that you are trying to avoid and that it would make economic sense for you to give the practice to them for free rather than close down, making them redundant and having to hand over the bag of gold to the insurer. It is not necessarily going to happen that way, of course. If they are not prepared to pay something for the practice, you may be looking for a merger or a sale and in those circumstances the new owner may not see the would-be partner as part of the new firm's future.

Targeting other firms

Merging with another practice is a very attractive way of solving the retirement conundrum. Care must be taken to ensure that the firm with which you propose to merge has a good reputation and is on a sound financial footing, something that is not particularly easy to do from the outside. Mergers that stand a better chance of success are where the practices concerned know one another reasonably well already. Friendships often occur between professionals, where one firm helps another out or partners know one another socially. The main threat of making it clear that you are thinking of retiring and would favour a merger with them is that they are quite likely to be a competitor and may not be particularly shy about letting other people know that you are thinking of retiring. If word gets out on the high street this can be the kiss of death for a practice. Before you know it, you will be finding that long-standing clients are instructing someone else and when you express disappointment they say: 'Oh, I didn't think you wanted the work as I heard you were retiring.' The best way to avoid this is to make your approach to the other firm on the basis that you are looking for a merger with them for other equally valid commercial reasons but with a view to facilitating your retirement at some other unspecified time in the future. If promising talks then arise your future intentions will be one of several different areas under discussion and in due course you can accelerate or delay your proposed leaving date depending on how you are enjoying life in the new firm, but at least you will be much further forward with your exit strategy than you were before. You may be able to float, at a very late stage in the talks, the proposition of an early exit from partnership into consultancy or a part time consultancy for a mutually agreeable period. The acquiring firm will thus have the security of knowing that your goodwill, experience and talents will be available to it for a known period but that ultimately it will succeed to your client base and the new firm will be the stronger for it.

Sale

Of all the various options, a sale is perhaps the most attractive. The difficulty is that there are not many buyers out in the marketplace at any given time. Potential buyers will include other solicitors' practices, other legal practices, such as licensed conveyancers and ABS, once the concept has got off the ground. Indeed, ABS may provide the answer to many a prospective retiring practitioner in the future and there are several other players who have stated early on in the process that they wish to get into the marketplace by acquiring suitable practices. Undoubtedly, for any organisation wishing to get a foothold in the legal marketplace, buying up firms is the fastest, if the most expensive, way of doing it.

The difficulty is in letting prospective buyers know that you are interested in selling your practice without telling the rest of the world, with the possible unfortunate consequences referred to above. The usual way of matching up prospective buyers and sellers is through an intermediary. There are certainly two well-known organisations specialising in the sale of legal practices and whose advertisements appear regularly in the legal press. Possibly because there are so few recognised specialists in this area, the fees for their services may be seen as too high. Like any third party involved in the sale of an enterprise, they will be looking for a percentage of the sale price achieved. However, they may not only be looking for that, but also for the fees involved for their time spent immersing themselves in the detail of your practice so that they are in a position to speak from first-hand knowledge to prospective buyers and these fees are not necessarily payable only in the event of a sale. You may therefore find yourself with a substantial bill and still not have sold the practice.

Apart from the recognised specialists, there are other organisations that can help you. Some legal employment agencies are also prepared to try to market your practice to possible interested firms or indeed individuals. As well as attempting to find an existing firm for you to merge with, often referred to in the trade as a 'bolt on', they will approach individuals who are looking to move firms, either because they are unhappy where they are or because they are being or have been made redundant. Taking over a practice in their own right may be something that they had not considered. Do not be particularly surprised if you have what on the face of it are expressions of great interest and enthusiasm at initial meetings only to find that when push comes to shove the individual simply does not have the bottle to go through with it. It is, after all, a huge step to be taking. If you go the sale route and can find a buyer a suitable form of sale agreement appears at **Appendix 17**.

Work in progress and repayment of capital

Many would-be buyers of a practice are put off by the substantial costs involved. The price you seek to achieve for your practice may appear to be relatively modest and affordable to the prospective buyer. What is not readily apparent are the other costs involved on top of the purchase price itself. They will assume that on takeover day whatever money comes in to the firm goes into the till and is theirs. It comes as something of a shock when you explain to them that at least for the first three or four months almost the whole of that money belongs to you. It is money earned by the old firm and represents payments due to you for work carried out by the old firm and which is only now being billed and paid. This often runs into many thousands of pounds. If the money then is not going to them but to you, how do they get paid? The simple answer is that they do not, not until the new firm has done some work, sent out its own bills and received the money in on them. It gets worse. 'What about the money on office account – can't I use that to pay my wages?', asks the prospective buyer. Well, no. First, as a new buyer you do not get any wages. You are no longer an employee. You are the boss. Bosses take draws, but they only take draws when there is the money available to do so. There is no money available out of the immediate income stream because that is work in progress which is going to the seller. There is no money in the office account because that is money which the seller either put there or left there and it belongs to them. Alternatively, at the point of handover the seller will draw all the money out leaving nothing in office account. If that course of action is taken, how does the buyer pay the rent and the staff, let alone take something for themselves? Answer: they put their own money in as their working capital or take out an overdraft. The original proposition for acquiring their own firm for an agreed price is now no longer looking quite so promising when the buyer realises that apart from finding a premium they are going to have to find a lot more money than they bargained for.

The fact is that buying a practice has much in common with setting up a brand new practice. When you set up a brand new practice you have all the associated set-up costs and because there is no work in progress you have to wait until jobs have come in and been processed before you can even bill them, let alone get paid for them Even with the relatively quick turnover of a conveyancing practice it is, on average, going to take at least eight weeks before the buyer can use the income stream as their own. With litigation, of course, it could be several months before the buyer is able to put in even an interim bill. So why then buy a practice as opposed to starting one yourself? The answer is that if you buy a practice you are likely to be trading from a site that has been known as a solicitor's practice for many years and you will have a set up that is already operating in terms of staff, equipment, procedures and the like, so that if it is a practice that has been well run you have a machine that is running like clockwork with a known track record and with people able to help you continue down the right pathways. The buyer of a practice will have a head start of about a year on where he or she would have been if they had started a new practice from scratch, possibly less if they are able to take a known and substantial client base with them from day one.

There are various regulatory requirements to be fulfilled with a sale of the practice which are summarised in the Law Society's practice note of 4 January 2012. They include the need to inform clients before the sale takes place to give them the option of instructing another firm – they may not like the sound of the people taking over or may feel that it will just not be the same without you there! There are also issues regarding file storage and informing the SRA of what is happening.

Most buyers will be keen for the retiring partner to remain with the practice for a period of at least six months in order to facilitate the handover of clients and to avoid clients leaving the practice because they are afraid that the new practice will not be run in the same way as the old in the future or that they may not get on with the new owner. The buyer will also want to draw upon the knowledge and experience of the seller in the right way to run the practice until they feel comfortable in their new role and are sufficiently confident to be able to take major decisions themselves, which may or may not accord with the way in which the seller has run the practice in the past. Once that transitional period has elapsed a decision can be taken on whether the parties mutually wish to continue and if so for how long. Ultimately there will come a point when, hopefully by mutual agreement, the arrangements can be terminated and retirement proper can take place. This is the point to which you have been heading all your professional life! Savour the moment!

Is it all it's cracked up to be?

Retirement does not mean all things to all men or women. Some people are forced into retirement whilst others choose it. For those that choose it a good many feel they have made a terrible mistake. The drop in income is huge and the life change is dramatic. No longer do you have a set routine, up at 8 am, in the office for 9.30 am, slave away at everyone's beck and call until closing time and then wonder if you dare slip away for an early night at 7 pm and feeling guilty if you don't take a pile of stuff home to do before bedtime. All that five days a week, every week and for some people even more than five days a week. The annual attempt to get away from it all is often a frenzied and unrewarding affair, with frantic activity trying to get everything in good order before you go away only to return a couple of weeks later to a pile of work that your locum or deputy has been unable to deal with in your absence and quite possibly one or two catastrophes that they have been unable to prevent but which you probably would have avoided.

For many people the shock to the system of retirement proves too much in one way or another. A great many people die within the first five years of retirement. The fact is that a certain amount of stress is good for the system. It keeps everything ticking over. For others for whom death does not set in, boredom does. The vast majority of police officers and service men and women who traditionally retire comparatively young almost immediately go out and get themselves another job despite the fact that their pensions are often more generous than the private sector and they have spouses who are still working, so there is no economic need for further employment. The plain fact is they cannot cope with sitting around and doing nothing and being a nobody after such a demanding career where they were the Mr or Mrs Big. For others, retirement is a panacea. Every day is like the weekend and yet the weekend never ends. So, is it all it's cracked up to be? Oh yes! Do it sooner rather than later.

21

Good luck!

Well, you have read the book, do you have the nerve 'to boldly go' where only a few have gone before? Many people consider setting up in practice on their own or starting a new firm with one or two others, but only a small proportion actually go through with it. If you do decide to take that great leap into the unknown then, if nothing else, it will be an enormously valuable experience. You will be a better person and quite possibly a better solicitor for it. Only those people who have taken that step fully appreciate the size of the undertaking and the considerable achievement and satisfaction of making a success of a practice that they have started themselves. It must be fairly close to the feeling someone gets who has built their own home.

Building a practice is not nearly so clear-cut, however. You are never quite sure when you have finished. Indeed, do you ever finish? There must come a point in time when the person who has built his own home feels confident that it is not going to fall down. It takes a long time before someone who has built their own practice manages to banish the phantoms of bankruptcy and failure from their everyday thoughts. There is no set time for sole practitioners to put away lists of expenses and billing figures and to abstain from the frenzied addition of the figures in a frantic attempt to convince themselves that their practice is still solvent. Indeed, such exercises should be part of the routine. The only difference is the reduction in intensity of the blind panic in which the calculations take place.

Be assured of two things. First, it is normal to feel that way, not just for a few months, but for a few years. The constant nagging doubt is a spectre called failure. No one likes to fail; the ever-present fear in the early years is that the practice will crumble and you will have to undergo the ignominy of admitting to your friends and colleagues that you could not make a go of it and have to look for a job. Do not let this put you off. You will not fail. Those practices that fold normally do so as a result of being too successful as solicitors, but lacking proper management that fails after a number of years to take corrective action in time. Anyway, you gave it a go while your friends did not.

Second, the fear and the doubt will pass. As one year builds on another, history is on your side. If you made it through last year, why should you not make it through this year, or the year after? With proper planning and management, you will keep the risks as small as possible and in as many different compartments as possible. Even if something does go wrong, the chances are that a quick damage limitation exercise will have the ship back on an even keel. There is no need to be afraid of failure if your failures are little ones. As the boss of the firm, it is part of your job to anticipate the dangers and failures, to make sure that you run only acceptable risks and that if the cards do not go your way, the result is something of a minor inconvenience rather than a catastrophic event.

Don't over stretch yourself and don't take big risks. Watch the pennies. Consider each new development carefully before undertaking it. Plan for failure. If it all went wrong, what would the consequences be and can you afford them? If not, do not take the risk.

Probably one of the biggest disadvantages of being in a small practice is that of isolation. In a larger firm, there is much greater interaction with other firms. Your partners will have friends who are partners in other practices of different sizes and types. Even if they do not know you, almost certainly your assistant solicitors, legal executives and your secretaries will have contacts within other firms. From these various contacts, you will get feedback as to how everyone else is doing. When you find that everyone else is in just a big a mess as you are, you begin to relax. Whether you should do or not is immaterial. Misery loves company. If things are going wrong for everyone else – and you are doing no more badly than anyone else – then you feel it is not really your fault.

As a sole practitioner or partner in a small firm, however, your lines of communication with other firms are much more restricted and when things begin to go wrong you tend to fear the worst and think it is the beginning of the end. With no one or very few people with whom you can share your problems and talk over your difficulties, you may well begin to panic. Your morale is likely to drop and before you know where you are, you are thinking of running down the shutters and handing in the keys to the landlord. Quite by chance you may be lucky enough to have a conversation with someone in another firm, who explains how their fee income has dropped by 50 per cent in the past month, which in itself was 30 per cent down on the previous month and how they are going to have to lay off 30 staff and have a crunch meeting with the bank next week that everyone is dreading. Suddenly, you feel normal. It is not that you are making a mess of things – it is just that market forces are operating against you. You may resist the temptation to tell your friend that you have just had to sack the cleaner and buy a mop and bucket for yourself, and that you have just managed to duck out of your crunch meeting with your bank manager and have put it off for a further three weeks in case the client gets the wrong idea.

With a bit of luck, the next phone call might produce what seems to be a promising client. Suddenly you feel you might persevere with the practice for another month. Next minute you look out of the window and the sun is shining and things do not seem quite as bad as they did a little while ago. You will have your failures but undoubtedly you will have your successes too. If you decide to start a new practice, you will be in for exciting times. Good luck and fasten your seat belt. If this book has done anything to ease the birth pangs involved in the delivery of your new practice into the turbulent world of clients, landlords, tax inspectors and similar irredeemable reprobates, then my labours in writing this book will have been most amply rewarded.

Appendices

Appendix 1

Specimen deed of partnership

THIS DEED OF PARTNERSHIP is made the Twenty-third day of November Two Thousand and Twelve and BETWEEN RAYMOND GREED (hereinafter called 'Mr Greed') of the first part ANDREW PLEASANT (hereinafter called 'Mr Pleasant') of the second part JOHN STRANGE (hereinafter called 'Mr Strange') of the third part and CHRISTOPHER DEVIOUS (hereinafter called 'Mr Devious') of the fourth part (and which persons are in this deed referred to as 'the Partners')

WHEREAS:

(1) The Partners (with other persons who have retired from partnership)[1] practised as Solicitors in partnership together at 1 Crooks Corner London WC2 under the firm name and style of GREED & CO. until the Thirtieth day of September Two Thousand and Twelve and the Partners have agreed to practise as Solicitors in partnership from the First day of October Two Thousand and Twelve

(2) The Partners have agreed to enter into this deed to record the terms on which they practise in partnership as Solicitors from the First day of October Two Thousand and Twelve

NOW THIS DEED WITNESSETH as follows:

1 THE Partners hereby agree to carry on the profession of Solicitors in partnership under the name of 'Greed Strange & Partners'

2 (1) THE partnership shall begin on the First day of October Two Thousand and Twelve
   (2) THE offices of the partnership shall be at 1 Crooks Corner London WC2 and at such other place or places as the Partners may from time to time agree

3 THE following property shall be deemed to be assets of the partnership and shall belong to the Partners in the proportions in which they shall from time to time share profits, that is to say:

   (1) The freehold office premises 1 Crooks Corner London WC2
   (2) Goodwill of the partnership business

4 (1) THE capital required for carrying on the partnership business shall be contributed from time to time by the Partners in shares to be agreed between them from time to time (but with the intention that ultimately it shall be contributed by the Partners equally)

(2) CAPITAL contributed by the Partners shall not carry interest unless otherwise agreed[(2)]

5 THE Bankers of the partnership are Solid Bank plc or as may otherwise be appointed by the Partners

6 ALL partnership monies not required for current expenses and securities for money shall as and when received be paid into the partnership bank to the credit of the partnership accounts and all monies and securities received by the partnership or by any Partner on behalf of any client or third person shall forthwith be paid to such client or third person or (as the case may require) shall forthwith be paid into a separate client account with the said bank and all cheques on any such accounts shall be drawn in the partnership name and may be so drawn by any Partner or person duly authorised by the Partners. Proper books of accounts and entries shall be kept and made by the Partners at any premises at which the partnership business shall be carried on and each Partner shall duly and punctually make full and proper entries of all business transacted by him on account of the partnership in accordance with such Rules as may be prescribed from time to time by the Law Society

7 EACH Partner shall devote the whole of his time and attention to the partnership business and no Partner shall without the consent of all the other Partners engage in any other business or hold any office or appointment PROVIDED ALWAYS that the emoluments from all offices and appointments held by any Partner during the partnership shall belong to the partnership

8 EACH Partner shall be entitled to four weeks' holiday in each year

9 IF any Partner shall:

(1) become bankrupt or insolvent or compound or make any arrangement with his creditors or
(2) grossly neglect the partnership business or
(3) commit or permit any serious wilful breach of the provisions hereof or
(4) be struck off the Roll of Solicitors

then and in any such case the other Partners may give to such Partner written notice requiring him to retire forthwith and upon receipt of such notice that Partner shall for the purpose of all the provisions hereof relating to the retirement of a Partner from the partnership be deemed to have retired from the partnership accordingly subject to such amendments as are necessary in consequence of such retiring Partner not retiring on the Thirtieth day of April in a year and provided also that the payment for goodwill under clause 17(1)(c) of this deed shall not apply

10   A Partner may be required to retire from the partnership upon being given not less than 12 months' written notice to that effect by all the other Partners (such notice to expire on the Thirtieth day of April of any year). The payment for goodwill under clause 17(1)(c) of this deed shall not apply unless the Partner has reached the age of 60 years by the expiration of the notice requiring his retirement[3]

11   NO Partner shall without the written consent of the other Partners:

(1)   enter into a contract with a trainee solicitor and any premium received in respect of a trainee shall belong to the partnership

(2)   pledge the credit of the partnership except in the normal course of partnership business or give credit to or conduct any business for any person company or firm after being forbidden in writing to do so by all the other Partners

(3)   engage directly or indirectly in any business or profession other than that of the partnership

(4)   engage or (except for gross misconduct) dismiss any clerk servant or other employee of the partnership

(5)   use any of the money goods or other partnership property except in the normal course of partnership business and for the benefit of the partnership

(6)   enter into or agree to enter into any contract for any goods or services exceeding the value of Five Hundred Pounds (£500) on behalf of the partnership

(7)   enter into any bond or become bail surety or security with or for any person or do or knowingly cause or permit or suffer partnership property or any part to be seized distrained upon or otherwise attached or executed upon

(8)   assign mortgage or charge his share of the partnership or any part of such share or make any other person a Partner in the partnership

12   EACH Partner shall at all time duly and punctually pay his private debts whether present or future and keep the Partners and partnership property indemnified therefrom

13   ON the Thirtieth day of April in every year or such other date as may be agreed a general account and balance sheet shall be taken and be made by Messrs Dodgey Accounting & Co. of 1 The Alleyway Fleecem Surrey Chartered Accountants (or by such other Chartered Accountants as may be agreed between the Partners) of all assets and liabilities of the partnership and of all the dealings and transactions of the partnership during the preceding twelve months and of all matters usually included in the accounts of a solicitor's practice and in taking such account a fair evaluation shall be made of all items requiring valuation and such account and balance sheet shall when signed by the Partners be binding on them save that if any manifest error shall be found therein and brought by any Partner to the attention of the other Partners within three calendar months after such signature the error shall be corrected

14 (1) THE profits of the partnership appearing in the yearly accounts shall be shared among the Partners in such proportions as they shall from time to time agree (provided that any one dissentient Partner shall be required to concur with the agreement reached by all the other Partners)

(2) EACH Partner may during the continuance of the partnership draw out of the partnership account at the Bank a monthly sum to be agreed with the other Partners on account of his share of profits PROVIDED THAT if when the said yearly account is taken at the end of the year it shall appear that any Partner has drawn any sum in excess of his share of the profits he shall forthwith repay such excess into the partnership accounts

15 (1) IN the case of the death of a Partner the surviving Partner or Partners shall as from the date of such death succeed to all of the assets of the partnership (including the goodwill) and the surviving Partner or Partners shall undertake all the debts liabilities and other obligations of the partnership and shall pay to the personal representatives of the deceased Partner the following sums (and no others) at the times set out below:

(a) within three months of the completion of the partnership accounts for the financial year current at the date of death a sum equal to the share of profits he would have earned in the months up to the date of death had he survived to the end of such year divided by twelve and multiplied by the number of months the deceased Partner survived in that year less his drawings and his share of the partnership's liability for Income Tax[4]

(b) by eight equal half-yearly instalments commencing six months after the date of death of the deceased Partner the amount of any capital sum standing to the credit of such deceased Partner in the books of account of the partnership together with the amount of any sum standing to the credit of the Current Account of such deceased Partner in the books of account of the partnership at the end of the financial year immediately prior to the financial year in which such deceased Partner dies PROVIDING nevertheless as follows:

(i) that any sums received by the surviving Partner or Partners from any Insurance Policy which the surviving Partner or Partners have or may have effected on the life of such deceased Partner shall be paid forthwith to the personal representatives of such deceased Partner as part or full payment of the sum due under sub-clause 15(1)(b) (but provided further that if the sum received by the surviving Partner or Partners under such Insurance Policy should exceed the sum due under this sub-clause the surplus after payment as aforesaid shall belong to the surviving Partner or Partners)

(ii) in the case of the death of a Partner named in the Schedule hereto the amount payable to the personal representatives of the deceased Partner shall be reduced by the sum set opposite his name in the Schedule hereto (being the nominal value of the Endowment Policy of Assurance effected or intended to be effected by him on his own life) whether or not such Policy shall in fact have been effected and whether or not the same shall have remained in full force and effect down to the date of the deceased Partner's death [(5)]

   (iii) pending payment to the personal representatives of such deceased Partner the net sum payable and from time to time remaining due shall carry interest at the rate of one per cent per annum over the base lending rate fixed by Solid Bank plc (with a minimum of five per cent) at the time such interest is payable and such interest shall be payable half-yearly at the times here before appointed by sub-clause (1)(b) of this clause

(2) As between two or more surviving Partners they shall be and become entitled to the assets of such deceased Partner in such shares as they shall agree (provided that any one dissentient Partner shall be required to concur with the agreement reached by all the other Partners) and the share of profits previously enjoyed by such deceased Partner shall be apportioned between such surviving Partners in like manner

16[(6)] IN the case of the death of a Partner the surviving Partner or Partners may in their absolute discretion if they think fit (but without being under any legal obligation so to do) make an ex gratia payment of a sum equivalent to one-third of the sum of the deceased Partner's share of profits in the preceding three completed years prior to his death such payment to be made to such dependant or dependants of the deceased Partner as the surviving Partner or Partners shall in their absolute discretion think fit and such payment shall be provided by the continuing Partners in the proportions in which they acquire the assets of such deceased Partner

17 (1) ANY one Partner may upon giving at least twelve months' notice in writing to that effect to the other Partners expiring on the Thirtieth day of April in any year retire from the partnership and upon his retirement the remaining Partner or Partners shall as and from the date of such retirement succeed to all the assets of the partnership (including the goodwill thereof) and the remaining Partner or Partners shall undertake all the debts liabilities and obligations of the partnership and shall pay to the retiring Partner (or as he may direct) the following sums at the times stated below (but no other payment whatsoever) that is to say:

   (a) by eight equal half-yearly instalments commencing six months after the date of such retirement the amount of any capital sum standing to the credit of such retiring Partner in the books of account of the partnership together with the amount of any sum standing to the credit of the Current Account of such retiring Partner in the books of account of the partnership at the end of the financial year immediately prior to the financial year at which end such retiring Partner retires PROVIDING nevertheless that pending payment to such retiring Partner the net sum payable and from time to time remaining due shall carry interest at the rate of one per cent per annum over the base lending rate fixed by Solid Bank plc (with a minimum of five per cent) at the time such interest is payable and such interest shall be payable half-yearly at the times hereinbefore appointed by sub-clause (1)(a) of this clause

(b) within three months of the completion of the yearly accounts for the financial year ending at the date of his retirement a sum equal to the proportion of the retiring Partner's share of the profits for such year (but deducting from such sum the amount of the retiring Partner's drawings during that year and his share of the partnership's liability for Income Tax) PROVIDED nevertheless that in the case of the retirement of a Partner named in the Schedule hereto the amounts payable to such retiring Partner under sub-clause (1)(c) of this clause shall be reduced by the sum set opposite his name in the Schedule hereto (being the nominal value of the Endowment Policy of Assurance effected by him on his own life) whether such Policy shall in fact have remained in full force and effect down to the date of such Partner's retirement

(c) in the event that the retiring Partner has reached the age of 60 by the expiration of his notice to retire from partnership by eight half-yearly instalments commencing six months after the date of such retirement a payment for goodwill of a sum equivalent to one-third of the sum of such retiring Partner's share of profits in the preceding three completed years prior to his retirement[7]

(2) As between two or more of the remaining Partners they shall be and become entitled to the share of partnership assets of such retiring Partner in such shares as they shall agree (provided that any one dissentient Partner shall be required to concur with the agreement reached by all the other Partners) and the share of profits previously enjoyed by such retiring Partner shall be apportioned between the remaining Partners in like manner and the amount payable to the retiring Partner under sub-clause 1(c) of this clause shall also be apportioned between the remaining Partners in like manner

18 UPON the retirement (from the Partnership howsoever occasioned) or death of any Partner he or his personal representatives shall if so requested in writing by the continuing or surviving Partner or Partners join with him or them in giving Her Majesty's Inspector of Taxes a notice under Section 154(2) of the Income and Corporation Taxes Act 1970 or any statutory replacement or modification thereof for the time being in force and the Partner so retiring or the personal representatives of such deceased Partner shall be indemnified by the continuing or surviving

Partner or Partners against any Income Tax which may be payable by him or them as a result of giving such notice in excess of the Income Tax which would have been payable if no such notice had been given

19 ANY Partner retiring from the partnership and receiving a payment for goodwill hereby covenants with the other Partners and each of them that he (the retiring Partner) will not in England or Wales practise privately as a Solicitor either by himself or as the Partner or employee of any other person or firm for a period of three years from the date of such retirement PROVIDED that nothing herein contained shall preclude him from acting for his relatives or any client for whom he shall have acted solely in an honorary capacity[8]

20 ALL disputes and questions whatsoever which shall either during the partnership or afterwards arise between the Partners or their respective representatives or between any Partners or Partner and the representatives of any other Partner concerning this deed or the construction or application thereof or any clause herein contained or any account valuation or division of assets debts or liabilities to be made hereunder or the rights duties or liabilities of any person under this deed shall be referred to a single arbitrator agreed upon between the parties or failing agreement by the President of the Law Society and be subject to the Arbitration Act 1996 or any statutory modification thereof

IN WITNESS whereof the parties hereto have set their hands and seals the day and year first above written

THE SCHEDULE above referred to

Name of Partner	Name of Life Company	No. of Policy	Nominal Value
Mr Greed	Fat Insurance Co. Ltd	CP33456	£30,000
Mr Pleasant	Nice Life Insurance Co. Ltd	A5639083	£30,000
Mr Strange	The Weird Life Assurance Co.	C3423543	£30,000
Mr Devious	Subtle Life Insurance Co.	C312456	£30,000

SIGNED SEALED and DELIVERED
by the said RAYMOND GREED
in the presence of:

SIGNED SEALED and DELIVERED
by the said ANDREW PLEASANT
in the presence of:

SIGNED SEALED and DELIVERED
by the said JOHN STRANGE
in the presence of:

SIGNED SEALED and DELIVERED
by the said CHRISTOPHER DEVIOUS
in the presence of:

Notes

(1) If appropriate.

(2) Or, 'shall carry interest at [*number*] per cent above the base lending rate of the partnership's Bankers prescribed from time to time'.

(3) This clause is an expulsion clause. The partner concerned need have committed no wrong and may simply have alienated him- or herself from his or her fellow partners. Careful thought should be given before including a clause of this kind in an agreement.

(4) The purpose of the clause is to give the deceased's estate a share of profit averaged out over the year rather than just the months up until death to avoid an artificially high figure if the months to death were exceptionally good or a low figure if exceptionally poor.

(5) If this clause is included, its effect can be draconian. It is designed to ensure that partners take out life policies for the benefit of their fellow partners and maintain the premiums since if not, the payment to the next of kin of the sums due under the deed is reduced by the sum which the policy would have yielded.

(6) Strictly speaking, such a clause is otiose, as it gives rise to no legal obligations. It may, however, provide comfort to some partners who would like the deed to be more generous on death. It also provides a means of escape if at the time of death the partnership is having a lean time as the payments are discretionary.

(7) The purpose of this formula is to take the average of three years' profits so that the goodwill payment is neither artificially inflated nor depressed by an unusually good or bad year.

(8) Whether this clause will stand the test of reasonableness for restraint of trade purposes will depend to some extent on the age of the retiring partner and the size of the goodwill payment. You may prefer to (a) make the covenant less onerous and (b) set out the restrictions in separate clauses to reduce the risk of the whole clause being struck down and the reasonable parts being thrown out along with the unreasonable.

Appendix 2

Specimen consultant's agreement

THIS AGREEMENT[1] is made the [*day*] day of [*month*] 2012 BETWEEN:

(1)   GREED & CO. of 1 Crooks Corner London WC2 ('the Partnership') and
(2)   RONALD EVERGREEN of 50 Long Road Enfield EN4 9PT ('the Consultant')

1. Definitions

In this Agreement the following expressions shall unless the context otherwise requires have the following meanings:

'the Termination Date' – the date of termination of this Agreement howsoever occasioned

'the Consultant's Duties' – the duties of the Consultant as specified in the First Schedule

2. Term

The Partnership shall retain the services of the Consultant and the Consultant shall carry out the Consultant's Duties from the date of this Agreement until the expiration of two years from such date[2]

3. Remuneration

The Consultant shall be paid a Consultancy Fee of £135 (together with Value Added Tax) in respect of each day spent in the performance of the Consultant's Duties payable on receipt of an appropriate invoice which shall be rendered at the end of each month

4. Expenses

The Partnership shall repay to the Consultant all travelling hotel and other out-of-pocket expenses reasonably and necessarily incurred by the Consultant in the performance of the Consultant's Duties upon suitable evidence of such expenditure being provided to the Partnership

5. Performance of duties

5.1   The Consultant shall perform the Consultant's Duties in a good, efficient and proper manner consistent with the standards expected of a professional person

5.2   Subject to clause 5.4, the Consultant shall be expected to work for such period as the Partnership reasonably considers necessary to devote to the Partnership for the proper performance of the Consultant's Duties

5.3   The Consultant shall:

    5.3.1   be required to work for not less than 150 working days each year

    5.3.2   not be required to work:

        5.3.2.1 during any holiday absence

        5.3.2.2 in the case of illness or accident in which case he shall notify the Partnership immediately and shall provide such evidence as to his illness or accident as the Partnership shall reasonably require

5.4   For the purposes of this clause, the Consultant shall in addition to the usual bank or public holidays be entitled to be absent for the purpose of holidays for five weeks in each calendar year commencing 1st January to be taken at such times as may reasonably be agreed between the parties[3]

6. Self-employed status[4]

The Consultant is engaged as a self-employed contractor. He is not and shall not be deemed to be an employee of the Partnership for any purpose whatsoever. The termination of this Agreement by the Partnership or the expiry of its term without renewal shall not in any circumstances constitute or be deemed to constitute a dismissal for any purposes

7. Authority

The Consultant shall not hold himself out as having power to nor shall he purport to bind the Partnership in any way whatsoever

8. Confidentiality

The Consultant shall not whether during the continuance of this Agreement or thereafter except in the proper course of his duties or as required by law use or divulge to any person, firm or company whatsoever and shall use his best endeavours to prevent the use or disclosure of any information concerning the businesses or finances of the Partnership, transactions or affairs of the Partnership or the names of or secrets of the clients of the Partnership which have or may come to his knowledge during the continuation of this Agreement

9. Outside interests

The Consultant shall not during the continuance of this Agreement be directly or indirectly interested or concerned (other than as a holder for investment purposes only of securities not exceeding 5 per cent in nominal value of the securities of that class) in any capacity or manner whatsoever and whether as principal or agent in any company trade or business without the written permission of the Partnership which shall not be unreasonably withheld

10. Termination by events of default

The Partnership may at any time and without prejudice to any rights or claims it may have against the Consultant by notice in writing terminate this Agreement forthwith and without any liability to pay any remuneration compensation or damages if at any time the Consultant shall:

10.1   be guilty of serious misconduct, commit a material breach of any of the terms of this Agreement or wilfully neglect to perform or (other than as a result of illness accident or other such incapacity) prove to be incapable of performing the Consultant's Duties or

10.2   become bankrupt or compound with his creditors or have any judgment against him which shall remain unsatisfied for more than one month or suffer execution against his effects or

10.3   commit any act of fraud or dishonesty (whether or not connected with the performance of the Consultant's Duties) or

10.4   be prevented as a result of illness, accident or other such incapacity from performing the Consultant's Duties for any period in excess of six consecutive months

10.5   be struck off the Roll of Solicitors or be suspended from practice

10.6   be guilty of any conduct which brings or is likely to bring the Partnership into disrepute in the eyes of the profession or its clients

11. Consultant's obligations upon termination

On the Termination Date the Consultant shall forthwith deliver to the Partnership all records, documents, accounts, letters and papers of every description (whether originals or copies) within his possession or control relating to the affairs and business of the Partnership and any other property belonging to the Partnership.[5]

12. Notices

Any notice:

12.1   shall be in writing
12.2   to be given to the Partnership shall be sufficiently served if either delivered personally to or sent by first class post to its usual trading address for the time being
12.3   to be given to the Consultant shall be sufficiently served if delivered to him personally or sent by first class post to his usual or last known address
12.4   if posted shall be deemed to have been served at the time when in the ordinary course of post such notice would have been received

13. Survival of covenants on termination

Notwithstanding the termination of this Agreement it shall remain in full force and effect insofar as the obligations of the Consultant that are expressed to operate or to have effect thereafter or are of a continuing nature are concerned and may be enforced against the Consultant accordingly

14. General

The provisions of the First and Second Schedules hereto form part of this Agreement which contains the whole of the terms agreed in respect of the Consultant's appointment as from the Commencement Date and is in substitution for any previous agreement or arrangement between the Consultant and the Partnership and shall only be capable of being varied by a supplemental agreement in writing signed by or on behalf of the parties hereto

Signed by
on behalf of the Partnership
and by the Consultant

THE FIRST SCHEDULE

The Consultant's Duties[6]

1.	To provide advice and assistance to the Partnership in connection with any matters relating to the business of the Partnership which the Partnership may refer to him

2.	To conduct the affairs of those clients of the Partnership as shall be referred to him by the Partnership PROVIDED ALWAYS that such matters shall be thin the reasonable sphere of competence and experience of the Consultant

THE SECOND SCHEDULE

Restrictive Covenants[7]

1.	The parties hereto agree and acknowledge as follows:

1.1	it is reasonable and necessary for the protection of the goodwill and trade connections of the Partnership that the Consultant should be restrained in the terms of the covenants hereinafter set out from making available or using for the benefit of himself or a competitor or potential competitor information which he has obtained and is likely to obtain in the course of his engagement as a Consultant to the Partnership and

1.2	after 12 months from the Termination Date the making available or use as aforesaid of the information will be less damaging to the goodwill and trade connections of the business by virtue of all or some parts of the information becoming redundant, non-confidential or out of date

2.	The Consultant accordingly covenants with the Partnership that in view of the circumstances referred to in clause 1 of this Schedule he will not without the prior written consent of the Partnership (such consent to be withheld only so far as may be reasonably necessary to protect the legitimate interests of the Partnership directly or indirectly):

2.1	at any time during a period of 12 months from the date of termination of this agreement by whatever means:

2.1.1	be engaged or concerned or interested or participate in or carry on business as or practise as a solicitor anywhere in England or Wales

2.1.2	solicit or entice in relation to a business which may in any way be in competition with the Partnership the custom of any person who at the date hereof or at any time during the period of 12 months prior to the date of termination of the agreement has been a client of the Partnership

3.   The Consultant hereby acknowledges and agrees with the Partnership that:

    3.1   each of the sub-paragraphs contained in paragraph 2 of this Schedule constitutes an entirely separate, severable and independent covenant by and restriction on him

    3.2   the duration, extent and application of each of the restrictions contained in paragraph 2 are no greater than is necessary for the protection of the goodwill and trade connections of the Partnership

    3.3   if any restriction contained in paragraph 2 shall be found void but would be valid if some part were deleted, such restriction shall apply with such deletion as may be necessary to make it valid and effective

    3.4   each of the covenants set out in paragraph 2 of this Schedule shall (without prejudice to any other rights or remedies of the Partnership) be enforceable by the Partnership against the Consultant by interlocutory injunction

Notes

(1) The agreement is for a self-employed consultant. You or the consultant may prefer the consultant to be an employee depending on the consultant's personal circumstances. The consultant may need to obtain an accountant's advice as to which status is preferable. In any event HMRC may conclude that the nature of the arrangement amounts to a contract of employment. Much will depend on the degree of control that the agreement gives to the firm over the consultant and whether in practice the consultant is free to take work elsewhere.

(2) This provides for a fixed term of two years. A longer term may be specified, or it can be converted into a 'rolling' agreement by adding, 'and thereafter shall continue until determined by either party serving at least six months' notice of termination on the other, unless otherwise determined in accordance with the terms of this agreement'.

(3) If the terms agreed include provision of a car paid for by the partnership it would be convenient to add in the terms as to who pays what. Current tax legislation may make this fiscally unattractive, since if self-employed, the consultant can deduct the cost of providing his own car from his tax bill as an expense.

(4) See note (1).

(5) If the consultant's terms include provision of a car, include here a clause for its return in a good and clean condition.

(6) The precise terms will need to be agreed with the consultant, but it is in the partnership's interests to have the clause reasonably wide. Alternatively, have one clause describing a narrow area which both parties expect to cover the area in which the consultant is expected to be employed and then a saving clause such as, '2. Such other duties as the

Consultant may reasonably be expected to carry out taking into account his particular skills and areas of experience'.

(7) The extent to which it is reasonable to require a consultant to give restrictive covenants at all is debatable. It will depend on the age of the consultant, whether he or she was formerly a partner in the firm and for how long and the likelihood of him or her being able to set up a competing practice and the level of damage thus inflicted. Bear in mind the clause as drafted precludes the consultant from earning a living for a year and a court will require to be satisfied this is reasonable on the facts before allowing it to stand. It may be safer to restrict the proximity to the firm's offices in which the consultant may practise rather than an absolute ban.

Appendix 3

Specimen business plan

Information required	Example plan
1. Name:	M.S.J. Smith Esq.
2. Practising as:	Martin Smith & Co.
3. Business address:	17–21 Shenley Road
	Borehamwood
	Herts WD6 1AD
4. Partnership/Sole trader:	Sole trader
5. Services offered:	The full range of contentious and non-contentious services normally associated with a 'High Street' type of practice. Investment business is not expected to be a major area of operation for the first two years.
6. Business start date:	Proposed start date: 1 December 2012
7. Business objectives:	To establish a wide client base incorporating both private and business clients and to provide a wide range of legal services to satisfy the needs of both. It is anticipated that the client base will initially consist of clients associated with a previous practice and thus outside the locality, with the balance shifting as the new practice becomes known. It is not intended to offer a service to legally aided clients as initially the firm will not have a franchise but merger with a franchised practice within three years is a possible strategy which will be decided at a later stage in the practice's development. Meanwhile the practice base will consist of private paying clients and it is intended that a strong practice will be developed in the field of family law.
8. Capital to be provided:	£30,000 to be introduced by M.S.J. Smith

9. Staff:	Position, Name, Age and Qualifications (if known), Start Date, Salary

1. Part-time Mrs Rachel Smith 01/12/12 Secretary and Book-keeper £5,000.00
2. Trainee Solicitor Paul Humphrey 01/03/12 £12,000.00

Services offered and potential market   Example plan

Services offered: (see Note 1)

Brief details of the services you are to provide should be given together with proposed charging structure (details of individual hourly rates and/or fixed fees).

Your market and potential: (see Note 1)

Indicate your likely clients, where they will come from and their potential.

Other competitors: (see Note 1)

Ascertain who they are likely to be and if possible their strengths and weaknesses together with estimated charges to clients.

Fee income and break-even figure:

Fee income level projected in first year: £42,000

Fee income break-even figure:

(This is equivalent to total overheads of the practice.)
Total overheads: £45,715

Note 1: With a solicitors' practice, this information need not be overly detailed. Bank managers will have a reasonably clear idea of what solicitors do. Show just enough information to demonstrate you have thought about the problems you are likely to face and are not expecting just to put your sign on the door and work to come flooding in.

MONTHLY PROFIT AND LOSS ACCOUNT FORECAST

Notes on budgeted figures

General comments

The budgeted monthly profit and loss account forecast is given purely as a guide and is not intended to account for every eventuality in respect of your practice. Many of the figures given are unrealistic. Every practice is unique and there are almost certain to be additional items that will need to be included in your forecast, and some in the example which you may not need.

The profit and loss account forecast is drawn up on an accruals basis. This means, for example, that rent which is shown in the cash flow forecast as paid on the usual quarter days, is paid in advance for the coming three-month period and, therefore, the cost in respect thereof is spread over those three months. Other items, however, are accounted for as the expenditure is incurred and such items may include motor expenses, periodicals and sundries.

In the forecast, it has been assumed that the practice is VAT-registered and, therefore, budgeted fee income and overhead costs are shown net of VAT

1. Fee income

Estimating fees chargeable throughout the first year, and the timing of the fees, are likely to be the most difficult figures to forecast. Consideration will need to be given to how quickly you expect to start undertaking chargeable work, the length of time that work is likely to take, the actual amount of work involved and when you are likely to be able to charge, possibly on account of final fees. This will depend on the circumstances relating to each individual practice.

In the example, fees are budgeted based on the fee income during the first year of a now well-established practice. As will be seen, initial fees chargeable are low, with peaks and troughs arising thereafter throughout the year, depending upon the timing and completion of the work.

2. Other income

Interest received

Large sums of money may well be held on clients' call accounts and interest received by the practice thereon. This interest is usually received twice yearly, in June and December, and is reflected accordingly in the budget on a receipts basis. The example shows no interest received to simplify the plan.

3. Overheads

Salaries and employment costs

Employment of staff will need to be given careful thought, particularly in relation to the projected level of fee income. In the example, the actual deductions for tax and insurance are either not shown or unrealistic in order to simplify the calculations and are calculated as follows:

(a) First three months:

	Monthly £
Part-time secretary at £5,000 per annum:	
Gross £5,000 ÷ 12	417
Employer's NI at 3.6%	15
Total	**432**

(b) After three months:

It is assumed that due to the increase in work load, the part-time secretary's hours need to be increased and one fee earner is taken on. The figures throughout the remaining nine months will then be:

	Monthly £
Part-time secretary now at £7,500 per annum:	
Gross £7,500 ÷ 12	625
Employer's NI at 5.6%	35
	660
Fee earner at £12,000 per annum:	
Gross £12,000 ÷ 12	1,000
Employer's NI at 10.2%	102
Total	**1,762**

(The employer's NI rate varies according to gross pay and is more complex than the example shows.)

4. Rent and rates

The offices are rented from a firm of accountants that has spare space, and rent and rates are £6,480 per annum, i.e. £1,620 per quarter, and are invoiced and payable on the usual quarter days in advance. However, for the purposes of the profit and loss account this needs to be spread over the applicable three-month period, giving a budgeted profit and loss account charge of £540 per month.

5. Property insurance

This is assumed to be payable once a year in advance, but in the profit and loss account is spread throughout the year. Insurance can often be paid in instalments throughout the year, although a charge may be made for this option.

6. Light and heat

Electricity and gas charges are often billed quarterly in arrears. The likely charge for each quarter needs to be spread over the appropriate three months and it needs to be borne in mind that charges are likely to be higher for the winter months than the summer months.

7. Property repairs

The occurrence of repairs will depend upon the condition of the property occupied and any budgeted figures will need to take this into account.

8. Equipment rental

Photocopier and other equipment rental totalling £450 is assumed to be payable quarterly in advance and is, therefore, spread over the applicable months at £150 per month. In addition, depending upon the type of agreement, there may be a maintenance charge payable depending upon machine usage.

9. Equipment maintenance

This will depend upon the condition of the equipment purchased and whether it is covered by guarantees. It may be in respect of equipment such as dictating machines, computers, faxes but this does need to be considered. A figure of £192 per annum, i.e. £16 per month, is used as an example.

10. Printing, postage and stationery

There will be some hefty expenditure incurred on set up, which in the example is made up as follows:

		£
(a)	Cost of setting up and printing 1,000 letterheads	225
(b)	Additional stationery: File covers and correspondence files Counsel's notebooks Copy paper for printer, photocopier, etc. Envelopes, pens, etc.	210
(c)	Document exchange joining fee, box charge and minimum usage charge	860
(d)	Postage stamps (three months' worth)	285
(e)	Law stationery forms (wide range of commonly used forms sufficient for three/six months)	200
(f)	50 interview/attendance note pads	90
(g)	Manual accounts system	740
Total		**2,610**

Throughout the year there will be odd bits and pieces of stationery required month by month. Every once in a while, items such as letterheads will need to be re-ordered.

11. Law library and books

On set up, there is likely to be substantial expenditure incurred, depending upon what you feel is essential as far as your own library is concerned. Thereafter, the expenditure may be minimal month by month, but again this will depend upon what you think you require.

12. Periodicals

Expenditure on newspapers and magazines, etc. is optional rather than necessary. You may wish to provide some reading material in your reception area for your clients while they are waiting to see you.

13. Advertising

As little or as much can be spent on advertising as you feel is required. It may be that you will want a concerted advertising campaign in the first month or two, and then you will just take a small advertising box in the local press each month, and from time to time depending on how the work is coming in have a more determined effort. For the long term you will need a properly thought out campaign involving entries in yearly directories.

14. Telephone

There will be initial connection charges to account for in setting up the telephone line and system. In the example £1,500 is assumed for this on the basis that a second-hand board is chosen rather than a rented system. Thereafter, the usual quarterly rental and call charges are likely to increase as the practice expands.

15. Motor expenses

Motor road fund tax and insurance is assumed to be accounted for in the first month. There will then be monthly running expenses, particularly fuel and oil, and depending upon the age and condition of the vehicle servicing and repair costs from time to time.

16. Accountancy

It has been assumed that a fee of £2,400 will be chargeable for preparation of the first year's accounts and reporting on those accounts in accordance with the Solicitors' Accounts Rules.

17. Subscriptions

Membership of the Law Society is free of charge. No other subscriptions have been assumed in this example.

18. Professional indemnity

An amount of £4,000 is assumed to be payable in advance as the premium to the insurer for the first year's PI cover. Many insurers will allow the premium to be paid by way of monthly instalments with a financing charge added, but see **Chapter 4** and **Appendix 4** for the basis on which a practice will be assessed and the importance of finding out at any early stage what the level of premium will be.

19. Bad debts

It is assumed that the collection of fees charged is well controlled, often with funds being provided by the client and held on clients' call account before the work is actually undertaken. While there is bound to be some experience of bad debts, for the sake of simplicity, this has been omitted from the example.

20. Sundry expenses

There are bound to be items not budgeted for above which crop up from time to time and it is usual to provide a figure month by month for such eventualities. The amount provided will depend upon how detailed you have already been in breaking down your overhead expenditure.

21. Depreciation

It is assumed that the furniture and office equipment are acquired on commencement of the practice and that no further assets are acquired or any assets disposed of during the rest of the first year. The motor vehicle is assumed to be owned by the proprietor and brought into the practice at its market value.

Details of the assets on set up are shown on the attached schedule together with depreciation rates and the calculations thereof.

Depreciation policy is a matter to be determined by each practice and would often be determined in discussions with the firm's accountants. The rates given in the example are therefore not necessarily the correct rates to use for your practice, but are merely an example of rates that could be used in suitable circumstances.

Fixed assets

Office furniture

No.	Description	£
4	4–drawer filing cabinet	400
5	Desks (second-hand)	300
2	Secretaries'/typists' chairs	60
1	Principal's chair	180

2	Client chairs	100
2	Fee earners' chairs	170
2	Storage cupboards for stationery	300
	Total	**1,510**

Depreciation Suggested rate: 10% on cost

Depreciation first year £1,510 10%	151
Monthly budgeted figure £151 ÷ 12	13

Office equipment

No.	Description	£
1	Copier/scanner	275
2	Word processing system: monitor with hard disk, keyboard, printer and Windows software	1,500
3	Fax machine	250
4	Dictating machines/transcribers with ancillary equipment (microphone/foot pedals/headsets, etc.)	1,234
	Total	**3,259**

Depreciation Suggested rate: 20% on cost

Depreciation first year £3,259 20% (actual figure is £651 but called £648 to eliminate fractions)	648
Monthly budgeted figure £648 ÷ 12	54

Motor vehicle

No.	Description	£
1	Second-hand Vauxhall Zafira 1.6 Elegance reg. no. MS 123	10,000

Depreciation Suggested rate: 25% on cost

Depreciation first year £10,000 25%	2,500
Monthly budgeted figure £2,500 ÷ 12	208

22. Net profit (loss)

After much careful consideration in order to produce these figures, the forecast will now show month by month whether you will be making a profit or a loss, together with an overall figure for the first year.

The example shows that the practice has in fact come out with a small loss of £3,715 for the year. The actual figure in respect of the practice on which this budget is based showed a somewhat larger loss for the first year, but is now well established and has since been trading profitably. You should, therefore, not become too concerned if the first year shows a small loss or little profit, as there are inevitable one-off set-up costs to be accounted for in the first year. The most important thing is to be objective in your forecasts and realistic about the figures used, especially in respect of the budgeted fee income.

MONTHLY CASH FLOW FORECAST

Notes on budgeted figures

General comments

Having produced a monthly profit and loss account forecast, the next stage is to produce a monthly cash flow forecast.

The figures shown in the cash flow forecast, although related to the figures given in the profit and loss account forecast, will not correlate on a month-by-month basis. This is due to the timing of cash inflows and outflows usually being quite different from fee invoices raised and expenses invoices received as shown in the profit and loss account forecast.

Various assumptions have to be made in producing the cash flow forecast and for the purposes of the example given those assumptions have been greatly simplified. For example, all fee income shown in the profit and loss account forecast is assumed to be collected together with the applicable VAT thereon, one month later. In reality, some of the fees may be collected during the month billed, some may be collected one, two or three, etc. months later.

VAT has been added to the fee income collected and similarly, where applicable, added to the overhead expenditure incurred.

(1) *Fee income (including vat)*

As mentioned above, fee income is assumed to be collected in the month following billing. No cash is assumed to be received in respect of the fee income although in practice you may receive some cash. The table below shows how the collection of fee income, as debtors, is calculated from the fee income figures forecast in the profit and loss account. The VAT rate is shown at the old rate of 17.5%. Most practices will be 'VAT neutral', paying out what they have collected in, and so the VAT percentage only affects cashflow whatever the particular rate may be.

Cash received

Profit and Loss Account

Month	VAT re Net debtors £	Debtors at 17.5% £	Total £	Cash flow month
0	–	–	–	1
1	1,000	175.00	1,175.00	2
2	2,000	350.00	2,350.00	3
3	2,750	481.25	3,231.25	4
4	2,000	350.00	2,350.00	5
5	5,500	962.50	6,462.50	6
6	6,750	1,181.25	7,931.25	7
7	4,000	700.00	4,700.00	8
8	6,500	1,137.50	7,637.50	9

Month	VAT re Net debtors £	Debtors at 17.5% £	Total £	Cash flow month
9	3,350	586.25	3,936.25	10
10	3,000	525.00	3,525.00	11
11	3,500	612.50	4,112.50	12
12	1,650	288.75	1938.75	Y/E Debtors
	42,000	**7,350.00**	**49,350.00**	

Other receipts

(2) *Capital introduced*

It is assumed in this example that £30,000 of the proprietor's own capital is introduced into the business as cash. It is also assumed that the proprietor already owned the motor vehicle introduced into the business. This has a market value of £10,000 and the proprietor will be given credit for the value of this vehicle in his capital account on the balance sheet. Therefore, the balance sheet will show total capital introduced of £40,000, being cash introduced of £30,000 and the market value of the motor vehicle introduced being £10,000.

(3) *Loans received*

If you are unable to introduce sufficient cash of your own in order to set the business up, you may need to borrow money, possibly from a bank or perhaps a relative or friend or some other lending source.

(4) *Disposals of assets*

No fixed assets have been disposed of in this example during the first year, but any cash received in respect of any such disposals would need to be shown here.

(5) *Interest received*

Interest will probably be received twice yearly, in June and December, in respect of monies held on client call accounts but has been removed from the cash flow and profit and loss forecasts to simplify them.

Payments

(6) *Drawings*

It is assumed that the proprietor draws a regular monthly sum of £1,500. However, in practice this may not be achievable and the proprietor's drawings will fluctuate from month to month, depending upon the practice cash flow month by month.

An essential exercise to carry out is to review your own personal expenditure and commitments in order to establish the level of drawings you require on a monthly basis to fund your personal lifestyle. This will be a vital consideration to bear in mind in considering the viability of your proposed business.

(7), (8) Salaries (net) and PAYE/NIC

Salaries are usually paid at or towards the end of the month during which the staff are employed. The calculations detailed below give a net pay figure but do not take account of actual tax and PAYE/NIC payable. The relevant rates and allowances for the year in question will need to be added to the calculations. Some deductions are made to provide realism.

(a) First three months:

		Monthly £
Gross salary		417.00
Net pay		369.26
Employer's NIC		15.00
Summary:	Net pay	369.26
	Add NIC	15.00
Total employer's cost		**432.00**

(b) After three months:

		Secretary Monthly £	Fee earner Monthly £
Gross salary		625.00	1,000.00
Net pay		510.51	754.16
Employer's NIC		35.00	102.10
Summary:	Net pay of both employees	1,264.67	
	Add NIC	497.43	
Total employer's cost		**1,762.10**	

(9) Fixed assets

Fixed assets are assumed to be bought and paid for in the first month as follows (as per fixed assets schedule).

	£
Office furniture	1,510
Office equipment	3,259
Subtotal	4,769
VAT @ 17.5%	834
Total	**5,603**

As mentioned above, it is assumed that the motor vehicle was owned by the proprietor and that this was introduced into the business at market value, therefore giving rise to no effect on the cash flow forecast. Also, if it is decided to buy rather than lease items such as a switchboard or photocopier, adjustments will need to be made to the schedules and the costings plan.

(10) *Rent and rates*

Rent and rates of £1,620 are assumed to be paid on the usual quarter days, with an additional amount of £450 being paid for the first 25 days of December.

(11) *Property insurance*

This is assumed to be payable once a year in advance in the first month.

(12) *Light and heat*

It is assumed that light and heat is payable quarterly in arrears, with VAT being accounted for as follows:

	Net £	VAT £	Total £
February	135.00	23.62	158.62
May	110.00	19.25	129.25
August	90.00	15.75	105.75
November	105.00	18.38	123.38
	440.00	**77.00**	**517.00**

(13) *Property repairs*

These are assumed to be payable one month after the invoice is received as follows:

	Net £	VAT £	Total £
April	100.00	17.50	117.50
August	100.00	17.50	117.50
	200.00	**35.00**	**235.00**

(14) *Equipment rental*

The rental of £450 net in respect of the photocopier is assumed to be payable quarterly in advance as follows:

	Net £	VAT £	Total £
December	450.00	78.75	528.75
March	450.00	78.75	528.75
June	450.00	78.75	528.75
September	450.00	78.75	528.75
	1,800.00	**315.00**	**2,115.00**

(15) *Equipment maintenance*

A charge of £192 annually in respect of the service contract for the fax is payable yearly in advance as follows:

	Net £	VAT £	Total £
December	192.00	33.60	225.60

(16) *Printing, postage and stationery*

It is assumed that printing and stationery is payable one month after receipt of invoice as follows:

	Net £	VAT £	Total £
December	185.00	–	185.00
January	1,475.00	249.38	1,724.38
February	65.00	2.63	67.63
March	65.00	2.62	67.62
April	215.00	28.87	243.87
May	65.00	2.63	67.63
June	65.00	2.62	67.62
July	65.00	2.63	67.63
August	215.00	28.88	243.88
September	65.00	2.62	67.62
October	65.00	2.63	67.63
Y/E creditor	230.00	31.49	261.49
	2,775.00	**357.00**	**3,132.00**

(17) *Law library and books*

Publications for the law library and books are assumed to be payable one month after the invoice is received. It should be noted that no VAT is chargeable on publications and books.

(18) *Advertising*

Advertising is assumed to be payable one month after the invoice is received as follows:

Cash flow month	Net £	VAT £	Total £
December	–	–	–
January	250.00	43.75	293.75
February	200.00	35.00	235.00
March	50.00	8.75	58.75
April	50.00	8.75	58.75
May	50.00	8.75	58.75
June	200.00	35.00	235.00

Cash flow month	Net £	VAT £	Total £
July	50.00	8.75	58.75
August	50.00	8.75	58.75
September	50.00	8.75	58.75
October	50.00	8.75	58.75
November	200.00	35.00	235.00
	1,200.00	**210.00**	**1,410.00**

(19) Telephone

The initial connection charges of £440 plus VAT are assumed to be invoiced and payable in December.

Thereafter, the usual quarterly rental and call charges are assumed to be invoiced quarterly in arrears and payable in the month the invoice is received as follows:

	Cash flow month	Net £	VAT £	Total £
(Connection charge)	December	440.00	77.00	517.00
	March	360.00	63.00	423.00
	June	525.00	91.88	616.88
	September	675.00	118.13	793.13
	Y/E creditor	825.00	144.37	969.37
		2,825.00	**494.38**	**3,319.38**

(20) Motor expenses

Motor expenses are assumed to be incurred and paid for in the same month and, for the cash flow forecast, are calculated as follows:

	Net £	VAT £	Total £	Memo – Tax & ins.
December	425.00	73.37	499.37	325.00
January	100.00	17.50	117.50	
February	100.00	17.50	117.50	
March	100.00	17.50	117.50	
April	100.00	17.50	117.50	
May	250.00	43.75	293.75	
June	100.00	17.50	117.50	
July	100.00	17.50	117.50	
August	100.00	17.50	117.50	
September	100.00	17.50	117.50	
October	100.00	17.50	117.50	
November	100.00	17.50	117.50	
	1,675.00	**292.12**	**1,968.12**	

No VAT is payable on car tax and car insurance.

(21) *Accountancy*

A provision of £200 per month has been shown in the profit and loss account forecast to give a total fee of £2,400 in respect of preparation of the first year's accounts and reporting thereon. It is assumed that all this work is carried out early on in the second year of the business, invoiced once the work is completed and the fee then payable, together with VAT thereon, sometime soon after the invoice date. Therefore, nothing is reflected in the cash flow forecast for the first year of business.

(22) *Subscriptions*

No subscriptions have been assumed in the profit and loss account forecast and, therefore, there is nothing to enter in the cash flow forecast.

(23) *Professional indemnity insurance premium*

An amount of £4,000 is assumed to be payable in advance, during December, in respect of the first year.

(24) *Bad debts*

Any adjustment in respect of expected bad debts would usually be shown by deducting the appropriate amounts from the forecast debtor collections. However, rather than complicate this forecast with bad debts, the amounts budgeted for in the profit and loss account forecast have been deliberately left out.

(25) *Petty cash (sundry expenses/periodicals)*

Sundry expenses and periodicals are assumed to be paid for in cash, being incurred as shown in the profit and loss account forecast. VAT is assumed to be payable on the sundry expenses of £50 per month, but no VAT would be payable on periodicals. The figures are calculated as follows:

	Net £	VAT £	Total £	Memo Non VAT
December	70.00	8.75	78.75	20.00
January	70.00	8.75	78.75	20.00
February	70.00	8.75	78.75	20.00
March	70.00	8.75	78.75	20.00
April	70.00	8.75	78.75	20.00
May	70.00	8.75	78.75	20.00
June	70.00	8.75	78.75	20.00
July	70.00	8.75	78.75	20.00
August	70.00	8.75	78.75	20.00
September	70.00	8.75	78.75	20.00
October	70.00	8.75	78.75	20.00
November	70.00	8.75	78.75	20.00
	840.00	**105.00**	**945.00**	**240.00**

(26) *Vat*

VAT is accountable to HMRC, usually on a quarterly basis and often arranged in line with the business year end. The VAT payable or repayable, as the case may be, is due one month after the quarterly VAT accounting period.

The VAT figures, due on fee income and reclaimable on expenditure, have been assembled from the work already carried out in respect of the cash flow forecast. Details of how the quarterly figures have been arrived at are shown on the attached VAT schedule.

It will be seen that VAT of £459 is repayable by HMRC in respect of the first VAT quarter to the end of February. This is not an unusual situation for the first quarter, as very often there will be some one-off large expenditures in respect of items such as fixed assets, telephone connection charges and printing and stationery set-up costs. At the same time, it is likely that fees invoiced for the first few months will be low.

Cash flow review

A. Total receipts:

The total receipts are shown month by month together with the total receipts for the year.

B. Total payments:

The total payments are shown month by month together with the total payments for the year.

C. Net cash flow (A – B):

This shows the net cash inflow or outflow month by month together with the total net cash inflow or outflow for the year, being a net cash inflow of £9,142.

D. Opening bank balance:

This gives the closing bank balance brought forward from the previous month. The total column shows a nil balance brought forward, which was the position at the start of the year prior to opening the bank account.

E. Closing bank balance (C/Line 27):

This gives the closing bank balance at the end of each month. As will be seen from the forecast, there is a healthy bank balance at the end of each month, which indicates that, with capital introduced of £30,000 at the start of the business, the business will have no cash flow difficulties throughout the first year. However, this does assume that actual cash receipts come in as budgeted and that there is no unforeseen additional expenditure.

The 'total' column shows a closing bank balance, at the end of the first year, of £9,142 and this ties in with the bank balance at the end of November. These two figures should be identical and this acts as a cross-check that no calculation errors have been made in the cash flow forecast.

Actual figures

When the business commences, the actual cash receipts and payments can be recorded month by month on the cash flow forecast and compared to the budgeted figures. This will enable the cash flow to be monitored each month and will be an indication of whether any problems are starting to come to light as regards the cash liquidity of the business.

Business premises

Details should be given of the proposed business premises. This should indicate whether they are freehold or leasehold, together with size in square feet.

If freehold, show the value of the property, giving the basis and date of valuation. Show the mortgage outstanding together with the name of the mortgagee, if applicable.

Give details of the rates payable.

If leasehold, indicate the lease terms together with the annual rental and rent review dates.

Example: A firm of accountants, operating in the High Street, have office space surplus to their requirements. Therefore, a sub-lease is to be taken out with these accountants to obtain 500 sq. ft of office space on a leasehold basis.

The annual rent payable, inclusive of rates, will be £6,480. The premises are to be leased for a period of 10 years initially, with a rent review after the end of the fifth year.

The firm is to be charged for light and heat, property insurance and internal and external repairs on a proportionate basis, being a ratio of 500 sq. ft out of a total of 3,000 sq. ft.

Office furniture

Office equipment

Motor vehicles

Details should be given of the office furniture, office equipment and motor vehicles to be acquired by the business, giving a brief description of each item, the number required and the anticipated cost.

Example: Details of the office furniture, office equipment and motor vehicles required by the business are given on the fixed assets schedule which accompanies the monthly profit and loss account forecast.

Assets available as security

If any assets are available to be given as security against a mortgage or loan, details of those assets should be given together with a valuation, including the basis and date thereof. A note should also be made as to whether these are business or personal assets.

Example: The business is to be financed entirely out of the proprietor's capital savings and, therefore, this section is not applicable.

Financial requirements

Details should be given of how the business is to be financed and whether this is to be provided from own resources, bank overdraft, bank loan or some other form of finance.

Example: The proprietor is to finance the business with £30,000 cash from his savings. In addition, the proprietor is to introduce his existing personal car into the business. The market value of this car at the commencement of business is £10,000.

In total, the proprietor has introduced £40,000 into the business and this will ensure, as can be seen from the cash flow forecast, that the business is self-financing. This will save on bank charges and interest that would otherwise be incurred were the business to operate and make use of a bank overdraft facility.

MARTIN SMITH AND CO
VAT ADDED TAX

	Dec £	Jan £	Feb £	Mar £	Apr £	May £	Jun £	Jul £	Aug £	Sep £	Oct £	Nov £
OUTPUT TAX												
Fee Income	175.00	350.00	481.25	350.00	962.50	1,181.25	700.00	1,137.50	586.25	525.00	612.50	288.75
Other												
TOTAL OUTPUT TAX	175.00	350.00	481.25	350.00	962.50	1,181.25	700.00	1,137.50	586.25	525.00	612.50	288.75
INPUT VAT												
Fixed Assets	834.00											
Light and Heat			23.62			19.25			15.75			18.38
Property Repairs					117.50				117.50			
Equipment Rental	78.75			78.75			78.75			78.75		
Equipment Maintenance	33.60											
Postage and Stationery	43.75	249.38	2.63	2.62	28.87	2.63	2.62	2.63	28.88	2.63	2.62	31.49
Advertising		35.00	8.75	8.75	8.75	35.00	8.75	8.75	8.75	8.75	35.00	8.75
Telephone	77.00			63.00			91.88			118.13		
Accountancy												
Motor Expenses	17.50	17.50	17.50	17.50	17.50	43.75	17.50	17.50	17.50	17.50	17.50	17.50
Petty Cash (Sundry Expenses)	8.75	8.75	8.75	8.75	8.75	8.75	8.75	8.75	8.75	8.75	8.75	8.75
TOTAL INPUT VAT	1,093.35	310.63	61.25	179.37	181.37	109.38	208.25	37.63	197.13	234.51	63.87	84.87
VAT PAYABLE/ REPAYABLE	(918.35)	39.37	420.00	170.63	781.13	1,071.87	491.75	1,099.87	389.12	290.49	548.63	203.88
QUARTERLY RETURN FIGURE			(458.98)			2,023.63			1,980.74			1,043.00
MONTH VAT PAYABLE/REPAYABLE				(458.98)			2,023.63			1,980.74		

MONTHLY PROFIT AND LOSS FORECAST

	Dec		Jan		Feb		Mar		Apr		May		Jun		Jul		Aug		Sep		Oct		Nov		Total
	Actual	Budget	Actual	Budget	Actual	Budget	Actual	Budget	Actual	Budget	Actual	Budget	Actual	Budget	Actual	Budget	Actual	Budget	Actual	Budget	Actual	Budget	Actual	Budget	Budget
FEE INCOME		1,000		2,000		2,750		2,000		5,500		6,750		4,000		6,500		3,350		3,000		3,500		1,650	**42,000**
OTHER INCOME																									
Interest																								–	–
TOTAL INCOME		1,000		2,000		2,750		2,000		5,500		6,750		4,000		6,500		3,350		3,000		3,500		1,650	**42,000**
OVERHEADS																									
Salaries and Employment Costs		432		432		432		1,762		1,762		1,762		1,762		1,762		1,762		1,762		1,762		1,762	**17,154**
Rent and Rates		540		540		540		540		540		540		540		540		540		540		540		540	**6,480**
Property Insurance		12		12		12		12		12		12		12		12		12		12		12		12	**144**
Light and Heat		45		45		45		37		37		36		30		30		30		35		35		35	**440**
Property Repairs										100								100							**200**
Equipment Rental		150		150		150		150		150		150		150		150		150		150		150		150	**1,800**
Equipment Maintenance		16		16		16		16		16		16		16		16		16		16		16		16	**192**
Printing, Postage and Stationery		185		1,475		65		65		215		65		65		65		215		65		65		65	**2,610**
Law Library and Books		500		30		30		30		30		30		30		30		30		30		30		30	**830**
Periodicals		250		200		50		50		50		200		50		50		50		50		200		50	**1,250**
Advertising		440		120		120		120		175		175		175		225		225		225		200		200	**2,400**
Telephone		425		100		100		100		100		250		100		100		100		100		100		100	**1,675**
Motor Expenses		200		200		200		200		200		200		200		200		200		200		200		200	**2,400**
Accountancy																									
Subscriptions																									
Professional																									
Insurances		333		333		334		333		333		334		333		333		334		333		333		334	**4,000**
Bad Debts																									
Sundry Expenses		70		70		70		70		70		70		70		70		70		70		70		70	**840**
Depreciation																									
Fixtures and Fittings		13		13		13		13		13		13		13		13		13		13		13		13	**156**
Office Equipment		54		54		54		54		54		54		54		54		54		54		54		54	**648**
Motor Vehicles		208		208		208		208		208		208		208		208		208		208		208		208	**2,496**
TOTAL OVERHEADS		3,873		3,998		2,439		3,760		4,065		4,115		3,808		3,858		4,109		3,863		3,988		3,839	**45,715**
NET PROFIT/(LOSS)		(2,873)		(1,998)		311		(1,760)		1,435		2,635		192		2,642		(759)		(863)		(488)		(2,189)	**(3,715)**

MARTIN SMITH AND CO
MONTHLY CASHFLOW FORECAST

	Dec Actual	Dec Budget	Jan Actual	Jan Budget	Feb Actual	Feb Budget	Mar Actual	Mar Budget	Apr Actual	Apr Budget	May Actual	May Budget	Jun Actual	Jun Budget	Jul Actual	Jul Budget	Aug Actual	Aug Budget	Sep Actual	Sep Budget	Oct Actual	Oct Budget	Nov Actual	Nov Budget	Total Budget
RECEIPTS																									
Fee Income (including VAT)																									
Debtors				1,175		2,350		3,232		2,350		6,463		7,931		4,700		7,638		3,937		3,525		4,113	47,414
Cash																									–
Capital introduced		30,000																							30,000
Loan Received																									–
Disposal of Assets																									–
Interest																									–
VAT Refund								459																	459
TOTAL RECEIPTS (A)		30,000		1,175		2,350		3,691		2,350		6,463		7,931		4,700		7,638		3,937		3,525		4,113	77,873
PAYMENTS																									
Drawings		1,500		1,500		1,500		1,500		1,500		1,500		1,500		1,500		1,500		1,500		1,500		1,500	18,000
Salaries (net)		369		369		369		1,265		1,265		1,265		1,265		1,265		1,265		1,265		1,265		1,265	12,492
PAYE/NIC				63		63		63		497		497		497		497		497		497		497		497	4,165
Fixed Assets		5,603																							5,603
Rent and Rates		2,070						1,620						1,620						1,620					6,930
Property Insurance		144																							144
Light and Heat						159						129						106						123	517
Property Repairs										117								118							235
Equipment Rental		529						529						529						529					2,116
Equipment Maintenance		226																							226
Printing, Postage and Stationery				185		1,724		68		68		244		68		68		68		244		68		68	2,873
Law Library and Books				500		30		30		30		30		30		30		30		30		30		30	800
Advertising				293		235		59		59		59		235		59		59		59		59		235	1,411
Telephone		517						423						617						793					2,350
Motor Expenses		442		118		118		118		118		294		118		118		118		118		118		118	1,916
Accountancy																									
Subscriptions																									
Professional Insurances		4,000																							4,000
Bad Debts																									
Petty Cash (Sundry Expenses/Periodicals)		79		79		79		79		79		79		79		79		79		79		79		79	948
VAT														2,024						1,981					4,005
TOTAL PAYMENTS (B)		15,479		3,107		4,277		5,754		3,733		4,097		8,582		3,616		3,840		8,715		3,616		3,915	68,731
NET CASH FLOW (A – B)		14,521		(1,932)		(1,927)		(2,063)		(1,383)		2,366		(651)		1,084		3,798		(4,778)		(91)		198	9,142
Opening Balance Brought Forward		–		14,521		12,589		10,662		8,599		7,216		9,582		8,931		10,015		13,813		9,035		8,944	–
Closing Balance Carried Forward		14,521		12,589		10,662		8,599		7,216		9,582		8,931		10,015		13,813		9,035		8,944		9,142	9,142

Appendix 4

Typical costing plan for setting up a small practice

Item	Cost (a, b)
Rent for 3 months	1,620
Office space for:	
1 principal, 1–2 fee earners and general office for 2 secretaries	
34.37 m² (370 sq. ft) and business rates and share of bills in shared	
offices (This does not allow for a waiting area and is the absolute	
minimum required – 46.45 m² (500 sq. ft) would be more realistic.)	
4 x 4-drawer filing cabinets	400
5 desks (second-hand)	300
2 secretaries'/typists' chairs	60
1 principal's chair	180
2 client chairs	100
2 fee earners' chairs	170
2 storage cupboards for stationery	300
1 desktop copier/scanner	275
2-terminal word processing system monitor with 500 GB hard disk,	
keyboard, laser printer + Windows software (c, d, e)	
(See specimen system in **Chapter 7**.)	1,686
1 fax machine (f)	100
One quarter's telephone line rental for fax and connection charge and	
call charges	190
Second-hand telephone system with 4 lines, switchboard and 5	
extensions (g)	
One quarter's rental + connection charge (outright purchase)	2,000
One principal's private telephone line + telephone	
(incl. connection charge, first 3 months' charges + purchase	
of handset)	235
Cost of setting up and printing 1,000 letterheads	400
Additional stationery:	
file covers and correspondence files, counsel's notebooks	
copy paper for printer, photocopier, etc.	
typewriter ribbons/envelopes/pens, etc.	210
3 months' rental of photocopier (h)	150
1 year membership of document exchange (one-off joining fee of £250,	
annual box charge £260, plus minimum estimated usage charge £350) (i)	860
3 months' worth postage stamps	285
4 dictating machines/transcribers, ancillary equipment (microphones/	
footpedals/headsets, etc.) (j)	1,234
Professional indemnity insurance premium (k)	4,000

Law stationery forms (wide range of commonly used forms, sufficient for 3–6 months)	500
50 interview/attendance note pads	90
Total	**15,345**

Notes

(a)   All figures are approximate. The object of the exercise is to give you some idea of what your initial set-up costs are likely to be. Depending on your budget, you may wish to be more lavish or frugal, but this gives you a baseline figure to work from. There will undoubtedly be items you can omit and others you must add, depending on scale of operation and your priorities. Use the plan as a basic shopping list and add or subtract to suit your own circumstances. If you have all the items in the plan when you open, you will at least be able to operate some kind of service. Allow a margin for error, so in the above example, assume set-up costs of £15,000 to £20,000 plus staff expenses.

(b)   All prices are exclusive of VAT. VAT will be payable at point of sale and so the money must be found initially, but you will be able to reclaim it in your first VAT quarter.

(c)   You may wish to have a facility at home so that either you or your spouse or both (if your spouse is employed in the business) can work from home. This will be especially useful during school holidays if you have young children, or if you need to get something done urgently out of hours. If you opt for this facility, allow for a proportion of the set-up costs, depending on how extensive a home facility is required.

(d)   There is no point now in buying second-hand computer equipment or printers. Today's machines are cheap, reliable and powerful.

(e)   Printers come in a variety of shapes and sizes (see **Chapter 7** for more detailed information on printers). *Inkjet* printers are quiet and produce a high quality product but not as good as a laser printer and are slower. They are a little cheaper than laser printers. *Laser printers* are the quietest, highest quality, a little more expensive and the fastest. They start at around £90 plus VAT, as opposed to £65 for an inkjet, so unless you are likely to have a constant need for a colour facility you are likely to opt for a laser printer.

(f)   Fax machines can vary in price and sophistication. They start from as little as £50. You could start by buying a cheap machine for the office and then after six to nine months take it home and upgrade to a more expensive machine for the office.

(g)   Substantial savings can be made on telephone systems. I would advise against too small a system. Too many sole or small practices set up with one or two telephone lines. As with other equipment, the decision to upgrade is constantly deferred. Clients who cannot get through are unlikely to return calls. If you expand the practice, you will be busy – possibly too busy – to get around to inspecting other telephone systems and unwilling to undergo the disruption caused by implementing a new system. Build a certain amount of expansion into your system from the start, hence five extensions when two are probably sufficient for immediate needs. Line connection charges are about £99 per line (so a three-line switchboard's connection charge would be £297) and are a one-off charge. Line rental charges are about £40 per quarter. When calculating yearly expenses, deduct the connection charge and add £160 annual rental and estimated call charges.

(h) A photocopier is a substantial investment, so a rental arrangement is likely to be the best answer. Alternatively, buy a small machine and take all your high volume copying to a professional copy shop. If you decide to buy instead of rent there are some good deals to be had on reconditioned machines from reputable suppliers. You can buy a reconditioned second-hand photocopier for about £2,000–£3,000.

(i) Document exchange joining fee £250 and box charge £260 per year. Usage charge invoiced six months later, based on level of incoming and outgoing items at approximately 50 per cent of cost of first-class post, subject to minimum charge of £350, entitling you to equivalent usage of £700 postage.

(j) By buying (or leasing) transcribers rather than dictating machines (transcribers can only play back, dictating machines can record *and* play back) you can lower your costs. If, however, the dictating machine breaks down you cannot plunder your secretary's machine to bridge the gap. Always have at least one machine more than you need. Murphy's Law will apply if you do not, and the machine will break down at the time you can least afford it to. Do not forget one or possibly two for home use. These can be your spare machines.

(k) This figure assumes PI insurers will treat the practice as one likely to bill £80,000 in the first year and with no previous adverse claims experience in relation to you or your former partners. If projected fee income is £45,000 the premium is likely to be in the region of £2,500. It is wise to get a written quotation. PI insurers' terms vary widely with some refusing to quote on a small start up practice. Make this one of the first items that you get an estimate for.

Appendix 5

Specimen letters for chasing unpaid bills

Letter 1

Dear Mr Ingrate,

Re: Outstanding account
      Date: 12 September 2012
      Amount: £448.00

My cashiers have reminded me that the above account remains outstanding. I would be most grateful if you would let me have a remittance in the next few days. A further copy of the account is enclosed for ease of reference.

Yours sincerely,

Letter 2

Dear Mr Ingrate,

Re: Outstanding account
      Date: 12 September 2012
      Amount: £448.00

I regret to note that my account is still outstanding despite an earlier reminder. In the circumstances, I would be grateful if you would let me have payment by return. May I remind you that interest is payable on overdue accounts. However, I will waive this requirement if payment is made as requested above. A further copy of the account is enclosed for your use.

Yours sincerely,

Letter 3

TW Ingrate, Esq.

Dear Sir,

Re: **Outstanding account**
       Date: 12 September 2012
       Amount: £448.00

We regret to note that the above account remains unpaid despite earlier reminders. We must inform you that unless this sum is paid to us within seven days from the date of this letter, together with interest of £*[amount]* making a total of £*[amount]*, proceedings for the recovery of the amount of the invoice, interest and costs are liable to be commenced against you without further notice.

Yours faithfully,

Appendix 6

Specimen claim form

Claim Form

In the Even Handed County Court	
Claim No.	

Claimant

Greed Strange & Partners (suing as a firm)

SEAL

Defendant(s)

Terence William Ingrate

Brief details of claim

In July 2012 the Claimants acted for the Defendant in their capacity as solicitors. The Defendant has failed to pay the Claimants' invoice for the work done.

Value

less than £5,000

Defendant's name and address	Mr T W Ingrate 1 St Andrew's Crescent HARROW Middlesex HA10 3NK		Amount claimed	448.00
			Court fee	50
			Solicitor's costs	50
			Total amount	548.00
			Issue date	

The court office at

is open between 10 am and 4 pm Monday to Friday. When corresponding with the court, please address forms or letters to the Court Manager and quote the claim number.

N1 Claim form (CPR Part 7) (10.00)   *Printed on behalf of The Court Service*

Claim No.	

Does, or will, your claim include any issues under the Human Rights Act 1998? ☐ Yes ☑ No

Particulars of Claim ~~(attached)(to follow)~~

1. At all material times the Claimants were a firm of solicitors and the Defendant was the Claimants' client. In July 2009 the Defendant instructed the Claimant to act on his behalf in his defence of various prosecutions before the Severe Magistrates' Court. The Claimants duly complied with the defendant's instructions.

2. On 12 September 2012 the Claimants rendered to the defendant an account numbered 523 in the sum of £448.00 (inclusive of VAT) in respect of work carried out. The Defendant has failed to make payment of the sum due.

3. The invoice was endorsed with notice informing the Defendant of his right to have the bill assessed by the Court under the provisions of the Solicitors Act 1974.

4. The Claimants claim interest on the sum owed at 8% per annum pursuant to Section 69 of the County Courts Act 1984.

AND THE CLAIMANTS CLAIM:-

1. The said sum of £448.00.

2. Interest thereon of £6.67 pursuant to Section 69 of the County Courts Act 1984 at 8% from 12 September 2012 to the date hereof being 68 days at the daily rate of £0.98.

3. Costs.

Statement of Truth

*(I believe)~~(The Claimant believes)~~ that the facts stated in these particulars of claim are true.
* ~~I am duly authorised by the claimant to sign this statement~~

Full name ___RAYMOND GREED___

Name of claimant's solicitor's firm _____

signed ___Raymond Greed___   position or office held ___Partner___
*(Claimant)~~(Litigation friend)(Claimant's solicitor)~~   (if signing on behalf of firm or company)

*delete as appropriate

Greed Strange & Partners
1 Crooks Corner
LONDON WC2

Tel 020 8666 6666
Fax 020 8777 7777

LDE 8888

Claimant's or claimant's solicitor's address to which documents or payments should be sent if different from overleaf including (if appropriate) details of DX, fax or e-mail.

Appendix 7

Specimen particulars of claim

IN THE EVEN HANDED COUNTY COURT

Case No.

BETWEEN: GREED STRANGE & PARTNERS (suing as a firm)

Claimants

– and –

TERENCE WILLIAM INGRATE

Defendant

Particulars of claim

1.   At all material times the Claimants were a firm of solicitors and the Defendant was the Claimants' client. In July 2012 the Defendant instructed the Claimants to act on his behalf in his defence of various prosecutions before The Severe Magistrates' Court. The Claimants duly complied with the Defendant's instructions.

2.   On 12 September 2012 the Claimants rendered to the Defendant an account numbered 523 in the sum of £448.00 (inclusive of VAT) in respect of the work carried out. The Defendant has failed to make payment of the sum due.

3.   The invoice was endorsed with a notice informing the Defendant of his right to have the bill assessed by the Court under the provisions of the Solicitors Act 1974.[1]

4.   The Claimants claim interest on the sum owed at 8 per cent per annum pursuant to Section 69 of the County Courts Act 1984.

And the claimants claim:

1.   The said sum of £448.00[(2)]
2.   Interest thereon of £6.67 pursuant to Section 69 of the County Courts Act 1984 at 8 per cent from 12 September 2012 to the date hereof being 68 days at a daily rate of £0.98.
3.   Costs.

Dated this 19th day of November 2012

GREED STRANGE & PARTNERS
1 Crooks Corner
LondonWC2
who will accept service of
proceedings herein at the
above address

To the District Judge of the Court
and to the Defendant

Notes

(1)   This notice is not a requirement in relation to contentious business. In the case of a non-contentious bill the right to require the claimant to obtain a certificate of fair remuneration before the bill can be sued on has been abolished, as has the fair remuneration procedure itself from 11 August 2009. The right of the client to be notified as to the charging of interest and the right to have the bill assessed are still requirements to be satisfied before proceedings on the bill can be brought. In any event Chapter 1, outcome 1.14 of the SRA Code of Conduct 2011 requires you to inform a client of their right to challenge or complain about your bill and the circumstances in which they may be liable to pay interest. The perfect place to do this is on the bill itself, although you should also have done this in your client care letter.

(2)   If the amount adjudged to be due is more than £5,000 you are entitled to interest on the judgment debt, in which case add as paragraphs 3 and 4:

3.   Interest on £[amount] as aforesaid at 8 per cent from the date hereof until judgment or sooner payment at a daily rate of £[amount].
4.   Costs.

Note: The sum to be inserted is the amount of the invoice, not the aggregate of the invoice total and the interest to date, i.e. you cannot claim interest on interest. In addition, the claim will now need to be issued in the National Civil Business Centre in Salford and not in your or the defendant's local county court.

Appendix 8

Software packages and services for law firms

The Law Society has until recently produced an annually updated publication *Software Solutions: A guide to integrated practice management software* for solicitors' practices lacking their own in-house IT resources, which covered accounts, practice management and case management products and services.

The 2008 edition featured 15 suppliers that passed a rigorous vetting process by the Law Society's selection panel in terms of product strategy, financial health and feedback from existing users. Each entry gave a description of the firm and its products; contact details; product pricing, features and hardware requirements; market share; verdicts both from the panel and an independent adviser; and market research ratings.

It is still available at **www.lawsociety.org.uk/productsandservices/ services/usingtechnology/softwaresolutions.law**.

An updated list of suppliers featured in the guide with their websites and contact telephone numbers is given below.

Name	Telephone	Website
Cognito Software Ltd	0121 314 7745	**www.cognitosoftware.co.uk**
DPS Software	0208 804 1022	**www.dpssoftware.co.uk**
Eclipse Legal Systems	01274 704100	**www.eclipselegal.co.uk**
IRIS Legal	01274 851577	**www.iris.co.uk**
Linetime	0113 250 0020	**www.linetime.co.uk**
OPSIS	0844 815 5751	**www.opsisltd.co.uk**
Quill Group Ltd	0161 236 2910	**www.quill.co.uk**
Select Legal Systems Ltd	01482 644 334	**www.selectlegal.co.uk**
Solicitors Own Software Ltd	01225 787700	**www.soslegal.co.uk**
TFB plc	01489 609000	**www.tfbplc.co.uk**

Appendix 9

Solicitors Act 1974, s.34 (Accountant's Report)

With consolidated amendments to December 2007.

34. Accountants' reports

(1) Every solicitor shall once in each period of twelve months ending with 31st October, unless the Council are satisfied that it is unnecessary for him to do so, deliver to the Society, whether by post or otherwise, a report signed by an accountant (in this section referred to as an 'accountant's report') and containing such information as may be prescribed by rules made by the Council under this section.

(2) An accountant's report shall be delivered to the Society not more than six months (or such other period as may be prescribed by rules made under this section) after the end of the accounting period for the purposes of that report.

(3) Subject to any rules made under this section, the accounting period for the purposes of an accountant's report –

(a) shall begin at the expiry of the last preceding accounting period for which an accountant's report has been delivered;
(b) shall cover not less than twelve months; and
(c) where possible, consistently with the preceding provisions of this section, shall correspond to a period or consecutive periods for which the accounts of the solicitor or his firm are ordinarily made up.

(4) The Council shall make rules to give effect to the provision of this section, and those rules shall prescribe –

(a) the qualification to be held by an accountant by whom an accountant's report is given;
(b) the information to be contained in an accountant's report
(c) the nature and extent of the examination to be made by an accountant of the books and accounts of a solicitor or his firm and of any other relevant documents with a view to the signing of an accountant's report;

(d) the form of an accountant's report; and

(e) the evidence, if any, which shall satisfy the Council that the delivery of an accountant's report is unnecessary and the cases in which such evidence is or is not required.

(5) Rules under this section may include provision –

(a) permitting in such special circumstances as may be defined by the rules a different accounting period from that specified in subsection (3); and

(b) regulating any matters of procedure or matters incidental, ancillary or supplemental to the provisions of this section.

(5A) Without prejudice to the generality of subsection (5)(b), rules under this section may make provision requiring a solicitor in advance of delivering an accountant's report to notify the Society of the period which is to be the accounting period for the purposes of that report in accordance with the preceding provisions of this section.

(6) If any solicitor fails to comply with the provisions of this section or of any rules made under it, a complaint in respect of that failure may be made to the Tribunal by or on behalf of the Society.

(7) A certificate under the hand of the Secretary of the Society shall, until the contrary is proved, be evidence that a solicitor has or, as the case may be, has not delivered to the Society an accountant's report or supplied any evidence required under this section or any rules made under it.

(8) Where a solicitor is exempt from rules under section 32 –

(a) nothing in this section shall apply to him unless he takes out a practising certificate;

(b) an accountant's report shall in no case deal with books, accounts or documents kept by him in the course of employment by virtue of which he is exempt from those rules; and

(c) no examination shall be made of any such books, accounts and documents under any rules made under this section.

Appendix 10

SRA Code of Conduct 2011, Chapter 7: Management of Your Business

Chapter 7: Management of your business

This chapter is about the management and supervision of your *firm* or *in-house practice*.

Everyone has a role to play in the efficient running of a business, although of course that role will depend on the individual's position within the organisation. However, overarching responsibility for the management of the business in the broadest sense rests with the *manager(s)*. The *manager(s)* should determine what arrangements are appropriate to meet the outcomes. Factors to be taken into account will include the size and complexity of the business; the number, experience and qualifications of the *employees*; the number of offices; and the nature of the work undertaken.

Where you are using a third party to provide services that you could provide, (often described as "outsourcing"), this chapter sets out the outcomes you need to achieve.

The outcomes in this chapter show how the *Principles* apply in the context of the management of your business.

Outcomes

You must achieve these outcomes:

O(7.1) you have a clear and effective governance structure and reporting lines;

O(7.2) you have effective systems and controls in place to achieve and comply with all the *Principles*, rules and outcomes and other requirements of the Handbook, where applicable;

O(7.3) you identify, monitor and manage risks to compliance with all the *Principles*, rules and outcomes and other requirements of the Handbook, if applicable to you, and take steps to address issues identified;

O(7.4) you maintain systems and controls for monitoring the financial stability of your *firm* and risks to money and *assets* entrusted to you by *clients* and others, and you take steps to address issues identified;

O(7.5) you comply with legislation applicable to your business, including anti-money laundering and data protection legislation;

O(7.6) you train individuals working in the *firm* to maintain a level of competence appropriate to their work and level of responsibility;

O(7.7) you comply with the statutory requirements for the direction and supervision of *reserved legal activities* and *immigration work*;

O(7.8) you have a system for supervising *clients'* matters, to include the regular checking of the quality of work by suitably competent and experienced people;

O(7.9) you do not outsource *reserved legal activities* to a *person* who is not authorised to conduct such activities;

O(7.10) subject to Outcome 7.9, where you outsource *legal activities* or any operational functions that are critical to the delivery of any *legal activities*, you ensure such outsourcing:

(a) does not adversely affect your ability to comply with, or the *SRA's* ability to monitor your compliance with, your obligations in the Handbook;

(b) is subject to contractual arrangements that enable the *SRA* or its agent to obtain information from, inspect the records (including electronic records) of, or enter the premises of, the third party, in relation to the outsourced activities or functions;

(c) does not alter your obligations towards your *clients*; and

(d) does not cause you to breach the conditions with which you must comply in order to be authorised and to remain so.

Indicative behaviours

Acting in the following way(s) may tend to show that you have achieved these outcomes and therefore complied with the *Principles*:

IB(7.1) safekeeping of documents and *assets* entrusted to the *firm*;

IB(7.2) controlling budgets, expenditure and cash flow;

IB(7.3) identifying and monitoring financial, operational and business continuity risks including *complaints*, credit risks and exposure, claims under legislation relating to matters such as data protection, IT failures and abuses, and damage to offices;

IB(7.4) making arrangements for the continuation of your *firm* in the event of absences and emergencies, for example holiday or sick leave, with the minimum interruption to *clients'* business.

In-house practice

Outcomes 7.5 and 7.7 apply to your *in-house practice*.

Outcomes 7.1 to 7.3, and 7.6 and 7.8 to 7.10 apply to you if you have management responsibilities.

Overseas practice

The outcomes in this chapter apply to your *overseas practice*.

Notes

(i) All of the chapters in the Code will be relevant to the management of your business, in particular those which require you to have systems and controls in place.

(ii) This chapter should also be read with the *SRA Authorisation Rules*, the SRA Financial Services (Conduct of Business) Rules 2001 and the *SRA Indemnity Insurance Rules*.

Appendix 11

SRA Code of Conduct 2011, Chapter 8: Publicity

Chapter 8: Publicity

This chapter is about the manner in which you publicise your *firm* or *in-house practice* or any other businesses. The overriding concern is that *publicity* is not misleading and is sufficiently informative to ensure that *clients* and others can make informed choices.

In your *publicity*, you must comply with statutory requirements and have regard to voluntary codes.

The outcomes in this chapter show how the *Principles* apply in the context of *publicity*.

Outcomes

You must achieve these outcomes:

O(8.1) your *publicity* in relation to your *firm* or *in-house practice* or for any other business is accurate and not misleading, and is not likely to diminish the trust the public places in you and in the provision of legal services;

O(8.2) your *publicity* relating to charges is clearly expressed and identifies whether VAT and *disbursements* are included;

O(8.3) you do not make unsolicited approaches in person or by telephone to *members of the public* in order to publicise your *firm* or *in-house practice* or another business;

O(8.4) *clients* and the public have appropriate information about you, your *firm* and how you are regulated;

O(8.5) your letterhead, website and e-mails show the words "authorised and regulated by the Solicitors Regulation Authority" and either the *firm's* registered name and number if it is an *LLP* or *company* or, if the *firm* is a *partnership* or *sole practitioner*, the name under which it is licensed/authorised by the *SRA* and the number allocated to it by the *SRA*.

Indicative behaviours

Acting in the following way(s) may tend to show that you have achieved these outcomes and therefore complied with the *Principles*:

IB(8.1) where you conduct other regulated activities your *publicity* discloses the manner in which you are regulated in relation to those activities;

IB(8.2) where your *firm* is an *MDP*, any *publicity* in relation to that *practice* makes clear which services are regulated legal services and which are not;

IB(8.3) any *publicity* intended for a jurisdiction outside England and Wales complies with the *Principles*, voluntary codes and the rules in force in that jurisdiction concerning *publicity*;

IB(8.4) where you and another business jointly market services, the nature of the services provided by each business is clear.

Acting in the following way(s) may tend to show that you have not achieved these outcomes and therefore not complied with the *Principles*:

IB(8.5) approaching people in the street, at ports of entry, in hospital or at the scene of an accident; including approaching people to conduct a survey which involves collecting contact details of potential *clients*, or otherwise promotes your *firm* or *in-house practice*;

IB(8.6) allowing any other *person* to conduct *publicity* for your *firm* or *in-house practice* in a way that would breach the *Principles*;

IB(8.7) advertising an estimated fee which is pitched at an unrealistically low level;

IB(8.8) describing overheads of your *firm* (such a normal postage, telephone calls and charges arising in respect of *client* due diligence under the Money Laundering Regulations 2007) as *disbursements* in your advertisements;

IB(8.9) advertising an estimated or fixed fee without making it clear that additional charges may be payable, if that is the case;

IB(8.10) using a name or description of your *firm* or *in-house practice* that includes the word "solicitor(s)" if none of the *managers* are *solicitors*;

IB(8.11) advertising your *firm* or *in-house practice* in a way that suggests that services provided by another business are provided by your *firm* or *in-house practice*;

IB(8.12) producing misleading information concerning the professional status of any *manager* or *employee* of your *firm* or *in-house practice*.

In-house practice

Outcomes 8.1 to 8.4 apply to your *in-house practice* unless it is clear from the context that the outcome is not relevant in your particular circumstances.

Overseas practice

Outcomes 8.1 and 8.4 apply to your *overseas practice*. In addition you must comply with the following outcome:

OP(8.1) *publicity* intended for a jurisdiction outside England and Wales must comply with any applicable law or rules regarding *lawyers' publicity* in the jurisdiction in which your office is based and the jurisdiction for which the *publicity* is intended.

Notes

(i) This chapter should be read in conjunction with Chapters 1 and 9.

Appendix 12

Arrangements on death of sole principal

[The following text appears as Principle 3.14 in *The Guide to the Professional Conduct of Solicitors 1999*, published by the Law Society. Note that the Guide applies to conduct issues occurring before 1 July 2007. For rules governing conduct after 1 July 2007, see the SRA Handbook at **www.sra.org.uk**.]

3.14 Arrangements on death of sole principal

A sole principal should make a will containing adequate provision for the running of the practice, after his or her death, by a solicitor who is admitted for at least three years and holds a current practising certificate.

Making arrangements

1   Clear instructions should be left by the sole principal to ensure that the executors are able to make arrangements immediately after his or her death to appoint a solicitor of sufficient seniority to run the practice, pending its disposal.
2   Although it is not essential to appoint a solicitor as executor, this would greatly facilitate the running of the practice. The will could include an authority for the solicitor-executor to purchase the practice if he or she desires.
3   An executor who is not a solicitor may not, as a sole signatory, sign cheques on the client account of the deceased's practice. For guidance on who can authorise withdrawals from client account see rule 23 of the Solicitors' Accounts Rules 1998 (Annex 28B at p.708).
4   In view of the provisions of rule 9 of the Solicitors' Incorporated Practice Rules 1988 (Annex 3D at p.122) it is advisable for a solicitor shareholder in a recognised body to appoint a solicitor as executor in respect of his or her shares.

Intervention

5   If no appointment of a suitable solicitor-manager is made, the Society may intervene in the practice in accordance with the provisions of

Schedule 1 to the Solicitors Act 1974 (Annex 30A, p.850). The powers of intervention are available where the Council have reason to suspect dishonesty on the part of the personal representatives, where there has been undue delay on the part of the personal representatives, or where the Schedule applied to the sole principal before his or her death. To avoid difficulties to clients following intervention, every effort should be made by the personal representatives to find a solicitor-manager. In cases of difficulty, the honorary secretary of the local law society may be able to help.

Intestacy

6 If a sole principal dies intestate, those entitled to apply for letters of administration strictly have no right to take active steps in administering the estate until so authorised. However, in these circumstances the prospective administrators are encouraged to nominate a manager for the practice before the grant is obtained.

7 Where there is a failure, within a reasonable time of death, to apply for a grant of representation in respect of the estate of a deceased sole principal (whether under a will or on intestacy), the court has power to protect the interests of the clients. In exercise of the discretion conferred by section 116 of the Supreme Court Act 1981, the court can make an order for a grant in respect of the deceased solicitor's estate in favour of a nominee or nominees of the Society. The grant may be general or limited depending on the circumstances and the power is in addition to that conferred on the Society by paragraph 11 of Schedule 1 to the Solicitors Act 1974 (see Annex 30A at p.854).

Appointment of a solicitor-manager

8 Where a solicitor-manager is appointed in respect of a deceased solicitor's practice, he or she becomes the sole principal and must comply personally with all professional obligations in relation to the practice.

Solicitor-manager's responsibilities

9 The solicitor-manager should take care to ensure that confidential information relating to the clients of the deceased sole principal is kept confidential and that any conflict of interest is avoided. (For conflict of interests see Chapter 15, p.313.)

10 The manager must personally exercise control over staff and must supervise or arrange for the supervision of the office(s) in accordance with rule 13 of the Solicitors' Practice Rules 1990 (see 3.08, p.73). The manager will conduct the practice for the personal representatives and pay the profits, less any remuneration agreed to be paid to him or her, to the estate.

Arrangements for remuneration of the manager are a matter between the manager and the personal representatives. The personal representatives are entitled to the professional profits earned during this period. Only in exceptional circumstances should these arrangements continue beyond the executor's year.

11 The manager must arrange for the stationery of the practice to be changed so that his or her name appears on the letterhead as the sole principal. He or she may be described as the manager of the firm.

12 The manager must inform the clients of the practice of the arrangements made – see 3.11, p.77 for details of the information that should be given to the clients. Further, Solicitors Indemnity Fund Limited and any insurers concerned (e.g. those providing top-up cover) should be advised so that cover will be in force for the solicitor-manager. Regulation and Information Services must also be notified of the arrangements (see p.xv for contact details).

13 The manager must comply with practice rule 15, and the Solicitors' Costs Information and Client Care Code (see Chapter 13, p.265).

Operation of client account

14 The sole principal's client account will be frozen on death. Fresh books must be opened immediately. They should be kept as the solicitor manager's books until the practice is disposed of or closed. The solicitor-manager will normally arrange with the sole principal's bank to open a new client account with an overdraft matching that of the existing client account. (See rule 22(8)(b) of the Solicitors' Accounts Rules 1998, Annex 28B at p.707.) The solicitor-manager must make arrangements for the former client account balances to be transferred to the new (overdrawn) client account as soon as the grant of representation is registered with the bank or building society. The solicitor-manager must not draw money from the new account in any circumstances where it would be improper to draw the same amount from the old account.

15 A similar arrangement can be made for office account purposes.

16 No further monies should be paid into the deceased principal's client account. Client's money received by the practice must be placed in the new account operated by the solicitor-manager. The solicitor-manager should encourage the personal representatives to supply an accountant's report up to the date of death. The solicitor-manager must deliver a separate report in respect of any other client monies which he or she has held in any other practice.

Investment business

17 The solicitor-manager should consider his or her position in relation to the Financial Services Act 1986. An investment business certificate which has been issued to a sole principal lapses on death. Therefore the solicitor-

manager must apply for an investment business certificate in his or her own name if he or she intends to conduct investment business. This is so even when the solicitor-manager holds separate authorisation in relation to another practice. Applications for an investment business certificate should be made to Regulation and Information Services. (See also Chapter 27, p.522.)

Sale of the practice

18 If the solicitor-manager purchases the practice from the personal representatives, he or she must not act for the personal representatives and must insist that they be independently advised in this transaction. Regulation and Information Services must be informed of the arrangements for the disposal or sale of the practice (see p.xv for contact details).

Appendix 13

Specimen holiday request form

Name: Paul Humphrey   **Entitlement:** 20 days 2012

Type of leave	From	To (inclusive)	No. of days	Balance	Authorised
Annual	25.06.12	26.06.12	2	18	R Greed
Annual	06.08.12	17.08.12	12	6	R Greed
Annual	23.08.12	Only	1	5	R Greed
Annual	22.11.12	23.11.12	2	3	R Greed
Annual	30.11.12	Only	1	2	R Greed

Appendix 14

Specimen proof of identity request

The law requires solicitors to obtain satisfactory evidence of the identity of their clients and sometimes people related to them. This is because solicitors who deal with money and property on behalf of their clients may be used by criminals wanting to launder money.

To comply with the law, we need to get evidence of your identity as soon as possible. It is our practice to ask to see two pieces of identification.

One must include your name and date of birth, for example, see list below:

- current signed passport
- birth certificate
- current photocard driver's licence
- current EEA member state identity card
- current identity card issued by the Electoral Office for Northern Ireland
- residence permit issued by the Home Office

Another must include your name and address, for example, see list below:

- benefit book or original notification letter from the DWP confirming the right to benefits
- council tax bill
- utility bill or statement, or a certificate from a utilities supplier confirming an arrangement to pay services on pre-payment terms
- a cheque or electronic transfer drawn on an account in the name of the client with a credit or financial institution regulated for the purposes of money laundering
- bank, building society or credit union statement or passbook containing current address
- solicitor's letter confirming recent house purchase or land registry confirmation of address
- local council or housing association rent card or tenancy agreement
- HMRC self-assessment statement or tax demand
- house or motor insurance certificate

If you cannot provide us with the specific identification requested, please contact us as soon as possible to discuss other ways to verify your identity.

We are professionally and legally obliged to keep your affairs confidential. However, solicitors may be required by statute to make a disclosure to the Serious Organised Crime Agency where they know or suspect that a transaction may involve money laundering or terrorist financing. If we make a disclosure in relation to your matter, we may not be able to tell you that a disclosure has been made. We may have to stop working on your matter for a period of time and may not be able to tell you why.

Appendix 15

Master checklist for setting up

Stage 1 – Preparation

1. Carry out an assessment of clients likely to follow you from an existing practice and how much their work is likely to be worth over a 12-month period. Check the position with regard to any restraint of trade covenants in your contract of employment or partnership deed, if relevant, and check the SRA Code of Conduct 2011 and consider whether or not you may write to the client in question asking for their support in the new practice. Consider checking with existing partners/employers as to whether they would object to you canvassing those clients or the work.

   Do not get too depressed at the outcome – when we sketched out the blueprint for our new firm in 1988 we reckoned on starting with eight clients and with an income of £8,000 in the first year. In the event, six clients followed, one of whom killed himself in the first month of the new firm!

2. Carry out a costing exercise as shown **Appendix 4** to work out the anticipated expenditure for the first year.

3. Start looking at areas from which you might start trading and make enquiries as to availability and cost of premises. Do not, at this stage, sign up to anything.

4. Put together a business plan, or ask your accountant to do so. If you need to appoint an accountant, make enquiries into suitable firms of accountants and ask them to make a presentation to you before making your choice.

5. Carry out a SWOT assessment of your business – Strengths, Weaknesses, Opportunities, Threats. Include possible threats from emerging competitors such as 'Tesco'-type law, banks and other large-scale players who have entered the market or may be about to and assess the likely impact on your businesses. Also include existing competitors in the area. Analyse what they do, how they do it and for how much, and identify ways in which you can successfully compete, always making sure that you will remain profitable in the process.

6. Identify possible new clients and start to develop relationships with them. Ask for meetings with them, socialise, have business lunches, etc.

and put a straight sales pitch to them. Tell them what you can do and why they should place their business with you. Take care not to infringe Chapter 8 outcomes on cold calling, etc. Depending on outcome, modify business plan and budgets, always taking a relatively conservative approach to the likely level of income generated. Many potential clients make encouraging noises but fail to deliver.

7. Consider the level of logistics support you will need – possible additional fee earners if you are likely to have a high level of work to start off with, bookkeeping and secretarial support, accountants. Have preliminary meetings with bankers about opening an account and what terms they can offer. Talk to more than one bank to get the best deal and ask to what extent they might be able to pass work to you.

8. Design notepaper. Ensure that it looks professional, and if necessary employ a graphic designer. Consider asking friends or family to do it for you. Ask yourself: What impression are you trying to create? What area of the market are you aiming at and does the notepaper convey that impression? Do you need a company logo? If so, will you design it yourself or engage a professional? Consider the name of your firm and make sure it complies with the SRA Code of Conduct 2011 and Chapter 8 outcomes. Look at other people's notepaper, pick out the good and bad points and adjust your approach accordingly. When you have mock-ups, show them to as many people as possible and ask for their comments.

9. Make enquiries of PI insurers or brokers about the likely level of premium. Contact telephone and broadband providers and obtain details of cost of line, availability and timescale. Investigate types of hardware, i.e. switchboards and handsets, the capabilities of each and the running costs as well as the capital set-up costs. Do not sign up to anything at this stage.

10. Investigate suitable IT hardware and software and consider who will be your IT advisors.

11. Investigate accounts package, make a preliminary choice and ask your accountant to advise on its suitability.

Stage 2 – Implementation

1. Enter into more detailed negotiations for office premises and if necessary agree terms of lease. It is generally unwise to commit to anything for any longer than two or three years. Bear in mind that whatever the length of the term, unless you are allowed to assign you are committing to paying the rent for the whole of that term, and even if you can assign you may be liable as a guarantor for your assignee or as the original tenant.

2. Select the likely start date in conjunction with accountants after having tax advice on implications of various dates.

3. Make a final decision on telephone and IT systems and arrange installation to coincide with the start of the lease. Ask the landlord if it will allow

the installation to take place a week before the lease commences. You never know, it might say yes!

4. If you are sure that the premises are yours, have notepaper and business cards printed (small quantities only at this stage) and a name-plate for display at premises and any other signage within the building made.

5. Finalise arrangements for additional members of staff. Be very conservative in your approach – staff are one of the most time-consuming and expensive resources of any business. Over-staffing at this stage could be fatal.

6. Select furniture and arrange for delivery to the new premises in time for opening day. Bear in mind that you will need a lead time of at least two days in order to unpack everything, arrange desks, get equipment set up and working and test everything out. Equipment will, of course, include computer systems, printers, faxes, etc.

7. Consider whether or not it is appropriate to set up a website at this stage. You will certainly need email but not necessarily a website. The website will advertise your practice, but you may need a couple of months in which to get a feel for the final direction in which your firm will be travelling and, having tested the market, where your strengths and weaknesses lie. Constructing a detailed website is time-consuming and at this stage time is very precious and the work is likely to be wasted if there is then a change of emphasis and the material on the website needs an extensive overhaul.

8. Obtain authorisation from the SRA for the commencement of a new practice. Notify HMRC and the Law Society of the details of the new practice and the likely commencement of trading. Obtain a VAT number. Firm up indemnity and public liability insurance and put in place.

9. Make the final appointment of bookkeeper, support staff, etc.

10. Implement the accounting system and ask your accountants to test it. Make sure you are there when they do it so that you can see for yourself how it will run and have an understanding of what it can do for you and how it can go wrong.

11. Investigate the cost of advertising and where and when suitable advertisements might be placed. Design a suitable advertisement and place in an appropriate medium. Adopt a conservative approach – advertising at this stage is something of an experiment, so do not spend large amounts of money testing the market to see what kind of response you get and do not tie yourself into long-term contracts. Depending on which market you are aiming at, it may not be appropriate to advertise at all.

12. Order suitable dictation/transcription systems.

13. Order supplies of tea, coffee, headache pills and Martin Smith's *Precedent Library* book!

14. Cross your fingers and anything else you think might work, put the kettle on and start hoping for the phone to ring. If it does not (and even if it does!), start telephoning everybody that you know to tell them that you

started trading and are hungry for work. After drinking tea, take a supply of business cards out and go for a walk down the high street and speak to as many local traders as possible to introduce yourself as the new solicitor on the block and ask them if there is anything you can do for them.

15. When the above item is completed, hurry back to the office to get started on all the new work you have picked up on your travels and return the phone calls you missed whilst out marketing.

Good luck!

Appendix 16

Expenditure checklist

[Figures given are averages. Insert correct figures.]

EXPENDITURE LIST	£
1. Housing	
Rent	595
Ground rent	
Service charge	
Mortgage instalments: repayment mortgage (please state net figure)	
Council tax	68
Water rates	16
General maintenance, repairs, decorations	
Cost of service of boiler/central heating system	
Substantial home improvements (e.g. extension, double glazing)	
Insurance: buildings	
Insurance: contents	8
Any other outgoings	
Total	687
2. Heat and light	
Gas	
Electricity	
Coal	33
Fuel oil	
Other	
Total	33
3. Food	
Groceries	346
Wines, spirits, beer and alcohol (for home consumption)	40
Total	386

4. Other household expenses	
Telephone	33
Newsagent	20
Domestic help	
Chemist	
Laundry and cleaning	65
Cleaning materials and other household requirements	
Stationery and postage	
TV, video and satellite/cable rental	
TV, video and satellite repairs	
TV licence	
Window cleaner	10
Other household expenses	5
Total	**133**
5. Garden	
Gardener	
Other help in garden/pool	
Plants, etc.	
Equipment	
Total	**0**
6. Pets	
Food	8
Vet and insurance	18
Boarding/kennels	
Total	**26**
7. Car	
Depreciation	16
Leasing payments	
Car licence	11
Insurance	24
Maintenance, repairs, replacements	20
Petrol and oil	151
Car wash/valet service	20
Parking expenses	
RAC membership	
Total	**242**

8. Employment expenses	
Fares	
Lunches	91
Special clothing and equipment	
Subscriptions for professional associations, unions, etc.	11
Total	**102**
9. Personal expenses	
Clothes	20
Jewellery	
Shoes	10
Hairdressing	
Cosmetics and toiletries	5
Optician	
Medical expenses including physiotherapy, osteopathy	
Dentist	10
Beautician	
Health clubs/tennis	
Tobacco/cigarettes	
Mobile phone	40
Spending money	150
Total	**235**
10. Sports, entertainment, hobbies, holidays	
Restaurant meals	130
Theatre, cinema, concerts	20
Other spectator events (e.g. sports)	60
Books, magazines	
CDs, tapes	22
Evening (and other) class fares	
Club subscriptions	
Hobby equipment (e.g. paints, leotards, golf clubs)	20
Holidays	100
Weekend breaks	50
Christmas expenses	55
Birthday and other gifts, parties, etc.	
Donations	
Total	**457**

11. Assurance, insurance and savings	
Life and endowment policies	112
Family protection	
Mortgage protection	
Sickness and accident, personal accident	
Medical insurance	
Other insurance (e.g. 'all risks', pets)	
Regular savings	
Pension contributions through salary	38
Total	150
12. Professional services	
Accountancy fees	
Legal fees	250
Total	250
13. Other items of expenditure	
Computer, stationery, ink cartridges, disks, Internet	10
Motor cycle running expenses	160
Bank account (additions)	
Total	170
14. Children's expenses	
School fees	
Fares to and from school	
Student grant contribution	
School meals	
Uniform and special clothing	
School trips	
Sports and other equipment	
Bicycle, motorbike, car	
Dancing lessons: fees, clothing, footwear	
Music lessons: fees, music, cost of instrument	
Riding lessons: fees, clothing, equipment	
Swimming lessons: fees, clothing, equipment	
Other special lessons	
Clubs/brownies/scouts/guides: subscription, hobbies, etc.	
Hobbies	
Toys	

Pocket money	
Clothing (other than for school)	17
Shoes	8
Hair appointments	
Theatre, cinema, concerts	10
Books, magazines	
CDs, DVDs	
Birthday parties	
Presents for others	
Stationery	
Holidays	
Computers	
Medical insurance	
Total	35
Grand Total	2,906

Appendix 17

Contract for sale of a solicitor's practice

Contract for Sale of [name] & Co, Solicitors

Dated:
Parties:

(1) 'Seller': [name] of [address] (hereinafter individually referred to as 'Mr [name]') and [name] of [address] (hereinafter individually referred to as 'Mr [name]')
(2) 'Buyer': [name] of [address]

1. Interpretation

In this agreement including the Schedules:

1.1 the following words and expressions have the following meanings, unless they are inconsistent with the context:

'**Assets**' the property, assets and rights of the Business to be purchased by the Buyer as described in clause 2.1

'**Business**' the business of a solicitors' practice carried on by the Seller under the trading name of '[name] & Co' at the Completion Date

'**Completion Date**' the close of business on [completion date]

'**Contracts**' the current contracts and engagements of the Seller in relation to the Business, but excluding contracts with employees

'**Creditors**' the aggregate amount owed by the Seller in connection with the Business to or in respect of trade creditors and accrued charges as recorded in the books of account of the Business at the Completion Date but not including liabilities for VAT or taxation on profits or chargeable gains

'**Employees**' the persons listed in Schedule 4 who, at the Completion Date, are employed by the Seller for the purposes of the Business

'**Excluded Assets**' the assets listed in Schedule 2 which are owned by the Seller but are not included in the sale to the Buyer

'**Fixed Assets**' all equipment, and other chattels on the Property or otherwise owned by the Seller at the Completion Date for the purpose of the Business

'**Goodwill**' the goodwill of the Seller in relation to the Business, together with the exclusive right for the Buyer or its assignee to represent itself as carrying on the Business in succession to the Seller, and all trade names associated with the Business

'**Liabilities**' the liabilities of the Business (other than the Creditors) outstanding at the Completion Date

'**Planning Acts**' as defined in the Town and Country Planning Act 1990, s.336

'**Property**' the leasehold premises leased by the Seller as listed in Part 1 of Schedule 1

'**Regulations**' the Transfer of Undertakings (Protection of Employment) Regulations 1981, SI 1981/1794

'**Work in Progress**' Work that has been carried out by the Seller in respect of client matters that is unbilled at the Completion Date and for which payment by the client subsequently is due

1.2 all references to a statutory provision shall be construed as including references to:

(a) any statutory modification, consolidation or re-enactment
(b) all statutory instruments or orders made pursuant to it
(c) any statutory provisions of which it is a modification, consolidation or re-enactment

1.3 except where the context otherwise requires, words denoting the singular include the plural and vice versa; words denoting any gender include all genders; words denoting persons include firms and corporations and vice versa

1.4 unless otherwise stated, a reference to a clause, sub-clause or Schedule is a reference to a clause or a sub-clause of, or a Schedule to, this agreement

1.5 clause headings are for ease of reference only and do not affect the construction of this agreement

2. Agreement for sale

2.1 Subject to the terms and conditions of this agreement, the Seller shall sell to the Buyer with full title guarantee and the Buyer shall purchase as at the Completion Date:

(a) the Business as a going concern and

(b) all the assets and rights owned by or under the control of the Seller and used in the conduct of the Business including, but without limitation:

   (i)   the Goodwill
   (ii) the Property
   (iii) the Fixed Assets
   (iv) the Contracts

but excluding the Excluded Assets and the Work in Progress

2.2 The provisions of Part 2 of Schedule 1 shall apply in relation to the sale of the Property

3. Purchase consideration

3.1 The consideration for the sale by the Seller of the Business and the Assets shall be the sum of £30,000 apportioned as set out in Schedule 3

3.2 A deposit of one thousand pounds shall be paid to the Seller on the signing of this agreement and shall be held as stakeholders

3.3 The consideration shall be inclusive of any VAT

4. Completion

4.1 The sale and purchase shall be completed on the [*completion date*] at the office of the Sellers or such other venue as shall be specified by them when the balance of the first tranche of £15,000 of the purchase consideration shall be paid by telegraphic transfer to Mr [*name*]'s account at Anytown Bank 222 Any Street London WC1 by no later than 2 pm. The balance of a further £15,000 shall be paid by standing order into the above account by fifteen equal monthly instalments of £1,000 the first of which shall be paid on [*date*] and thereafter on the first day of each month

4.2 The Seller shall cause to be delivered or (if so requested by the Buyer) made available to the Buyer:

(a) such documents as are required by the Buyer to complete the sale and purchase of the Assets and vest title to the Assets in the Buyer, including (but without limitation) an assignment of the Goodwill

(b) all payroll records and information relating to clients and suppliers relevant computer programs and other books and documents which relate to the Business

(c) all records of National Insurance and PAYE relating to all the Employees duly completed and up to date

4.3 The Buyer shall from the Completion Date represent himself as being the successor practice to the business formerly conducted by the Sellers and shall keep the Sellers indemnified from all liability for the cost of providing professional indemnity insurance run off cover for a period of six years from the date of Completion. In the event of a claim arising during the period of three years from the Completion Date in respect of a loss to a client or former client caused by a negligent act or omission alleged to have occurred during a period prior to the Completion Date the Sellers shall be liable for payment of the excess (if any) payable for each such claim and shall indemnify the Buyer for such excesses as are paid by him but subject to a maximum excess of £5,000 per claim and a maximum total payment of £15,000 in any one year. The Sellers jointly and severally warrant to the Buyer that they have disclosed to the Buyer all existing claims to their knowledge and that they are not aware of any other current or potential claims. In the event of any such claim arising they shall provide to the Buyer such information and assistance as is requested by the Buyer and or the insurers to resolve the claim and no claim shall be settled by the Buyer without the Seller being fully consulted and giving their consent and in the event of a disagreement over settlement the matter shall be decided by an independent arbitrator agreed by the parties or appointed by the President for the time being of the law Society in default of agreement at the joint expense of the parties

4.4 The Sellers shall indemnify the Buyer from all liability in respect of any findings or awards of compensation or penalties imposed by any professional body in respect of any claims by clients or former clients of the Business relating to matters conducted by the Sellers prior to the Completion Date and which do not fall for payment under the Professional Indemnity Insurance arrangements maintained by the Buyer

4.4.1 The Buyer shall employ Mr [*name*] for a period of one year from the Completion Date as a Salaried Partner at a salary of not less than £30,000 per annum in return for Mr [*name*] working a three-day week totalling a maximum of 30 hours per week and with four weeks' paid holiday in addition to the usual Bank Holidays and shall provide him with a complete indemnity for all liabilities of the Business incurred after the Completion Date by entering into an Indemnity in the form contained in Schedule 5 hereto

4.5 The Buyer shall retain the services of Mr [*name*] as a Consultant for a period of six months at a salary of not less than £30,000 per annum in return for Mr [*name*] working a three-day week totalling a maximum of 30 hours per week and with four weeks' paid holiday in addition to the usual Bank Holidays and shall provide him with a complete indemnity for all liabilities of the Business incurred after the Completion Date. Mr [*name*] shall be responsible for his own tax affairs and National Insurance liability. The Buyer shall contribute one-half of the fee payable by Mr [*name*] in respect of his practising certificate for the period 2011/12

5. Representations

5.1 All the terms of this agreement between the parties hereto are deemed to be contained in this agreement and no statement representation or description whether made by the Seller or by his Agent on his behalf in writing or orally or contained in any literature advertising or other matter issued by or on behalf of the Seller shall form part of this agreement or have any effect thereon or be deemed to be a representation or condition inducing the same save the Seller's written replies to enquiries and written communications between the parties and the copies of the accounts of the Seller prepared by [name] and Co. for the last three financial years

6. Creditors and liabilities

6.1 The Seller shall promptly discharge the Creditors and Liabilities and notwithstanding completion of the purchase of the Business shall be responsible for all debts payable by and claims outstanding against it at the Completion Date whether made known to the Seller or apparent at that stage or not including all wages, sums payable under taxation statutes, rent and other expenses

7. Employees

7.1 The Seller warrants that he has complied with the provisions of regulation 10 of the Regulations
7.2 All salaries and other emoluments, including holiday pay, tax and National Insurance payments and contributions to retirement benefit schemes, relating to the Employees shall be borne by the Seller up to the Completion Date and all necessary apportionments shall be made
7.3 Mr [name] shall indemnify the Buyer for all liability in respect of [name of employee] for payment of a redundancy payment or liability for acts of unfair dismissal or discrimination of any nature which have occurred prior to completion including the costs of defending any claims brought in relation to those matters

8. Title and apportionments

8.1 Subject to the provisions of Schedule 1 relating to the Property, the Seller shall take all necessary steps and cooperate fully with the Buyer to ensure that he obtains the full benefit of the Business and Assets and shall execute such documents and assignments and take such other steps (or procure other necessary parties so to do) as are necessary or appropriate for vesting in the Buyer all his rights and interests in the Assets and the benefit of all contracts currently enjoyed by the Seller and the Business

8.2 All rents, rates, gas, water, electricity and telephone charges and other outgoings relating to or payable in respect of the Business up to the Completion Date shall be borne by the Seller and as from the Completion Date shall be borne by the Buyer and all periodical payments receivable in respect of the Business up to that time shall belong to and be payable to the Seller and as from that time shall belong to and be payable to the Buyer. Such outgoings and payments receivable shall if necessary be apportioned accordingly, provided that any such outgoings or payments receivable which are referable to the extent of the use of any property or right shall be apportioned according to the extent of such use.

8.3 The Seller shall indemnify the Buyer in respect of any liability in respect of VAT matters up to the Completion Date for any VAT which should have been charged and was not or the Seller has otherwise failed to account to HM Revenue and Customs for VAT collected or due and in respect of any penalties imposed for failure to comply with VAT regulations. Any VAT collected after the Completion Date shall be accounted for and apportioned between the Buyer and Seller as they may agree or in default of agreement as advised by Messrs [name] & Co., accountants

8.4 Where any amounts not otherwise specifically provided for in this agreement fall to be apportioned under this agreement, the Seller shall provide the Buyer with full details of the apportionments, together with supporting vouchers or similar documentation, and in the absence of dispute the appropriate payment shall be made by or to the Seller forthwith. If the amount of any apportionment is in dispute, the issue shall be decided by a jointly instructed Chartered Surveyor appointed by the parties (and in default of agreement by the President for the time being of the Royal Institution of Chartered Surveyors) whose fees shall be borne jointly by the parties in the first instance and thereafter in accordance with the Surveyor's decision. The amount determined in accordance with this provision shall be paid within 14 days of the determination, together with interest calculated on a daily basis (as well after as before judgment), from the Completion Date until the date of actual payment, at the rate of 4 per cent per annum above the base rate from time to time of Any Bank plc. In the case of the Work in Progress bills delivered after the Completion Date shall be apportioned as the Parties agree and in default of agreement shall be determined by Messrs [name] and Co., Chartered Accountants, whose decision shall be binding upon the Parties and whose costs shall be borne as [name] and Co, shall decide

8.5 The sums due to the Sellers by way of work in progress shall be paid by the Buyer to the Seller within 14 days of receipt by the Business of the monies due from the client of the Business. The Seller shall have full access to the books of account of the Business for the purposes of calculating the Work in Progress and monitoring the receipt of monies due

9. Future activities

9.1 For the purpose of assuring to the Buyer the full benefit of the Business the Seller shall not:

(a) at any time disclose to any person or use for any purpose and shall use all reasonable endeavours to prevent the publication or disclosure of any information concerning the Business

(b) for a period of two years after the Completion Date either on his own account or through any other person directly or indirectly solicit, interfere with or endeavour to entice away from the Buyer any person who is now or has, during the two years preceding the Completion Date, been a client, client or employee of, or in the habit of dealing with, the Seller in relation to the Business

(c) for a period of one year after the Completion Date or the date of ceasing employment and or consultancy (whichever is the later), either on his own account, or in partnership or as an agent, consultant or employee of another person or firm practice or through any other person directly or indirectly operate or take part in a business which competes with the Business within a radius of two miles of the Property

9.2 The Seller shall promptly refer to the Buyer all enquiries relating to the Business which the Seller may in future receive

10. Information

The Seller shall preserve all information, records and other documents relating to the Excluded Assets for a period of not less than three years and upon reasonable notice by the Buyer make such information, records and documents available for inspection by the Buyer or its authorised agents at reasonable times during normal business hours. During the period of his employment as a Salaried Partner Mr [name] shall have access to the books of account of the practice and shall be permitted to take and retain copies of such records

11. Costs

All expenses incurred by or on behalf of the parties, including all fees of agents, solicitors and accountants, employed by either of the parties in connection with the negotiation, preparation and execution of this agreement shall be borne solely by the party which incurred them

12. Communications

12.1 All communications between the parties with respect to this agreement shall be delivered by hand or sent by first class post to the address of the addressee as set out in this agreement, or to such other address (being in England and Wales) as the addressee may from time to time have notified for the purpose of this clause, or sent by facsimile transmission (with confirmation by letter posted first class within 24 hours)

12.2 Communications shall be deemed to have been received:

   (a) if sent by first class post: three business days after posting exclusive of the day of posting

   (b) if delivered by hand: on the day of delivery

   (c) if sent by facsimile transmission: at the time of transmission

12.3 In proving service:

   (a) by delivery by hand: it shall be necessary only to produce a receipt for the communication signed by or on behalf of the addressee

   (b) by post: it shall be necessary only to prove that the communication, or letter of confirmation, was contained in an envelope which was pre-paid duly addressed and posted in accordance with this clause

   (c) by facsimile transmission: it shall be necessary only to produce the transmission slip

   (d) service by email shall not count as good service

13. Entire agreement and schedules

13.1 This agreement and the Schedules constitute the entire agreement and understanding between the parties with respect to all matters which are referred to

13.2 The Schedules form part of this agreement

13.3 This agreement binds each party's successors and assigns

14. Invalidity

If any term or provision in this agreement shall in whole or in part be held to any extent to be illegal or unenforceable under any enactment or rule of law, that term or provision or part shall to that extent be deemed not to form part of this agreement and the enforceability of the remainder of this agreement shall not be affected

15. Proper law

The construction, validity and performance of this agreement shall be governed by the laws of England and Wales

AS WITNESS the hands of the Seller and of the Buyer the day and year first above written

SCHEDULE 1

Part 1 Leasehold property

ALL THAT leasehold property situate at [*address of property*] as the same is comprised in a lease ('the Lease') dated [*date*] and made between [*names of parties to the lease*]

Part 2 Conditions of Sale

Mr [*name*] shall execute a Deed of Assignment of the lease to the Premises to the Buyer at the Buyer's request subject to the Licence to Assign of the landlord and in the meantime shall hold the Lease on trust for the Buyer

SCHEDULE 2

Excluded assets

Cash in hand or at the bank or Building Society

Any amounts recoverable in respect of taxation attributable to periods ended on or before the Completion Date

The antique book case at the Property in Mr [*name*]'s room

SCHEDULE 3

Total consideration

Total consideration	£30,000
comprising:	
Goodwill	£29,999
Leasehold property	£1

SCHEDULE 4

Employees

[*name*] of [*address*] born [*date of birth*], date of commencement of employment [*date*], conveyancing executive

    [*name*] of [*address*] born [*date of birth*], date of commencement of employment [*date*], legal secretary

SCHEDULE 5

Indemnity

THIS DEED OF INDEMNITY is made this [*day*] day of [*month*] 2012 BETWEEN
    [*name*] of [*address*] ('Mr [*name*]') and [*name*] of [*address*] ('Mr [*name*]') of the one part and Mr [*name*]of [*address*] ('Mr [*name*]') of the other part
    WHEREAS:

(1) Mr [*name*] has taken Mr [*name*] into partnership (as salaried partner) and intends to employ Mr [*name*] as a Consultant in the practice of Solicitors at [*practice address*] and otherwise as may be required
(2) Mr [*name*] will be held out to third parties to be liable to pay the debts and liabilities of the partnership and there is a risk that Mr [*name*] may erroneously be thought by third parties to be similarly responsible
(3) Mr [*name*] has agreed that Mr [*name*] and Mr [*name*] are entitled to the following indemnity

NOW IT IS HEREBY AGREED as follows:
    Mr [*name*] hereby agrees with Mr [*name*] and Mr [*name*] and each of them to pay and discharge all liabilities of the partnership incurred after the Completion Date and to keep Mr [*name*] and Mr [*name*] and their respective personal representatives indemnified against all such liabilities and against all claims proceedings costs demands and expenses in respect thereof

SIGNED AS A DEED by the said

[*name*]

In the presence of

SIGNED AS A DEED by the said

[*name*]

In the presence of

SIGNED AS A DEED by the said

In the presence of

Commentary

This precedent assumes that there is a two-partner firm where both partners intend retiring in the near future. One is intending to retire within six months of the completion date and the other in one to two years from completion once a replacement has been found. The retiring partner has employed his wife in the practice, who will also be retired at around the same time as her husband, but as an employee of the practice there are redundancy and unfair dismissal issues. The Buyer is not keen on shouldering such a burden and so to facilitate the sale the wife has agreed to look to the retiring partner to bear that burden rather than the incoming new owner. In effect she has agreed to forgo her redundancy entitlement to soothe the path for them both to stop working. The only other employee, a legal secretary, has agreed to remain and the new practice will shoulder the redundancy liability, as indeed it has to under the Transfer of Undertakings (Protection of Employment) Regulations 1981.

Note the provisions as to repayment of capital and of work in progress. Clearly, it is in the interests of the buyer to spread out those payments over as long a period as possible and in the retiring partner's interests to have the money over the shortest possible time frame. It will be a question of the bargaining position of the parties as to the exact terms of the deal that are agreed. There is also a provision for the outgoing partners to have access to the books of account in order to see what is happening within the firm during the transitional period. Quite apart from wanting to know what client's bills are being paid so that the time when work in progress might be paid, there may be continuing ethical and professional issues if either are held out to the public as a principal during that time. If either of the partners who intends gradually to withdraw from the practice is held out as a partner, albeit a salaried partner, he or she will remain liable for acts of dishonesty within the practice and for failure to comply with other professional rules of conduct. This need on their part to know what is happening financially within the firm may clash with the incoming buyer's wish to keep such matters private.

It may suit the new owner and the partner who wishes to retire at a later stage to leave the partner *in situ* and to have an informal agreement that he or she will retire after a year or two depending on how things are going, thus avoiding the creation of a sole practice, which the new owner may prefer as some lenders and insurers discriminate against sole practitioners. This involves a high degree of trust on both their parts and carries substantial risks, but can work in the right circumstances where a partner wants to retire, although not immediately, and must at least make some plans for an exit strategy.

Bibliography

Software Solutions: A guide to integrated practice management software (Law Society, annually). The 2009 edition is still available online at **www.lawsociety.org.uk/documents/downloads/softwaresolutionsguide2009.pdf**.

The books listed below are published by Law Society Publishing and are available at the Law Society Business Centre and good legal bookshops, or by direct mail through Prolog (0870 850 1422) or via the website **www.lawsociety.org.uk/bookshop**. For further information on these and other titles published by Law Society Publishing, please see the website.

The Solicitor's Handbook 2012 (Andrew Hopper QC and Gregory Treverton-Jones QC, 2011)
The Law Society's Directory of Solicitors and Barristers (annually)
Lexcel Client Care Toolkit, 2nd edn (Law Society, 2011)
Lexcel Risk Management Toolkit (Law Society, 2011)
Lexcel People Management Toolkit (Law Society, 2011)
Lexcel Information Management Toolkit (Law Society, 2011)
Lexcel Business Continuity Planning Toolkit (Law Society, 2011)
Lexcel Financial Management and Business Planning Handbook (Law Society, 2011)
Conveyancing Quality Scheme Toolkit, 2nd edn (Law Society, 2012)
Marketing Legal Services, 2nd edn (David Monk and Alastair Moyes, 2011)
Managing People in a Legal Business (ed. Jill Andrew, 2010)
Precedent Library for the General Practitioner, 2nd edn (Martin Smith, 2009)
Profitability and Law Firm Management, 2nd edn (Andrew Otterburn, 2007)
Solicitors and the Accounts Rules, 3rd edn (Peter Camp, 2011)
Solicitors' Accounts Manual, 12th edn (SRA, 2011)
Outcomes-focused Regulation (Andrew Hopper QC and Gregory Treverton-Jones QC, 2011)
Solicitors and Money Laundering, 3rd edn (Peter Camp, 2008)

Useful contacts

HM Courts and Tribunals Service
Website: **www.justice.gov.uk/about/hmcts**

Financial Services Authority
25 The North Colonnade
Canary Wharf
London E14 5HS
Tel: 020 7066 1000
Website: **www.fsa.gov.uk**

HM Revenue and Customs
Website: **www.hmrc.gov.uk**

Law Society
113 Chancery Lane
London WC2A 1PL
Switchboard: 020 7242 1222
Practice Advice: 0870 606 2522
Website: **www.lawsociety.org.uk**

Office Team Legal and Professional Services (formerly OyezStraker)
OfficeTeam Ltd
Unit 4
500 Purley Way
Croydon
Surrey
CR0 4NZ
Tel: 020 8774 3415
Website: www.officeteam.co.uk/officeteam/products_services/legal_and_
professional_services/

Peapod Solutions Ltd
1 Castle Business Village
Station Road
Hampton TW12 2BX
Tel: 0845 683 2517
Website: **www.legaloffice.com**

QuarryHouse Computer Systems
Devonshire House, Manor Way
Borehamwood WD6 1QQ
Tel: 020 3468 2070
Fax: 020 3432 7686
E-mail: george.rendall@quarryhouse.co.uk
Website: **www.quarryhouse.co.uk**

Sole Practitioners Group
113 Chancery Lane,
London WC2A 1PL
Tel: 020 7320 5801
Website: **www.spg.uk.com**

Solicitors' Assistance Scheme
Tel: 020 7117 8811
Website: **www.thesas.org.uk**

Solicitors Regulation Authority
Tel: 0870 606 2555
Professional Ethics: 0870 606 2577
Website: **www.sra.org.uk**

Law Society accreditation schemes: CQS and Lexcel

Part of the marketing plan for your new business should include careful consideration of whether membership to the Law Society's accreditation schemes is necessary or indeed required (e.g. for the purposes of Legal Services Commission funding).

In this section, we shall explore what options are available to you and why you should consider becoming a member.

Accreditation schemes available

As well as numerous membership networks (otherwise known as Sections) available at the Law Society, there are many accreditation schemes that individual practitioners and practices can join.

Accreditation schemes for individual practitioners include children law, criminal litigation, clinical negligence, family law, mental health, personal injury, planning law and many others. By accrediting as an individual practitioner you earn special recognition for your expertise in specific areas of law.

The Law Society operates these individual practitioner accreditation schemes in order to:

- promote high standards in legal service provision;
- ensure that consumers are easily able to identify legal practitioners with proven competency in given areas of law;
- help consumers to make informed choices;
- offer solicitors and firms use of a recognisable brand;
- provide information for courts, statutory bodies and other professionals; and
- ensure that scheme members maintain relevant standards of competency and expertise, by means of periodic reselection and re-accreditation.

When setting up your legal practice you need to have regard to accreditation schemes for practices. We have explored below two accreditation schemes, the Conveyancing Quality Scheme and Lexcel.

Conveyancing Quality Scheme

The Conveyancing Quality Scheme (CQS) was launched in late 2010 and its purpose is to provide a recognised quality standard for residential conveyancing practices. Achievement of membership establishes a level of credibility for member practices with stakeholders (regulators, lenders, insurers and consumers) based upon three key areas:

- the integrity of the senior responsible officer and other key conveyancing staff. The senior responsible officer is an individual at the practice accountable to the Law Society for membership to the scheme;
- the practice's adherence to good Core Practice Management Standards; and
- adherence to prudent and efficient conveyancing procedures through the Law Society Conveyancing Protocol.

The CQS creates a trusted community of conveyancers which will deter fraud and drive up standards in conveyancing year on year.

The benefits of being a member

There are many benefits to being a member of the CQS.

The main benefit, of course, is that a member is part of a trusted community of conveyancers that stakeholders such as lenders have confidence in. Further evidence suggests that having the CQS badge has increased members' marketing ability to members of the public, which has resulted in an increased client intake. Other benefits include:

- use of CQS branding on letterheads and websites;
- entry on to the Law Society website with a search tool for members of the public;
- quarterly CQS e-newsletter, including news and features;
- CQS events; and
- exclusive PI insurance product offering.

Further benefits being developed include making online technical solutions such as smart forms available to CQS firms and their clients; further promotion of the scheme to the public; affinity products and solutions; and CQS materials for members to give to clients.

Becoming a member– requirements and process

In order to make an application to the scheme, the applicant practice must be regulated by the Solicitors Regulation Authority.

The practice applying also has to undertake residential conveyancing work and nominate a senior responsible officer (SRO) and head of conveyancing (HOC) for the purposes of the scheme.

Application to the scheme is made through an application form, which is available on the Law Society's website (**www.lawsociety.org.uk**). The form is split into two main elements: provenance and excellence.

In relation to provenance, the applicant is asked to provide information on details of the practice's constitution, the number of managers, financial information relating to residential conveyancing for the previous three years, information on referral fees, complaints and PI insurance claims history and other.

In relation to excellence, the applicant is asked to confirm whether it has various policies and procedures under four Core Practice Management Standards: financial management, supervision and operation risk management, client care and file and case management.

Along with the application, the applicant must submit to the CQS office the practice's PI insurance policy schedule and claims summaries for the previous five years, accounts reports where they are qualified, details on complaints and the CPD record for relevant persons. Details of all relevant people for the purposes of the application must be included, that is, all those that are: managers/partners at the firm, qualified conveyancers (such as solicitors, FILEX or licensed conveyancers), non-qualified conveyancers, key support staff and accounts staff.

At the time the application is submitted, the SRO must either have completed basic disclosure checks (Criminal Records Bureau checks) or have instigated obtaining them, for themselves, the HOC, managers and qualified conveyancers. Results of those checks will need to be provided to the CQS team before the application can proceed.

Once all information has been provided, the CQS team will consider the application and the information provided and conduct further checks. For example, identity checks are carried out on the SRO, HOC and managers. A credit check is carried out on the practice and should the score be below an accepted level a bank reference will be obtained. Additional checks include the inspection of SRA records (in relation to practicing certificates and any conditions, complaints and regulatory investigations), checking records with FILEX and the Council of Licensed Conveyancers, as appropriate, considering CPD records. Further analysis is conducted in relation to PI insurance claims, complaints, regulatory investigations and so on.

Once all information has been considered, a decision is taken to accredit, defer (for up to 12 months) or reject a practice's application for membership. If the application is deferred or rejected, the CQS office will set out the reasons why the practice has not met the required standards and any corrective action that is to be taken.

Upon becoming a member, the practice agreement signed by the applicant at the outset comes into force. This agreement sets out the obligations upon the practice during membership and includes (amongst other things) that the practice agrees to update the CQS office every six months in respect of complaints, to adhere to the Conveyancing Protocol and that all relevant members of staff will undertake mandatory training. The training which is mandatory is set by the CQS Office.

Applying as a new practice

As a new practice, providing some of the information described above will be difficult as it will not have yet occurred. For example, three-years figure for the number of residential conveyancing transactions, five years' PI insurance claims history, complaints history and so on.

Being a newly formed practice is not a bar to becoming a member of the CQS. However, full information must still be provided.

If the practice has recently been formed, the CQS office will encourage the applicant to provide a copy of the business plan provided to the applicant's PI insurers together with a business forecast for the next 12/24/36 months. The business forecast should include a forecast for the business as a whole, with the residential conveyancing forecast shown as a percentage of that forecast.

All practices need to ensure that they have in place the required Core Practice Management Standards as set out in the application form. If the applicant finds when completing this part of the application form that they are responding 'No' or 'Working towards' to a number of the Core Practice Management Standards, we recommend that the applicant purchases the CQS Toolkit (available online from the website) and/or contacts practice advice solicitors for advice on how to set up, implement and embed these processes.

Applying as a newly formed practice should not be a daunting task – essentially, the CQS office needs to be assured that the financial standing, business model and effective management of the newly formed practice is in place. The more information an applicant is able to provide the better.

CQS success and future

At the beginning of 2012, there had been more than 1,6000 applications to the scheme more than 1,000 had been accredited. Of those accredited, an additional 600 branch offices are in place, making a total of 1,600 CQS 'outlets'. With the first practice to be accredited in February 2011, the CQS has gained over 1,000 members in less than 12 months and therefore has created that trusted community very quickly. The Law Society aims to double its membership within the same time frame.

Stakeholder buy-in to the scheme has been equally successful, with Santander making CQS a prerequisite for new members and others (such as Nationwide) confirming that anyone removed from their panel must have CQS before they will be reinstated.

Anecdotal evidence has suggested that being a member of the CQS has reduced PI insurance premiums outside of the PI insurance scheme for CQS members that the Society facilitated and, further, that business for those that are CQS members has increased.

Further stakeholder engagement activities are planned in 2012, which should lead to data sharing with the lenders thereby making CQS a panel management tool and further marketing is planned to raise awareness of the CQS with the public.

So the question is why would you not want your practice to be a member of the CQS? Further, if your practice has Lexcel, you are already part-way there.

For more information

If you have any questions regarding the Conveyancing Quality Scheme, please contact the CQS office via e-mail (cqs@lawsociety.org.uk) or telephone (+44 (0)20 7316 5550).

Lexcel Practice Management Standard

The Lexcel scheme is the only legally focused standard available to any size or type of legal practice in the world. There are currently over 1,000 accredited practices, from sole practitioners to large law firms, and in-house legal departments in public and commercial sectors.

Benefits of Lexcel accreditation

Benefits of working towards and gaining accreditation include:

*   increased operational efficiencies;
*   improved competitive advantage;
*   improved client care and customer service;
*   more effective risk management;
*   support to create a positive staff culture; and
*   the potential to reduce PI insurance premiums.

The standard

Reviews and revisions of the scheme are made on a regular basis to ensure Lexcel remains relevant for the legal profession. The current version of the standard is Lexcel v5.

The standard and scheme are reviewed regularly to ensure Lexcel remains relevant for legal practices. Practices can currently apply to and be assessed against Lexcel v4.1. Lexcel v5 was launched on 31 October 2011. Compliance requirements for Lexcel v5 are as follows:

- 1 January 2012 – optional compliance for all assessments;
- 1 July 2012 onwards – mandatory compliance for all assessments.

Management

Lexcel is managed by the Lexcel office of the Law Society of England and Wales. The Lexcel office administers and reviews all applications, oversees and manages the assessment process, promotes the scheme and develops the standard, scheme and all associated products. The Law Society of England and Wales is the only body with authority to award Lexcel accreditation.

The Lexcel Panel has overarching responsibility for the Lexcel standard and regularly provides advice to the Lexcel office on applications and the scheme's processes. The panel comprises legal professionals from every size and type of practice.

Applicants

Lexcel can be applied for by any legal practice in any jurisdiction in the world. Practices whose head office is in England and Wales must be members of the Law Society of England and Wales. The definition of a legal practice for the purposes of Lexcel is either:

- a law practice in the form of partnerships, limited liability partnerships, sole practices and incorporated law firms; or
- an in-house legal department, including practices within corporate, public sector and government organisations.

Practices with multiple offices can apply by jurisdiction. For example, a law firm with five offices across England must submit one application and be assessed across all five offices.

Cost of accreditation

There are three main costs of applying for accreditation. These are:

- resource cost – how much it will take to work towards compliance using either internal resources or engaging with external experts;
- application fees – paid to the Law Society when submitting an application form and dependent on the size of your practice;
- assessment fees – paid to a Lexcel assessment body and dependent on the size of your practice.

The application process

The first action any practice should take is to complete the free Lexcel self-assessment checklist. This simple tool will help identify where you are compliant or non-compliant, as well as areas for improvement or development. For practices applying for the first time, the checklist provides a good gauge on how near to compliance the practice is.

There are key steps in the Lexcel process which must be adhered to when submitting an application and undertaking assessment. In brief, these are:

1.	Ensure the requirements are embedded.	All requirements must be in place at least three months before the date of assessment.
2.	Arrange an assessment date.	Between three months and four weeks before an assessment.
3.	Submit a Lexcel application form with all required information.	Four-week turnaround.
4.	Wait for approval.	Practices must not have an assessment without receiving approval to proceed to assessment from the Lexcel office.
5.	If approval given, undertake an assessment.	Duration depends on size of practice.
6.	Assessor submits assessment report.	Within two weeks of last on-site day to Lexcel office.
7.	Complete any corrective action.	Three weeks for minor non-compliances, three months for major non-compliances.
8.	Assessor submits corrective action report.	Within two weeks of non-compliance deadline.
9.	Lexcel office reviews reports.	Four-week turnaround.
10.	Lexcel office issues decision.	As part of step 9.

The application form

Practices must complete a Lexcel application form and send it in to the Lexcel office. All sections of the form must be completed and received by the Lexcel office no later than four weeks before an assessment. The form must include:

- sign off by the most senior person in the practice, e.g. managing partner or legal director;
- details of any complaint or conduct matter that has arisen at the practice. This must include information such as regulator investigations or visits, complaints from a client that were dealt with internally or referred to the relevant complaint body;
- PI insurance details, including claims and notifications, from the practice's broker or insurer;
- adverse publicity information which may bring the accreditation scheme or the Law Society's brands into disrepute;
- Staff list including names, job titles, department, location and date of joining.

Note: checks are completed on all initial applicants irrespective of whether disclosure has been made. A random sample of 20 per cent of re-accreditation applications who state there are no matters will also be checked. Any non-disclosure or misrepresentation may result in an automatic suspension of an application, renewal or award of accreditation.

Approval to proceed to assessment

The Lexcel office will issue one of three decisions following the review of each application form:

- approval to proceed – this means a practice can undertake its assessment;
- refuse Lexcel – an applicant is able to refer its application to the Lexcel Panel; or
- suspend application – a factor is affecting the practice's application which requires it to await an outcome prior to a decision being issued, e.g. outcome of an SRA investigation.

Lexcel assessment bodies and assessors

Assessment bodies

Assessments are conducted by independent licensed assessment bodies. Lexcel assessors are employed by licensed assessment bodies. Assessment bodies are not allowed to provide consultancy and assessment services to the same practice. For details of the Lexcel assessment bodies, see: **www.law-society.org.uk/productsandservices/lexcel/assessors.page**.

Assessor

Assessors are all bound to ensure that the assessment is conducted in a compliant, confidential and independent manner. Each assessor must be contracted with a licensed assessment body, have relevant experience and have undertaken all preparatory requirements as laid out by the Lexcel office to maintain assessor status.

Assessment timescales

Factors affecting durations

The duration and sample guidelines apply to the practice as a whole. The total number of fee earners and support staff must be added across all branch offices.

The main factors affecting the length of the assessment are the number of:

- staff;
- practice areas; and
- other quality standards held (e.g. Investors in People or ISO9001).

Duration and sample guidelines

Lexcel assessments must follow the Lexcel duration and sample guidelines. The Lexcel duration and sample tables to calculate timings are available via the Lexcel website at: **www.lawsociety.org.uk/lexcel**.

Preparation and report writing time

Preparing for an assessment is an important element of the assessment process. Assessors should allow a between half and one day for preparation and report writing of initial, annual maintenance visits (AMVs) and full re-assessments.

Travel time

The Lexcel guidelines do not reflect travel time to and from the on-site assessment. If the practice has multiple offices the assessment body and practice should agree how much time will be allocated to the assessor for travel and the associated cost.

Offices and work areas

All offices and work areas must be included in all initial assessments, AMVs and full re-assessments. It is compulsory for all offices to be visited by the assessor. Interviews and file samples must also cover each office.

In very exceptional circumstances, it may be possible to conduct telephone interviews and view documentation and files remotely, rather than attending an office. This request must be submitted to the Lexcel office for review before any agreement with the client. The Lexcel office will approve, decline or amend the request.

Types of assessment

Initial assessments

All offices and practice areas must be included in the assessment. It is also mandatory that the assessor checks that all requirements of the Lexcel standard are being complied with.

Practices submitting an initial application must ensure the Lexcel requirements have been embedded for at least three months at the time of their assessment. This is to ensure that there is sufficient evidence for the assessor to evaluate if all the requirements are correctly understood and embedded within the practice.

Annual maintenance visits (AMV) Years 1 and 2

During AMVs the assessor must include all offices and practice areas in the assessment. All requirements in sections 6, 7 and 8 of the Lexcel standard must be assessed. In addition, any areas where non-compliance was found at the previous assessment must be reviewed.

For AMV1s, the assessor may tailor how they assess sections 1 to 5 of the standard to help the practice get the most benefit from the assessment. For example, if the practice has a very sound three-year business plan, the assessor may choose not to assess those sections of the Lexcel standard and focus on the areas that the practice was less strong on. For AMV2s, the assessor will need to assess any requirements from sections 1 to 5 that were not assessed during the AMV1.

The onsite AMV1 or AMV2 takes approximately half the time of an initial assessment.

Full re-assessment

On the third anniversary of the practice's initial award, a full re-assessment is required. This needs to take place in the month that it was initially awarded or the previous or following month, for example, if the practice was awarded in June, then its AMV 1 may take place in May, June or July.

The assessor must include all offices and practice areas in the re-assessment, and all the requirements of the standard must be assessed.

A full re-assessment takes the same length of time as an initial assessment.

Joint assessments and passporting arrangements

There is a degree of synergy between Lexcel and IiP, ISO9001:2008 and the SQM. Practices that want multiple accreditation awards should consider undertaking simultaneous assessments. This typically reduces the overall duration of an assessment and, thus, reduces expenditure.

Alternatively, practices can passport into Lexcel, particularly if they have undertaken another accreditation assessment within the past six months.

The overlaps and passporting grids can be found on the Lexcel website at (**www.lawsociety.org.uk/lexcel**).

Outcome of assessment

It is the responsibility of the assessor to evaluate the evidence available and reach a conclusion about the recommendation he or she wishes to make. The four outcomes that the assessor can recommend are as follows:

- assessment is premature (initial applications only) – the practice has little evidence to support its meet Lexcel's requirements and corrective action will require more than six months' work. The practice will need to re-apply ensuring no assessment is booked within six months of the last day of its initial assessment;

- major non-compliance – the practice cannot produce evidence to demonstrate that it meets a requirement of the Lexcel standard and corrective action will take between 21 days and three months to rectify, or it is deemed necessary for the assessor to revisit the practice as documentary evidence will be inadequate to demonstrate compliance;
- minor non-compliances – the practice cannot produce evidence to demonstrate that it meets a requirement of the Lexcel standard and corrective action can be undertaken within 21 days by providing the assessor with documentary evidence;
- award or renew accreditation – the practice has produced evidence to confirm it meets all the requirements in the Lexcel standard.

Note: even one instance of a practice not producing evidence of compliance against a requirement of the Lexcel standard must give rise to a non-compliance, for example, there is one file where the client was not informed of the status of the fee earner.

Corrective action

Documentary evidence

The corrective action the practice takes must address the cause of the non-compliance arising. Assessors must agree with the practice the type and level of detail required for the corrective action to be deemed acceptable.

Revisit

If documentary evidence alone is not sufficient to determine whether a major non-compliance has been rectified, a revisit may be necessary. This is for the assessor to decide but clear communication between the assessor, assessment body and client is essential. If a revisit is necessary, the assessor will limit the assessment to the areas of non-compliance found at the original assessment.

Reports

There are two types of reports that must be completed for a Lexcel assessment:

- assessment reports – the assessor must complete the assessment report for all Lexcel assessments;
- corrective action reports – a corrective action report must be completed if minor or major non-compliances have been raised. If the practice addresses the minor non-compliances before the assessor has completed the assessment, the assessor may include this information in the assessment report.

Assessors must clearly state the evidence they have witnessed to close the non-compliance on the assessment report, below where the non-compliances have been raised.

Final decision on accreditation application

The Lexcel office will review the assessment report and corrective action report. One of two final decisions on an application will be given:

- award of Lexcel accreditation – practice is sent confirmation of accreditation and an award pack; or
- refuse Lexcel – practice is not awarded Lexcel. The Lexcel office will contact the practice directly to confirm the decision and next actions.

Only the Lexcel office can award/re-award practices. The practice's assessment body will be informed of the award/re-award when the practice is notified.

Termination

The Law Society reserves the right to terminate or suspend accreditation at any time for any reasonable reason. The practice will not be entitled to be reimbursed for any sums paid in respect of the application fee.

Appeals

Practices have the right to appeal decisions made by the Lexcel office and/or assessors recommendations. See the Lexcel website for details.

For more information

If you have any questions regarding the Lexcel scheme, contact the Lexcel office via email: (lexcel@lawsociety.org.uk) or telephone (+44 (0)20 7320 5933).

Index